The Writing of Violence in
the Middle East

Suspensions: Contemporary Middle Eastern and Islamicate Thought
This series interrupts standardized discourses involving the Middle East and the Islamicate world by introducing creative and emerging ideas. The incisive works included in this series provide a counterpoint to the reigning canons of theory, theology, philosophy, literature, and criticism through investigations of vast experiential typologies—such as violence, mourning, vulnerability, tension, and humour—in light of contemporary Middle Eastern and Islamicate thought.

Forthcoming:

Hostage Spaces of the Contemporary Islamicate World: Phantom Territoriality, Dejan Lukic

The Poetics of Mourning in the Middle East: Elegies, Alina Gharabegian

The Writing of Violence in the Middle East

Inflictions

Jason Bahbak Mohaghegh

Suspensions: Contemporary Middle Eastern and Islamicate Thought

continuum

Continuum International Publishing Group

The Tower Building	80 Maiden Lane
11 York Road	Suite 704
London SE1 7NX	New York NY 10038

www.continuumbooks.com

British Library Cataloguing-in-Publication Data
A catalogue record for this book is available from the British Library.

ISBN: HB: 978-1-4411-0630-8

Library of Congress Cataloging-in-Publication Data
Mohaghegh, Jason Bahbak, 1979-
The writing of violence in the Middle East: inflictions/Jason Bahbak Mohaghegh.
    p. cm. – (Suspensions)
Includes bibliographical references (p.) and index.
ISBN 978-1-4411-0630-8 (hardcover)
1. Middle Eastern literature – History and criticism – Theory, etc. 2. Violence in literature. 3. Literature, Experimental. I. Title.

PJ307.M643 2011
809´.8956 – dc23

2011027652

Typeset by Newgen Imaging Systems Pvt Ltd, Chennai, India
Printed and bound in Great Britain

For the grandfather's shadow . . .

Contents

Series Foreword

Poets, artists, theologians, philosophers, and mystics in the Middle East and Islamicate world have been interrogating notions of desire, madness, sensuality, solitude, death, time, space, etc. for centuries, thus constituting an expansive and ever-mutating intellectual landscape. Like all theory and creative outpouring, then, theirs is its own vital constellation—a construction cobbled together from singular visceral experiences, intellectual ruins, novel aesthetic techniques, social-political-ideological detours, and premonitions of a future—built and torn down (partially or in toto), and rebuilt again with slight and severe variations. The horizons shift, and frequently leave those who dare traverse these lands bewildered and vulnerable.

Consequently, these thinkers and their visionary ideas largely remain unknown, or worse, mispronounced and misrepresented in the so-called Western world. In the hands of imperialistic frameworks, a select few are deemed worthy of notice and are spoken on behalf of, or rather *about*. Their ideas are simplified into mere social formulae and empirical scholarly categories. Whereas so-called Western philosophers and writers are given full leniency to contemplate the most incisive or abstract ideas, non-Western thinkers, especially those located in the imagined realms of the Middle East and Islamicate world, are reduced to speaking of purely political histories or monolithic cultural narratives. In other words, they are distorted and contorted to fit within hegemonic paradigms that steal away their more captivating potentials.

Contributors to this series provide a counterpoint to the reigning canons of theory, theology, philosophy, literature, and criticism through investigations of the vast experiential typologies of such regions. Each volume in the series acts as a "suspension" in the sense that the authors will position contemporary thought in an enigmatic new terrain of inquiry, where it will be compelled to confront unforeseen works of critical and creative imagination. These analyses will not only highlight the full range of current intellectual and artistic trends and their benefits for the citizens of these phantom spheres, but also argue that the ideas themselves are borderless, and thus of great relevance to all citizens of the world.

Jason Bahbak Mohaghegh
and Lucian Stone

Preface

VIOLENCE, EAST/WEST

WEST   EAST

Thinking (disaster) vs. Guarding (quarrel)
Universality (nature) vs. Narrowness (half-death)
Myth (boundary) vs. Strangeness (cloud)
Incarnation (the god) vs. Invincibility (the butcher)
Nausea (crust) vs. Disdain (fumes)
Hell (interruption) vs. Night (mystery)
Weapons-Systems (communication) vs. Knives (slashing)
Time-Murder (overhanging) vs. Microscopic Time (waiting)
Paralysis (supplication) vs. Immateriality (inflammation)
Hallowing (the rock) vs. Tasting (the skull)
Smoothness (the plateaus) vs. Arcing (the hills)
Gravity (scandal) vs. Mockery (arrogance)
Iron (courage) vs. Oil (sleep)
Withering (the sands) vs. Ravaging (the stars)
Noise (dissonance) vs. Untelling (tirade)
Flagellation (the cure) vs. Fastening (the shutdown)
Breaching (air) vs. Crumbling (wind)
Transgression (falling) vs. Submergence (spinning)
Questions (the battle) vs. Omens (the flight)
Paradox (attacks) vs. Poetics (gallows)
Sliding (the point) vs. Trading (the pitfall)
The Double (grimacing) vs. The Shadow (sinking)
Agony (pillage) vs. Ferocity (massacre)
Revelation (the cellar) vs. Artificiality (the mountain)
Articles (passion) vs. Ice (vigilantism)
Abjection (revolt) vs. Laceration (adventure)
Hurt (the madman) vs. Guilt (the hooded)
Extinction (silence) vs. Cancellation (counsel)

And within this, some will be made infamous . . . Writing has now come face-to-face with a most crucial juncture: to negotiate with the inescapable presence of violence (amidst extreme hazards). As such, this book entrenches itself in the domain of Middle Eastern thought so as to stage a powerful conversation on questions of cruelty, evil, vengeance, madness, and betrayal. Through an erratic comparative approach, one can track this increasingly volatile landscape from many positions, decoding some of the most intricate ideas, techniques, styles, and approaches of its literary-philosophical vanguard in a dangerous era. To accomplish the task, this work traverses new wave texts that illustrate the rising patterns and trends in operation across the region, particularly with regard to their views on violence as an embedded and amorphous fixture of textual practice. Occupying a supreme focus are thinkers of dynamic war-like manifestations, all of whom reflect an elaborate potential destiny of the writing-act as it takes on its more perilous orientations in our time.

Beyond the narrow judgment of violence as a purely tragic reality, these philosopher-poets—in states of exile, prison, revolution, martyrdom, and battle—come to wager with the more elusive, inspiring, and even ecstatic dimensions that rest at the heart of a visceral universe of imagination. It is through this convoluted and controversial thematic plane, one charged with endless dark turns, that this project renders its record of voices and movements drawn from the inner circles of yet another East. By exploring the most cutting-edge provinces of writing from this vast trans-cultural front, the aim is to reveal many of the experimental outlooks in play across such outsider spaces, as captivating gestures that could redefine our understanding of violence and its now-unstoppable relationship to world literature.

Such labyrinthine realms will be tested, crossed, and mapped through the expressions of its forerunners (to seek what palpitates). This will lead to singular perceptions of violence as a fatalistic motion, counterbalance, and creative prism, all the while allowing for a striking question to advance itself: *What does it mean for a work to become accursed, and with it to give rise to an afflicted textual event?* In response, we will delineate the topic's widening corridors, weighing its varied orchestrations and implications, its fascinating archetypes, and thereby trailing it into such obscure conceptual compartments as: threat, annihilation, sharpening, deception, rage, and assassination. The ultimate intent is to unlock the possibility for an affirmative encounter with the seemingly limitless force and scope of such cosmologies of thought, one that enhances a certain existential complexity and discloses pathways of speculation (however maleficent in nature).

We begin at the end of the world, where certain authors move toward their own dread, misfortune, and infinite mortality, where the poets keep bad company and hold court with the wrong ones time and again (discredited guests, discredited hosts). Here writing is asked to walk its lowest parlors, the obsidian circus of possibilities, and keep vigil over excruciation.

Violence is the last empire of the imaginary (to seek what is farthest, most hostile, in coarse settings). From this point, it is necessary to commence a sinuous exchange between sectors, to throw the critical-creative gaze across a tensed East/West axis, juxtaposing select passages from the so-called Middle Eastern front with, across, and against those of the so-called Western narrative. They will enter into contestation, juggling respective forms of malice, nothing-ness, carving, suspicion, anger, myth, and hypocrisy. These alignments, strung across fragile theoretical tightropes, transmitting their distinct passcodes to one another like back-alley whispers, will enable this project to develop a ver-satile arsenal and collection of entry-points (unknown barbaric principles). This is not dialectics; this is irrelevant catastrophe, for though the West forever stands as the First World, the East is never the Second or Third World, but rather the Seventh or Twelfth now becoming a Zero-World (insurgent waves of obsolescence). More than this, the incessant counterpoint, with fragments placed opposite one another, will herald a long-awaited challenge, each inter-face in actuality a combative round, a cutting showdown of traditions/icono-clasms for which the right to survival remains an elusive hard-won prize. This is not dialogue; this is rivalry, strife, self-testing, the electricity of sectarian vio-lence transposed across 28 opening spheres. One from the East, one from the West; one falls, one succeeds, on the back of the other. There seems no other way: the aftermath of such contemporary instincts must locate itself in adver-sity, competition, struggle, and intolerance. And so, it is through the verses below that one finds a theater for provocation and illusory civilizational war-fare (enemy territoriality). Violent words necessitate violent methodologies.

I. Thinking (Disaster) vs. Guarding (Quarrel)

To think the disaster (if this is possible, and it is not possible inasmuch as we suspect that the disaster is thought) is to have no longer any future in which to think it. —Maurice Blanchot[1]

* * *

Gaze upon this world:
—from one end to the other—
That within the soft sheets of its ruinous deep sleep
it is alienated to itself

And gaze upon us:
Awakened,
Sobered to our own desolation.
Infuriated and quarrelsome

We stand guard over our own bitterness.
We are the fanged wardens of our own pain,
So that we do not default on the black frame of duty that we have placed around it.
—Ahmad Shamlu[2]

In the supposed West, violence came in the robes of a stagnating crisis: the death of the knowing subject, for which mourning, testimony, and witnessing were the last remaining options, leaving an age of evacuated neutrality and loss, the groundlessness of modernity's victim (consciousness slung down). Mass forfeiture. The ever-slipping logic of passivity, acquiescence, self-induced defeat, and semi-noble suicide have taken hold here (there is wretchedness in such integrity).

In the new East, violence came with the mandate of a critical assignment: the conscription of the acting ante-subject, for which entrancement, severity, and constraint became the posture of an all-encompassing obligation, creating an age of guardians, caretakers, guarantors, attendants for whom imperatives of waking, alertness, and duty forged a mindset of unending diligence (the angriest task). Thus the apparatus of self was ever-tightened, amidst the strict commissioning of the protectorate, those who would watch the road, transfixed, staunch, tormented-unto-calmness, who would quarrel with the evasion of Man and God and substitute it with the rigid gaze of the one who will not lose (there is integrity in such wretchedness).

II. Universality (Nature) vs. Narrowness (Half-Death)

This is a war universe. War all the time. That is its nature. There may be other universes based on all sorts of other principles, but ours seems to be based on war and games. —William Burroughs[3]

* * *

Winds shift against us. The southern wind blows with our enemies.
The passage narrows.
We flash victory signs in the darkness, so the darkness may glitter . . .
For the thousandth time we write on the last breath of air. We die so they do not prevail!
We live our death. This half-death is our triumph. —Mahmoud Darwish[4]

In the supposed West, violent thought still ponders itself in universal tones, wondering after the essence, the natural, however damned, decrepit, misleading, beholden to the image of a pre-given visitation (that this had to happen), contemplating signals of a foregone catastrophic conclusion, reading ill-born

constellations in prayer of a solution. The vision is always planetary and millenarian, as if there were still incorporeal answers to visceral questions, for they
see themselves as the inheritors of this unright world.

In the new East, violent thought aligns itself with the ultimate sliver, the
outnumbered minor segments who wait in ambush of the universal; these are
not the heirs of the world but the unformed outsider coalition, the starved, the
ragged, those of the narrow drift to whom all are opposed (enemy-relation-
ality), for whom nature itself sends death-threats. The vision is always extraneous, vicious, offensive-defensive, practitioners of the counter-strike, whose
self-willed perishing comes at the price of existence itself (for the East knows
that they are not of this world, and that this world must not prevail).

III. Myth (Boundary) vs. Strangeness (Cloud)

*If mythic violence is lawmaking, divine violence is law-destroying; if the former sets
boundaries, then the latter boundlessly destroys them; if mythic violence brings at once
guilt and retribution, divine violence only expiates; if the former threatens, the latter
strikes; if the former is bloody, the latter is lethal without spilling blood.* —Walter
Benjamin[5]

* * *

This is what I am: No, I am not from the age of decline
I am the hour of dreadful agitation and shaking loose of minds
This is what I am—A cloud passed by
Pregnant with a hurricane of madness
Ostentation rushes by beneath my window. The others say:
"He tends the herd of his eyelids,
He unites strangeness with strangeness."
This is what I am: Uniting strangeness with strangeness. —Adonis[6]

In the supposed West, violence remains a metaphysical relic, fathered in transcendent zones, descending from above, imposing itself as an infinite, traceless
exchange between myth and divinity. Thus it is always vague, ethereal, spread
across impossibility-principles, a negation-instinct that leaves thought to dwell
in absence/otherness (the cowardice of alterity), purging everything solid, as
a hiding-place from the now-famished tyrannies of past discourse (laws once
built up must fall down). Tired of blood, they reinvent the void (as if hollow-
ness were not its own endangerment).

In the new East, violence happens (in excessive displays), takes place (across
countless lines), asserts itself as an ever-present spark of disorientation (it

breathes, subsumes, and takes over what it wants through confounding plans). If there is abstraction, it is not from emptiness but from complexity (intricate vertigo), as violence spreads itself across undeniable occasions, a vast continuum yet apparent in the most precise inflections of the wrist (acute terror). No apologies, no withdrawals, no recantations of poorly lived histories, just a continuous unifying pact with strangeness (agitation, lunacy, hurricane). What exit, sanctuary, or retreat, when the vapors themselves announce such strength?

IV. Incarnation (The God) vs. Invincibility (The Butcher)

To kill God. The master of mirrors. The father of gardens.
Pushed by I do not know what mad, unsuspected force. With my hands.
For my salvation and the world's. To kill God.
Through you the world will be avenged . . .
Ungrained night. Night of murder.
I shall not extend the deadline. —Edmond Jabès[7]

* * *

When I was a child
I fell into a pit
But didn't die;
I sank in a pond
when I was young, but did not die;
and now, God help us—
one of my habits is running
into battalions of mines
along the border,
as my songs
and the days of my youth are dispersed:
here a flower,
there a scream;
and yet,
I do not die!
They butchered me
on the doorstep
like a lamb for the feast—
thrombosis in the veins of petroleum.
In God's name
they slit my throat
from ear to ear
a thousand times,

and each time
my dripping blood would swing
back and forth
like the feet of a man
hanged from a gallows. —Taha Muhammad Ali[8]

In the supposed West, violence is focused against celestial icons, punishing their ability to mirror, playing out the ceremonial rebellion of the incarnation against the original, against the unconditional rulings of the onlooker, that which saw too much (shame), raking the frail contract of the genesis (confrontation of likenesses), to heal the sorrow of pure derivation, amidst narratives of waning grace (they still dabble in souls), the once-anointed echo now becoming the sour backlash (condemned resemblance), and with no recourse but to stride headlong against the master (so feared that it became unpronounceable).

In the new East, violence begins from unmapped sites, for the origin does not parallel the emergence (unidentified)—no imitations, no emulative trap—for the gods could not see these ones (they live in the gaps of omniscience), and in this way endured, outdid, and unstrung themselves from a bitter showdown with the supreme, instead gaining a monstrous, abominable immortality, one based in disfigurement (to be unclaimed), in reckless anthems of orphanhood (there is no business, no debt, no covenant with the skies). They never became documented citizens, these non-belongings, with nothing to live up to (savage irresponsibility), free to make deals with whomever/whenever, remaining eternally accented, without acknowledgment, ownership, or command (arcane immunities are born of this untouched status), intrinsically mal-suited (for there is nothing intrinsic), attached only to a renegade standard of invincibility. This culminates at the storefront of the butcher (all writers are butchers here)—figures of precision, particularity, rhythm; it is all evident in the descriptive specificity, where battalions, mines, and ripped throats are romantically interspersed with songs and petals (foul lyricism).

In the West, murder has a deadline (to kill the One); in the East, it is an ongoing function (to kill everyone).

V. Nausea (Crust) vs. Disdain (Fumes)

I am physically nauseated by commonplace humanity, which is the only kind there is.
All of this leaves me with the impression of a monstrous and vile animal created in
the chaos of dreams, out of desire's soggy crusts, out of sensations' chewed-up leftovers.
—Fernando Pessoa[9]

* * *

Anyone who remains idle in our world is despised
And this despair, this discomfort, is disdainful
Morning has dawned and we must ignite the fire,
Burn the enemies,
That perhaps its fumes may reach the sky of the devil
Or within his windmill distance itself from our land
Morning has dawned . . .
Alas the day of the corrupters is as dim as midnight. —Khosrow Golesorkhi[10]

In the supposed West, antihumanism proves a useless luxury of spectatorship, congealing at safe distances, stamped upon fake pedestals, where the superior hurl righteous nausea down and across the backs of the amassed. The rabble, the herd, the they: such uninvolved terminologies of sickening (writing here has long been an agoraphobic condition), vile expressions that never go beyond words, remaining enclosed in interior revulsions (the perch), anti-pathic voicings that never keep their promise in the beautiful matrix of action, that never enact aversion, never brand the appalled look of centuries on the naked skin of the blameworthy.

In the new East, an inexorable trigger is pulled, for all loathing demands immediacy (one works in the devil's windmill)—there is no hesitation, no discomfort in approaching, in following the line of abhorrence right into the other's lungs: to shatter the interval, where repulsion electrifies the will to burn, where disgust is compressed into an unstoppable arm. It is never given the time to burden, to consolidate into a chronic illness (how long has the West been suggesting, wishing, and theorizing the Death of Man . . . and still they live?). No, in the East, this species is met with uncompromising ignition (one sees through the distaste), in order to fulfill the expense/detriment of perception, and so they bring trouble, scalding, peaceless fumes, and the unforgiving dawn (the disdainful clear the land).

VI. Hell (Interruption) vs. Night (Mystery)

Praised be the nightmare, for it reminds us that we have the power to create Hell.
—Jorge Luis Borges[11]

* * *

When dawn broke, we were all staring at each other in amazement, wondering: How did we stay alive? How did we survive that night? We'd spent a night during which bombs, explosives, and rockets had been galloping around our house as if the elements had gone mad . . . It was as if the sounds of the explosives had a mysterious, drug-like effect. —Ghada Samman[12]

In the supposed West, the nightmare is defined as a hellish interruption, a striation, disjuncture, and shock-value, where one resists diametrical threats, such that even when self-licensed it operates within a scared dialectic, freezing consciousness in static polarizations. This nightmare petrifies the mind, loosening images of abnormality, making thought stand across from the unthinkable, in order to produce a unidirectional vibration. Here flight becomes improbable, determining surrender through forcibly extracted pangs, and the dreamer grows uneven, rickety, tremulous, drenched, and shaken. But is the shudder the most powerful device? Is this wavering (the darting of pupils, the fluctuation of pulse, the vacillation of limbs) an optimal engagement with fright?

In the new East, the night saturates to the point of accompaniment (liquidity, circularity), leaving a perpetual inseparability between the inner and the outer, self and space, imagination and reality. Thus the mind conspires with the violence surrounding; when brought before the death-squads, it hallucinates into the event (unclear which comes first), embellishes the episode, poeticizes atrocity (for atrocity is inherently poetic), adding components, aiding its cause, stimulating its greatness, and actively fictionalizing the most horrendous parts of its appearance (to make it better by envisioning it worse than itself). Can one grapple with this: that in harrowing states of religious cleansing, civil uprising, imperialist bombing, amidst the flying reign of bullets, amidst tangible missiles, within torture-chambers, one would begin to flirt with untruth, amend trivial details, disturb facticity, and begin to lie in ways that only exacerbate the so-called actual occurrence? For this is how trauma, oppression, and repression are outstripped—in the East, violence must become a mutual convulsion, wherein thought catapults, rushes, and over-tempts the abysmal event, where consciousness throws dice at the edge of all things.

In the West, one shivers beneath the nightmare (to submit to the unknown); in the East, one shivers with anticipation throughout the night (to intensify the mystery).

VII. Weapons-Systems (Communication) vs. Knives (Slashing)

The first weapons system was determined by obstruction, that is to say, ramparts, shields, the size of the elephant . . . Next came weapons of destruction, particularly artillery which changed everything, and up to thermonuclear devices . . . The third series of weapons-systems, though, has not been neutralized, and that's the weaponry of communication. —Paul Virilio[13]

* * *

I'd like to slash with my knife the sneaking lies that are your enemy
without a word to anyone
with a black knife embossed with beavers' teeth
to be the assassin of a gray world without love
assassin
of your snaky ways
with a black knife
surrendering celebrations to the garden of black roses
black
pitch black
your assassin. —Namik Kuyumcu[14]

In the supposed West, violence becomes increasingly symbolic, virtual, techno-logical, favoring mediation, genocidal efficiency, and atrophic bodies that diffuse acidic information (ideology-stricken). There is only an impersonal, anonymous, complacent rehearsal, heaped together in rugged strata . . . toward pure anaesthetization (the civilian).

In the new East, a fourth weapons-system remains: that of *invasion/excision* (slashing instruments). There is nothing primitive about the hand-crafted blade, the knife's curvature, its angles, its snaking, its gentle guidance, the way it punctures the grayness (without justification). It is to shift the criterion of arms back to a singular trust and sensuality—to learn the weight, the grip, the touch, the labor, the ornamentation, a protocol of swiftness, sleekness, coordination, elegance, and rapidity. The razor slides, returns, sheathes, and motions back again, in a circuitous transaction (the professional).

In the West, violence undergoes mounting compartmentalization (tech-nicality); in the East, there is still the prospect of overarching manipulation (expertise).

VIII. Time-Murder (Overhanging) vs. Microscopic Time (Waiting)

My mission is to kill time, and time's to kill me in its turn . . . How comfortable one is among murderers. —Emile Cioran[15]

* * *

Since I've been in jail
the world has turned around the sun ten times
And if you ask the earth, it will say:
"It's not worth mentioning,

a microscopic time."
And if you ask me, I will say:
"It's ten years of my life." —Nazim Hikmet[16]

In the supposed West, time remains a fearsome adversary (the intimidated), leaving consciousness hunted, evading the swinging scythes of expiration, in a standstill of death-stares. The totalitarian imminence of time—as that which has already happened (too late), is always happening (omnipresent), and is yet to happen (on the way), gives it the semblance of an ambitious, overhanging thirst. Here time takes the first turn (birth), and the last turn (finality), gaining a cheater's advantage, and thereby wins the existential game (fraud). One can only hold out for so long, before the unavoidable takes its maximal sedating hold, before the pre-approved concession of the sigh (regret), the laying down of once-tensed hands, the mellowing of once-clenched teeth, and capitulation to the tilted ordinance (one just follows orders here).

In the new East, there are antidotes to the authoritarian syndromes of time: forgetting (one can neglect time), acceleration (one can move at velocities that surpass time), reversal (one can turn back the hands of time), transposition (one can substitute the segments of time: past-becoming-future, future-becoming-present, present-becoming-past). More than this, though, there is the unbelievable approach of waiting, whereby a lone consciousness sits in place, prompts fate to take a seat alongside itself, watches the lead bars incessantly, and proceeds to outlast time itself (the customer). Far from the pounding domain of the chronological (the objective clock of everyone), this one brings time into hyper-individuated captivity, locks it in the experience of a single, ever-constricting jail-cell, makes it claim the seconds of every client, one by one, counting each ragged transpiration in a microscopic calculus. And, once there, once trapped in this microcosmic lens, where every instant wields the slanting, abolition, and resurgence of a ludicrous martyr (the one who dies constantly, only to bounce back, declare itself, and die again), time itself loses the taste, finding itself over-occupied, over-worked, arrested by frivolous errands, and choking on the same elastic spirits it has come to compile (to alienate, disqualify, and give too much, until it quits). To test the threshold of time's impatience.

In the West, one flails for a while, in a kind of theatrical revolt, before the head bows and thought marches forward to the same altar as the others; in the East, one shows unswerving hospitality to time, feeds it precisely what it asks for, in compact tragic feasts, ingrains the climax as a sequence of diminutive boundless mortalities, until time's stomach distends and its mind stutters in a bookkeeper's anguish (hyper-chronicling). The death of a being is easy enough to claim, record, and resolve; but the death of this waiting one, the one who computes the loaded sunsets, who sifts through the miniscule closings, the exactness of the straight lines on the cell walls that verify the slow years, necessitates a meticulous, painstaking score (insisting too much, taking too long, subordinating its distressed collector to an infinitesimal archive).

IX. Paralysis (Supplication) vs. Immateriality
(Inflammation)

I imagine two kinds of Violence.
The victim of the first kind is led astray.
It is the Violence of a rapid train at the moment of the death of the despairing person who willfully threw himself on the tracks.
The second kind is that of the serpent or the spider, that of an element which is irreconcilable to the order wherein the possibility of being is given, which turns you to stone. It does not confound but slips; it dispossesses, it paralyzes, it fascinates before you might oppose anything to it. —Georges Bataille[17]

* * *

The thought struck me with horror. I rose, threw off the cloak and stood in front of the mirror. My cheeks were inflamed to the color of the meat that hangs in front of the butchers' shops. My beard was disheveled. And yet there was something immaterial, something fascinating, in the reflection that I saw . . . It was as though everything that was heavy, earthy and human in me had melted away. —Sadeq Hedayat[18]

In the supposed West, violent fascination reveals itself in the wake of a stunned, prostrated supplicant, the one whose gaping expression is a ventriloquism of the extreme limit of non-knowledge, the one who becomes jammed, disenfranchised, shackled, and clawed by the irreconcilable. Thus one is given the depiction of an immovable sphere, the torso usurped by the inflexible travesties of the serpent/the spider (to be caught and held down), for which paralysis, dispossession, and unopposable gloom commingle to forge their thorns.

In the new East, violent fascination reveals itself as an incendiary propulsion (that which grows heated), leading to outrageous inflammation, the one of unremitting melting (the power of that which can shed itself, de-layer, wiping away entire molecular sheets). Thus one is given the depiction of maligned skin, tender unveilings of the hideous (raw, marked, irradiated), always going beneath to find worse outcomes (disheveled underpinnings), the complicated geography of scar-tissue, tangential cross-cuts, crimson tattoos, where the reflection (no longer earthly, heavy, cloaked) wears incomprehensibility as a kind of face.

In the West, one is conquered by perplexity (the request); in the East, one incurs amazement at all turns (through deformation/malformation).

X. Hallowing (The Rock) vs. Tasting (The Skull)

You should have eyes that always seek an enemy—your enemy. And some of you hate at first sight. Your enemy you shall seek, your war you shall wage—for your thoughts. And if your thought be vanquished, then your honesty should still find cause for triumph in that. You should love peace as a means to new wars—and the short peace more than the long. To you I do not recommend work but struggle . . . You say it is the good cause that hallows even war? I say unto you: it is the good war that hallows any cause.

O my brothers, am I cruel? But I say: what is falling, we should still push. Everything today falls and decays: who would check it? But I—I even want to push it further.
—Friedrich Nietzsche[19]

* * *

I opened your head
To read your thoughts.
I devoured your eyes
To taste your sight.
I drank your blood
To know your wants
And made of your shivering body
My nourishment. —Joyce Mansour[20]

In the supposed West, the riddle follows: that one should live untimely in order to die at the right time. This springs from a certain feeling that things have not gone far enough, requiring further pressure, exertion, and struggle. The result is an air of confidence and starkness, the shoulder lodged against the profound weight of rock/world, straining uphill, the long-term imperative of the one with work still sprawling before them (to seek triumph).

In the new East, the riddle follows: that one should have the right timing in order to make other things die at the wrong time. This springs from a certain feeling that things have gone too far (corpsed over), the standing edifices of world mangled already, beyond futility, requiring only the vampiric arrival of the one who will devour, taste, and drink from the tipped vessels of the elders, as old vestiges supply young motives (antisocial evolution). The unwelcomed caller, of despicable customs, who rakes, exploits, gorges, brings the last stages of consumption (forced conversion, forced invigoration), and thereby ends the masquerade.

In the West, one strives (expenditure); in the East, one infiltrates (assailment).

XI. Smoothness (The Plateaus) vs. Arcing (The Hills)

Nomad existence has for "affects" the weapons of a war machine . . . Learning to undo things, and to undo oneself, is proper to the war machine: the "not-doing" of the warrior, the undoing of the subject. A movement of decoding runs through the war machine . . . effectuated in the Void, not in nothingness, but in the smooth of the void where there is no longer any goal: attacks, counterattacks, and headlong plunges.
—Gilles Deleuze and Felix Guattari[21]

* * *

To your fire-tempered sticks,
and on with your sweat wrung shirts,
get to your horses. —Suleyman Cobanoglu[22]

In the supposed West, existential positions are systematically undone, turned into self-stringing affects, the archaeology of Being now deciphered, un-sutured, and re-assembled in schizoid patterns. No longer the psychoanalytic vestiges of the unconscious, no longer the despotic fortifications of consciousness, for there is no one left to haul such burdens—instead, immanent machinic desires find their plane of consistency in a kind of mystical detachment, sailing between sense and nonsense, attuned only to roving bodies without organs.

In the new East, there are still bold existential typologies that supersede the quicksand of Being: the swordsman, the horseman, the runner, the spear-thrower, the archer. These are figures of urgency, zeal, and near-perfect animation, those of kindred javelins who hasten, charge, and launch across rough frontiers, those of lethal gamesmanship (malevolent playfulness). The swordsman: one of rampant symmetries and perforations (the saber). The horseman: one of hurried balance (the mount), pseudo-animality (the reins), and forward bolting (the gallop). The runner: one of speed, pacing, and proper exhalation, and who pulverizes the soil (apocalyptic courier). The spear-thrower: one of arcing, horrific vectors, and impetuous bouts, who heaves, flows, joins verticality and horizontality toward the one grand target (heart-penetration). The archer: one who worships aim alone, who sets sights, inhales, flexes, swears oaths to the air, and directs the bow accordingly, and for whom ontological purpose has been ousted by the need for accuracy (graceful onslaught).

In the West, one speaks of uninhabited plateaus; in the East, there are still those leaner kinds who walk the hills.

XII. Gravity (Scandal) vs. Mockery (Arrogance)

He was no liar, admitted the truth and said that he was cruel. Human beings, did you
hear that? He dares to say it again with his trembling pen. So it is a power stronger than
will . . . Curse! Could a stone escape from the laws of gravity? Impossible. Impossible,
for evil to form an alliance with good. That is what I was saying in the above lines.
—Comte de Lautreamont[23]

* * *

perhaps I am a red snake.
a snake with a scorpion asleep on its forked tongue.
a snake protected by the night.
one that scares pretty children.
gets them accustomed to capping.
red bodies extending towards red channels.
I see red spots of lust.
red love songs.
in red barrel organs
they are playing love songs.
I am a red gangster.
I carry red weapons. —Kucuk Iskender[24]

In the supposed West, violence entails a subsequent admission (confession)—
coated explanations and references of its controversy, scandal, and stigma.
Truth-telling has not been banished, its brooding, somber gravity yet to be
discarded even from the dominion of unholy traits—one still trembles, asking for every flake of sympathy and absolution, demarcations of forgiveness,
exonerated minutes, and the hope for utter acquittal. Hence, the most bastard allusions come with their repentance, contrition, and prevailing call to
judgment.

In the new East, violence requires arrogance (declaration): the swagger, the
boast, the taunt (criminal pride), to rile the war-spirit, where illicit language
spits, mars, and hails discomfort (the progenitor). One becomes slick-tongued
(neo-charlatanism), spawning half-breed dialects of provocation, venom, and
mockery—an idiomatic program of obscenity, villainy, and comical thug inter-
ventions, run by those of wicked under-royalty and bohemian aristocracy (the
felon, the dealer).

In the West, the iniquitous rationalize their crooked tendencies (oration);
in the East, there is an ironic conceit of self-promotion (for the kings are the
brazen ones, with the reddest hearts on the street).

XIII. Iron (Courage) vs. Oil (Sleep)

The cosmos of iron is not an immediately accessible universe. To approach it one must love fire, hardness, and strength. It is recognizable only through creative acts nurtured with courage. —Gaston Bachelard[25]

* * *

Here
every button is connected to a generator
it's the work of iron and the arm
at every corner a steel giant
sleeps on the oily floor
spewing a world of fume
there's an old friendship between patience
and tuberculosis in the chests of men. —Manouchehr Neyestani[26]

In the supposed West, one paints a utopian containment, where fire does not spread but rather boxes itself in a philosophical enclosure, or within the paradisiac safety of an artistic flourish. This capsule, where asceticism and privation hide in the swinging arms of the ironsmith, this evocative insularity, at once shielded and remote, houses itself within a sculptor's inner forge (stoves, candles, flames, hammers), contented with its own bottled sublimities.

In the new East, one paints a post-dystopic chill (most are asleep), the factory where fume and oil fashion their own intriguing saga, shower their pestilence, where the gloved ones, under surveillance (poor supervision), dismantle the contraptions (valves, pipes, gears, handles, dials). A regulated web of emission, viscosity, and bareness, where thought drains and scorns its labor (the thresher).

In the West, violence can still discover its islands of courageous tranquility (the cosmos); in the East, violence is filtered through wires, cables, and linked afflictions (the generator).

XIV. Withering (The Sands) vs. Ravaging (The Stars)

Dying, I called to my executioners so I could bite the butts of their rifles. I called plagues to suffocate me with sand, blood. Misfortune was my god. I lay in the mud. I withered in criminal air. And I even tricked madness more than once. —Arthur Rimbaud[27]

* * *

The magician, poet
And warrior loved me
Offered his sacrifice
Built his obelisk
Where he recorded
His spells and the wafting
Scent of the motion
Of wind and stars.
Names he inscribed
Of flowers in my far country.
He wept at my grave
Sprinkled the book of a slaughtered child . . .
They sell me into slavery
While I wait for my labor pains
In the cities of the East
Ravaged by whirlwinds. —'Abd al-Wahhab al-Bayyati[28]

In the supposed West, one aspires to become "the vanquished," to costume oneself in apostasy, paranoia, and filth-ridden phenomenologies. One inverts the established hierarchies of sanctity, such that the absolute bottom alone validates (putrescence), one wishes to be thrown down and poured upon, stacking withered injustices (the piles). And still, this is nothing more than the sentimental relaxation of the winner, the one for whom things have come too easy and therefore bids robbery (dereliction); it is the last sought-after prize (counter-opulence): to ask for killers, plagues, suffocation, misfortune, and madness, when all along everything had been granted (wallowing).

In the new East, there is only "the vanquishing," before which one remains endlessly available. It is no longer about the success, truce, or defeat (the whirlwind), but rather the most obstinate attempt to stay, to take as long as possible before the destructive moment, to extend the duration (of the inevitable) as a kind of defiant elongation of the full moon. This is its own inescapable process: to internalize the snake-bite of the event, to be wanted by the undesirable force (the anti-beloved), and thus to solicit, entice, and hook the one that chases ceaselessly. One retaliates by becoming the treasured item. For they know the whereabouts of the obelisk, have read the book of the slaughtered child, have recited its spells, have seen slavery, stars, and graveyards, and have lain flowers as a vouching (beneath the columns).

In the West, there is the ravishing option of becoming-unborn, reveling in feigned bankruptcy (the unworthy); in the East, there is no such delight, only this coasting across subdued rivulets, waiting long enough for the over-inscribed to ravage itself and the other (mutual strangulation).

XV. Noise (Dissonance) vs. Untelling (Tirade)

Noise against noise. Noise against weapon. Noise is a weapon that, at times, dispenses with weapons. To take up space, to take the place, that is the whole point . . . One must start with the fury, one must, truly, start with the noise, battle, and racket, but one must, furthermore, start from the fury of multiplicities. —Michel Serres[29]

* * *

I would have liked to tell you
The story of a nightingale that died.
I would have liked to tell you
The story . . .
Had they not slit my lips. —Samih al-Qasim[30]

In the supposed West, one finds a dissonant era, where the turbulence, overlap, and entanglement of the now punctuates itself as a rattle. This is the symptom of its clamor, its mercurial aggravation, the loose chaos that has riveted an age, that dispenses its conflicting modes . . . a period of unreadable loudness and atonality, saying nothing, speaking to no one (random acoustic fury).

In the new East, one finds the removed narrative (deletion), where the unsaid becomes its own roar, ovation, and sonic eruption. This is where the untelling answers back, as tirade, in raving invectives, across three particular soundscapes: the shriek, the wail, and the moan (auditory epidemics). The shriek: morphologies of suddenness; the wail: morphologies of sadness; the moan: morphologies of incredible pain/pleasure. Here the understated is its own percussion (we will speak of the drums later).

In the West, one is advised to note the frantic din (as indicator); in the East, one is advised to note the implied denunciation that nevertheless precipitates its blaring, slit-mouthed legend (the reverberation of what might have been sung . . . before "they" came).

XVI. Flagellation (The Cure) vs. Fastening (The Shutdown)

It was his fate . . . to be abandoned to the malice of mankind and the physical laws of force . . . The thing he most feared, however, was flagellation, for this was the standard cure administered in those days against excesses of the imagination. —Gerard de Nerval[31]

* * *

Barking
panting
homeless
rabid wind
bit furiously
on a piece of crumpled newspaper
in the dead eye of a blind alley.
My eyes
heavy with an acrid dust
were forced shut.
My heart did not beat
and my faith
saluted death in a poem.
I was dead
and my veins
like dark steel straps
were fastened around my carcass. —Nosrat Rahmani[32]

In the supposed West, one flees the whip (excoriation), its lightning-reach curling across the convenient surface of the back, the legs, the heels, as a drastic humiliation-exercise (fifty . . . one hundred . . . one thousand). One fathoms this scourge through its most capital scenes: the implements (rods, coils, cords), the locations (the pillar, the stake, the public square), the arrangement of the body (stripped, knotted, tied), the reaction of the beaten (fainting, writhing, weeping), the treatment of the received blows (washing, rinsing, stitching), and the remainder of disciplinary scars where one cannot see them (unenlightened areas).

In the new East, one reveres the strap (instigation), for here it provides a dampened, murkier sentence: to establish a euphoric, anti-solipsistic sphere whose main destiny is to be punctured, besieged, and mutilated. And still, this seamless flogging is its own commemoration (the procession), where the charismatic, the resplendent, and the auratic show their devotion . . . half-rigor, half-glamour . . . where the chosen issue salutations through the spilling of their veins (glorious acridity).

In the West, flagellation arises from the misdeed; in the East, it is an adulation (of the fastening, the shutdown, and the unmistakable carcass).

XVII. Breaching (Air) vs. Crumbling (Wind)

Cast down the walls. Breach and breathe. Inhalation. Breath, inside and outside. This concerns the thorax. The muscular walls of the rib-cage, of the defenses of the thorax, exposed to the winds. Your breath has been set free, not taken away. An understatement:

mouth to mouth contact with distance, as though with an infinity of air. And because the walls are down, there is no swelling. —Jean-Francois Lyotard[33]

* * *

*In my small night, ah
the wind has a date with the leaves of the trees
in my small night there is agony of destruction
listen
do you hear the darkness blowing?
I look upon this bliss as a stranger
I am addicted to my despair.
Listen
do you hear the darkness blowing?
Something is passing in the night
the moon is restless and red
and over this rooftop
where crumbling is a constant fear
clouds, like a procession of mourners
seem to be waiting for the moment of rain.
A moment
and then nothing
night shudders beyond this window
and the earth winds to a halt
beyond this window
something unknown is watching you and me.* —Forugh Farrokhzad[34]

In the supposed West, one is caught amidst aerial streams, the body flung from side to side, and yet within this turmoil somehow muttering to oneself of liberation (emancipation-as-luck). This is its haphazard reception of the infinite, a gift based on accident, indeterminacy, and undeserved inheritance. No birthright, no heritage, no deciding legacy, just the perverse freedom of the beggar, ever-trailing casual donations to the bystander (postmodern slave morality).

In the new East, one is made into an elemental champion, vanguard of quaking and epochal dances, as sensuality cooperates with the leaves to create vascular dilemmas. This is its own synesthetic juncture: where darkness blows, clouds mourn, night quivers, and despair is ingested as a supple drug. No, this one is not the assistant, the partisan, or the minion of incoming winds (subservience) but rather their protégé (instruction), the one of the most observant preparation (grooming), for which there is always the assumption of a gradual throne-taking.

In the West, one kneels in vagrancy before atmospheric flares, pawning one's own becoming to residual chance (rainfall); in the East, one researches, reports, and schedules the appointment (to become the awarded), sitting in its addictive spaces of longing (the balcony, the rooftop) for the endowment.

XVIII. Transgression (Falling) vs. Submergence (Spinning)

Transgression carries the limit right to the limit of its being; transgression forces the limit to face the fact of its imminent disappearance, to find in itself what it excludes (perhaps, to be more exact, to recognize itself for the first time), to experience its positive truth in its downward fall? And yet, toward what is transgression unleashed in its movement of pure violence, if not that which imprisons it, toward the limit and those elements it contains? —Michel Foucault[35]

* * *

From the world submerged beneath the ground, in a maze
carved out from iron, cement and stone
where the spider of fear and boredom
spins out its threads along silent paths, and there is no escape
In death's labyrinth, where humans perish
longing for life
where sound disappears spinning as though the ages gasped
through you
You are here . . . What is it you sing to the graves? —Mahmoud al-Buraikan[36]

In the supposed West, one seeks the erotic blast of the limit (the gouging of eyes), for it is a question of transgressive momentum that leads to the voyeuristic impasse of exclusion (to see what has been erased). This is its ripe contestation (overturning), one that treads beyond sovereignty, subversion, and contradiction and into the all-permitting orbit of a white globe, where communication falters and the negative plunges from its rim toward the solar depths.

In the new East, one seeks the delayed victory, committed by the one whose wrongful death can curse the living: this is no tactful extortion, but rather an outright subterfuge, whereby the figure once-crushed now sits in submergence (the shelter, the stable, the lair), awaiting a seismic reckoning, and then spins back from this later vantage (the second labyrinth) to bring its nocturnal glare (dusk). There is no useful diversion here: it comes for them, from the end of days (ascription), from the cracked lips of an anti-sage (the one of defective messages).

In the West, one seeks the cavern of transparency, implosion, and effacement; in the East, vendettas are outlined, entombed for a while, and then
upheld in the gasping afterwards.

XIX. Questions (The Battle) vs. Omens (The Flight)

*We are all fighting a battle. (If, attacked by the ultimate question, I reach out behind
me for weapons, I cannot choose which of those weapons I will have, and even if I
could choose, I should be bound to choose some that don't belong to me, for we all
have only one store of weapons.* —Franz Kafka[37]

* * *

In the sunset sky
On the graying bay
Glide a thousand skiffs, black and sinister . . .
A thousand friends of a daylong flight
a thousand comrades noisy and morose
a thousand beaks, claws, back from action
a thousand stomachs filled with carrion. —Mehdi Akhavan-Saless[38]

In the supposed West, one battles with further obscurity, where perception
caves to doubt and clueless guessing, where one consorts with hunger artists,
metamorphic insects, officers, and vultures, where the backdrop, foreground,
and floor give way to growing unfamiliarity (what does not belong), becoming lost amidst the castles, penal colonies, forests, and courthouses, each its
own room of fake assumption (there is always something that did not happen there). Such is the index of an unrescued will: to clutch for stored arms
through warehouses of complete triviality.

In the new East, one navigates obscurity through signposts (expatriations,
migrations, trespasses), reads the tidings (the above-written), and success-
fully deposits perception into premonition. Though there is no proposal in
the radical nowhere, one survives through intuition, intimation, instinct,
and mood; this is not superstition but sinister improvisation, snatching
advice from meteorological, geological, and physiological remnants (the
admonition).

In the West, there is only helpless unintelligibility (scouring behind for
the not-night); in the East, one tempers consciousness to receive otherwise
encrypted notifications and omens.

XX. Paradox (Attacks) vs. Poetics (Gallows)

Anything that purges the accursed share in itself signs its own death warrant. This is the theorem of the accursed share. The energy of the accursed share, and its violence, are expressions of the principle of Evil. Beneath the transparency of the consensus lies the opacity of evil—the tenacity, obsessiveness and irreducibility of the evil whose contrary energy is at work everywhere: in the malfunctioning of things, in viral attacks, in the acceleration of processes and in their wildly chaotic effects, in the overriding of causes, in excess and paradox, in radical foreignness, in strange attractors, in linkless chains of events. —Jean Baudrillard[39]

* * *

Always these gallows,
This crowd, the eyes
that meet and turn away,
these daggers of defeat
that hide in the bricks of this house,
in seasons to come,
in the very seeds of fruit. —Fu'ad Rifqa[40]

In the supposed West, the accursed still seeks a dwelling, replacing the incapable shell of Man with the unquenchable appetite of the image, the simulation, and the occurrence (object-voracity). Thus one comes upon the recent radioactivity of the thing, which extradites doom and proliferates intelligent metastasis, across viral trails, and beneath which humanity becomes merely another contender, given its portion, allocation, and percentages like anyone else, a marginalized candidate in this bad lottery (paradoxical cards), and with nothing left at stake amidst the insatiability, pretending, and exoticism of contagious drives.

In the new East, the poetic imagination is itself the payment of the accursed share; the writing-act becomes the scaffold, opportunity, and banned acumen of evil; it transports the nefarious energies through its words (literary ailment). These are sophisticated pieces, closer to incantation (the forbidden), each line its own expectant gallows, as the author plays scribe to the unruly, the wayward, and the concocted numinous, laying eroded bricks in the house, poisoned seeds in the fruit, and envisaging the daggered seasons ahead.

In the West, evil is handed over to synthetic attractions; in the East, it finds itself engraved, harvested, and smuggled in well-monitored textual riots.

XXI. Sliding (The Point) vs. Trading (The Arch)

I consider myself in my minutiae. I put my finger on the precise point of the fault, the unadmitted slide. For the mind is more reptilian than you yourselves, messieurs, it slips away snakelike, to the point where it damages our language, I mean it leaves it in suspense. —Antonin Artaud[41]

* * *

Stalls, their lips held tight
because
night it is, night
underneath an arch where an opaque mist
rises in a dance
a crowd of men
stooped over
from inside their cloaks
eyes fixed at the eclipsed arch
the ghastly call of the nightwatch
set their figures trembling with fear
the bazaar is fraught with nightmare
fear and hope in constant strife
atop shadowy waves.
Pathways lead nowhere, pitfalls all around
filled with treachery
filled with deception
the bazaar grins at all dread
the bazaar is entranced in the darkness of night. —Manouchehr Sheibani[42]

In the supposed West, the pale evidence of damage must remain buried; it slips from view into censored quarters (the underpasses); it miniaturizes, adulterates, or quarantines its traces, becoming an unadmitted particle, a suspended infection in the forsaken interstices of the word (stammering), shot through the narrow serpentines of consciousness and entrenched in an unnoticed oblivion-point (the disregarded).

In the new East, treacheries are hoarded, bartered, negotiated in the rows of a dreadful marketplace. The bazaar is our model: where violence becomes a sold artifact, where jealousy, envy, cunning, and strife are produced, advertised, and transferred, always changing hands (accessibility), where the translucent deception of the merchants (slyness) combines with the corrupt patrol of the nightwatchman (bribery), where connections, clubs, and underhanded grins hold sway, amidst the beckoning of open storefronts (the pitfall), the stooped backs of owners who peddle the shine, glint, and luster of assorted wares (hyper-appearance), where all things are cheapened, obtainable for purchase, littered across the most circumspect aisles.

In the West, whatever harms must be raced through an anorexic episode, relegated to protective diminishments and indentations; in the East, whatever harms can be bought, switched, and traded, relegated to widening lattices of greed.

XXII. The Double (Grimacing) vs. The Shadow (Sinking)

An enemy that is one with our own intimate being, an enemy that is indistinguishable and inseparable from ourselves . . . The double that wears our own face as its mask. The face that is gradually obliterated and transformed into an immense mocking grimace. The devil. The clown. This thing that I am not. This thing that I am. A marytrissible apparition. —Octavio Paz[43]

* * *

Nighttime when everything's shadow is upside down
The upset sea
Is sunk in its own waves;
Each timid shadow has slunk off to some corner,
Toward the hurrying fugitives of the waves.
A hidden shadow
Swells up from a path.
This shadow on its course
Won't glance at the other shadows on the shore. —Nima Yushij[44]

In the supposed West, there is the double: the apparition that looks directly at the human (grimacing), as a divulgence of twin miseries, an exposure of ageless deprivation, the lack introduced by mirror stages, the covetous grappling of symbolic, imaginary, and real spheres. This dislocation leaves things unwell, mired in split inclinations (partial), such that the duplicated ones can never bring more than prohibition.

In the new East, there is the shadow: the apparition that looks away from the human (disinterest), calls forth the tides, distributes the waves, drafting expulsion-letters, and therein overthrows with an almost surgical rashness. This is not the parergon that under-writes the dominant text (it does not slink in corners)—this one is unstrung, anomalous, predatory, the one of cautious placement, all the while remaining unconcerned (callousness). This is the privilege of the one who sits above the shores (statuesque), as a satellite, upon its own slab, within its own slot (the vault), and confirms the facility and prowess of the uncaring.

In the West, defacement is a matter of returning sameness; in the East, defacement is a blank commencement.

XXIII. Agony (Pillage) vs. Ferocity (Massacre)

This elation produces in us the brutal strength to face the agony of a universe not made for our contentment and indemnification. From inhuman distances, with the fearsome farsightedness of birds of prey we see that sinister spectacle of stupidities and deceits, pillage and tortures that is the history of our species. —Alphonso Lingis[45]

* * *

Animals recently set free
have been growing more ferocious daily
pouncing on children and the sick
in alleys.
There are rumors, other news: they say
a great famine, plague, massacres . . .
When the dawn arrives
with its carts piled with ammunition
my neighbors bang their heads
against doors,
a sign of complete servility
or unbearable pain. —Sargon Boulus[46]

In the supposed West, one perceives violence as a historical vandalism—this cataclysmic influence is no deflection, no decoy, but rather scrawls the experience of "life itself." In this way, there can be no argumentation, objection, or bargaining (no lanterns can stave off this forthcoming), for a picture solidifies itself of a foregone conclusion of what is (grayness). This farsightedness becomes a voluminous indictment of the species (all are sinful), for which there remains neither a teleological summit nor even a theory of perpetual decline, just the mock elation of having recognized a recurring pathology of ignorance, boredom, and waste.

In the new East, violence is wrought only by those of elite ahistoricality, those of immemorial daring and the middle-exodus, who chisel against tradition (anti-dynasticism). These are the oncoming hordes, those of influx, insurrection, and ransack (ferocity), those of jaws, scalps, and leather (massacre), those who harbor, hover, and prowl (the beastly), and whose rural athleticism disputes the metropolis. They descend first as rumors, from wooded areas (the jungle), through city gates, not heathens, not crusaders, but different installations (the marauder, the bounty hunter), those without station, those who bring disappointment, famine, and pure malefaction.

In the West, violence resigns itself to a world-historical condition; in the East, violence does its work against the many at the hands of nameless droves (there are no customs).

XXIV. Revelation (The Cellar) vs. Artificiality (The Mountain)

She waits. A picture of terrible solitude reveals itself to her: a cellar with empty bottles—and all in white. In the midst of the bottles is her son's head, inclined to one side . . . He has hanged himself . . . She is unaware that she is suffering from hallucinations. In her present state, the most incredible, hitherto unseen things become reality, so that when these images appear to her in the night sky, they are really there.
—Unica Zurn[47]

* * *

The two great masters didn't then realize that the reason for this haziness was the blindness that had begun to descend upon them, nor did they realize it after both had gone completely blind, rather they attributed the haziness to having been duped by the Khan, and hence they died believing dreams were more beautiful than pictures. In the dead of night in the cold Treasury room, as I turned pages with frozen fingers and gazed upon the pictures in books that I'd dreamed of for forty years, I knew I was much happier than the artists in this pitiless story. —Orhan Pamuk[48]

In the supposed West, occultism is registered with a surprise-factor, full of panting, teardrops, and disconsolation; it lingers in unlit cellars amidst decapitated forms (dismay), leaving one aghast, partly awakened before parodic revelations. This acephalic sentience, forever puzzled and unpersuaded, can never move beyond headlessness.

In the new East, otherworldliness is a well-plotted half-ruse, mixing the ancient world of hieroglyphs, tablets, and astrological devices with the futural world of supernatural abilities, powders, and numerological manifestations. This astonishment takes place amidst artificial elevations, within the trickery of the mountain, fusing many things beneath its carnivalesque domes: performance (hypnotic spectacle), magnification (commotion), rotating showcases of bravery and acrobatic leadership (travelers, puppeteers, musician-spies), aggrandizement (the marvel), sparkling (the flash), panoramic entertainment (the circus), and potent opiates (the kindling).

In the West, there are no such festivals; in the East, all become magnetic accomplices.

XXV. Articles (Passion) vs. Ice (Vigilantism)

It was then that I developed a violent passion for objects, for inanimate things. By objects I don't mean all those useful articles. . .no, I fell in love only with raw matter, primary matter itself. I surrounded myself with the most heteroclite articles . . . I spent days turning them this way and that, touching them, smelling them. I rearranged them a thousand times a day. —Blaise Cendrars[49]

* * *

Reflection Machine: You have to have been juvenile to let yourself go like that, to write like that and at that cost: whenever you want to write down your thoughts you swerve out of control, you've got too much hate boiling over, too much fear when a little cold blood would do you well, too much accumulated resentment when you need to look at things coldly, with a head that is cold and clear as steel, cold as ice, when you need a will of steel . . . cold-bloodedness . . . cold-bloodedness above all else. —Réda Bensmaia[50]

In the supposed West, violence upholds its sado-masochistic errors: the first is the contemptuous epitome of reason (idealism), the one who serves maiming alone, as the premier axiom, and for whom each individual casualty is nothing more than a dispensable fraction, proving the hypothesis (formality), another variable in the mathematical equivalence of nature's serial mortification; the second calls every passerby to sweet discipleship (transcription), teaches the doctrine of transience, stinging, and aching, across many sessions of affectionate persecution (indulgence).

In the new East, violence is more convinced of its ways (it does not cower), for this is its manner of escalation: to become perilously shallow, to ridicule emotion (caustic) and take upon itself the frost-bound tone of eventuality. Hence one becomes a proponent of a certain chilling vigilantism: so far beyond the ethical, this rare other stoicism, this unapproachable dexterity (the standoff), where there is no accountability beyond one's own scathing fingers (the hit-man).

In the West, the aroused look to preserve (permanence); in the East, the iced look to dispatch (assassination).

XXVI. Abjection (Revolt) vs. Laceration (adventure)

There looms, within abjection, one of those violent, dark revolts of being, directed against a threat that seems to emanate from an exorbitant outside or inside, ejected beyond the scope of the possible, the tolerable, the thinkable. It lies there, quite close, but it cannot be assimilated. It beseeches, worries, and fascinates desire, which, nevertheless, does not let itself be seduced. —Julia Kristeva[51]

* * *

Decay is an artificializing process that is promulgated on the substratum of all modes of survival (beings). In other words, decay—unlike death—is not external to survival, for it perpetuates itself on the substratum of survival, in order to indefinitely postpone death and absolute disappearance. In decay, the being survives by blurring into other beings . . . In no way does decay wipe out or terminate; on the contrary it keeps alive. —Reza Negarestani[52]

In the supposed West, decadence sets itself along an uncrossable barrier (what cannot be lured), assuming all kinds of prevented skills (the obstruction), and thereby reinforces the requirements of proper taste (what cannot be absorbed). There is a density here (against suffusion), as abjection thwarts seduction . . .

In the new East, decay provides an invitation to enter, pierce, and encroach (it opens the crevice). There is only contravention (the doorway), for the living is a temporary façade, while the dying is the advent—it is no human affair, for they were made to be savored, and to nourish the others that come later (the parasitic, crouching ones). A novel makeup: that of cremation (flecks, grains, debris), dehydration (softness, wetness, aridity), laceration (fissures, tissue, marrow, hole-complexes), demolition (becoming-clay, the shipwrecked body), excavation (necrophilic adventurism), exhumation (teratology), vermiculation (crawling, defilement), and miasmic dispersion (dust, fog, mist).

In the West, some things remain too dismal for release; in the East, there are only disproportionate ratios of closeness.

XXVII. Hurt (The Madman) vs. Guilt (The Hooded)

He who hides his madman dies voiceless.
He who leaves a trace, leaves a wound.
He who has rejected his demons badgers us to death with his angels.
To understand, the intelligence must get itself dirty. Above all, before it even gets dirty, it has to get hurt. —Henri Michaux[53]

* * *

That earthquake which shook the house
one night turned everything upside down.
Flame-like it burned the sleeping world
and bloodied the ash gray of morning.
It is here where I see
the brow of old age in the mirror of the cup.
The pages of the book of my fate

I see in the full garbage can.
I see myself a millennium-old executioner
guilty of killing the days. —Nader Naderpour[54]

In the supposed West, there is a certain type of madman (throbbing): the populace's demonic envoy, the one who smears dirt upon the countenance, who plays the sacrificial victim, in order to elucidate the wound, hurt, and fragility of the rest (deconstitution).

In the new East, there is a certain type of executioner (slaying): the one of unofficial inversions, who levels guilt (thoroughness), feared most by all state appendages (no servant, no officer), the hooded one who nevertheless operates with flagrancy (the lever).

XXVIII. Extinction (Silence) vs. Cancellation (Counsel)

Is it possible, is that the possible thing at last, the extinction of this black nothing and its impossible shades, the end of the farce of making and the silencing of silence, it wonders, that voice which is silence, or it's me, there's no telling . . . —Samuel Beckett[55]

* * *

I and my brother against my cousin, I and my cousin against the stranger . . . —Bedouin Proverb[56]

In the supposed West, one seeks the just process of extinction (silent volition) . . .

In the new East, there is an expression that outclasses blood-lines, communal ties, and kinship rites; these are the lengths of more dire affiliations (vitiation-brotherhood). Cancellation is a preemptive strike against breath itself, wound through torrential intimacy (supra-tribalism), fiendish solidarity (the luminaries), mean camaraderie (the precursors), and abusing confederations (the counsel) . . .

In the West, one wonders when it will be over; in the East, one realizes it was over a long time ago (before this even started) . . .

Chapter 0

Zero-World Consciousness

ZERO-WORLD CONSCIOUSNESS
(desperation, idolatry, crowdedness)

COSMOLOGY
(the stranger, the foreigner, the opponent, the intruder, the visitor)

SIGHTLESSNESS
(solitude, suddenness, tightening, illumination)

THRESHOLD
(inevitability, adornment, insane pressure)

ENTANGLEMENT
(redness, rancor, contempt)

FACTIONALISM I
(vulnerability, extinguishing, malevolent inspiration)

FACTIONALISM II
(conspiracy, asylum, atmosphere)

FIRST IMMORTALITY
(subsidence, conscription, draining)

ENCHANTMENT
(the nightmare, the mirage, the reflection, the hallucination, the simulation,
the memory, the story, the vision, the fantasy, the dream)

One of the incomparable powers of new Middle Eastern literature rests in its ability to build zero-worlds.

The zero-world is a convoluted thought-scape, one that can be animated by a single concept and eliminated by another (all are vindictive). It is the extraordinary rite through which a fugitive consciousness trains itself to circumvent history, solidifies its own prism, and then disbands in the wake of the next invading figment. Any affect can steal the ruling logic for a while: speed, pain, noise, anger, smoothness (each can ransom the zero-world to their own calligraphies). They prove formidable while they stand, monumental and self-exalting; they can impose, coerce, and violate at will, guided by nothing more than a fleeting aphorism—one slender thematic axis enough to warrant the subordination of lives. These are aerial tyrannies . . . explosive, transient, and self-forgetting, erasing their own iconographies, betraying their own alignments, in the face of new ciphers. In this respect, they remain harsh, extravagant, raptorial, and entirely disloyal. They yield insatiate thirsts that can be derailed by the sheer announcement of another curiosity, occurrence, or stronghold.

We must become students of this volatility, and ask after the settings of the zero-world. What are its exact parameters, how does it coordinate its territoriality, and where is it in relation to the real (beneath, beyond, within)? Is it subterranean (an underground), exilic (an outside), or infinitesimal (a pocket)? Perhaps it is none of these sectors, but rather a kind of spatial-sensorial transmission, one that is passed along, between, and through oblique messages: whispers, murmurs, rustlings, insinuations, interludes, hints, and scraps of paper. It builds its camp in the diagonal exposures of the allusion, in folkloric layers of passion and treachery. In this sense, the zero-world is a sort of debris; it is a relic of the listener, delivered and misdelivered; it switches owners continually, inviting patterns of reproduction, embellishment, and diffusion.

And why do some gravitate toward this precinct? What ethos attracts the concentration of these select authors? Beyond the traditional outposts of literature and philosophy, one finds the long-neglected, un-theorized terrain of *desperation*—thus we turn to its mania, panic, and valor, so as to reformulate this experience as an elite stance (the advantaged). As will be discussed later, it is the ragged, vitriolic tenants of desperation alone, those most undersupplied and inconsolable, who have enough voracity for the risk entailed here. Such is the link between imagination and avarice.

Furthermore, the zero-world is neither a utopian promise nor a dystopian ideology—instead, it is a device of *idolatry*. As a result, one must remain wakeful when an author of this caliber introduces a new item to the forefront, for here the object is restored to a certain fanaticism (the false worship of ornamentation). And this, in turn, brings a shocking automaticity to the spectrum of action (to prostrate, flinch, cringe, flee, and convulse). Such is the link between imagination and an unforeseen devotion to the thing.

It is for this primary reason that the zero-world also strays from all asceticism; it is never the wasteland, but always an overture toward *crowdedness*—it drags in the clamor, the density, and the stirring of opposing squads. It induces its own overpopulation through incurable and abrasive contact. Such is the link between imagination and self-antagonizing collectivity.

Principle 0. Cosmology: Zero-World Consciousness Must Envisage Its Own Cosmology . . .

The function of a zero-world literature is to cradle a host of unwanted archetypes, to fashion a clear stage for the arrival of the stranger, the foreigner, the opponent, the intruder, and the visitor. Thus the seemingly vague premise of a zero-world is no abstraction: it is the dueling performativity of these new ranks, orders, gangs, and breeds, ascending and descending across one another with competing articulations of dread and desire. One must watch after the slight differentiation of movements here, so as to know with whom one deals at any given moment—the stranger: the one of half-resemblances, who appears, encounters, and defamiliarizes the matrix of the known; the foreigner: the one of misleading accents, who reaps, mal-adjusts, and pollutes the regime of meaning; the opponent: the one of sinister intentions, who glares, waits, and undermines the right to existence; the intruder: the one of fluid perimeters, who nears, slinks, and punctures the operation of everydayness; the visitor: the one of overused invitations, who indulges, stays, and abuses the ceremony in play. And more than this, each carries its own hold upon the realm of sensation: some seek obsession, where the sliver universalizes itself, and the mind is left to follow endlessly; some seek fascination, where originality shows its true potential, turning the unlike into a paralytic agent; some seek seduction, where one tips the sliding scales of closeness and distance, and all thoughts convene a formula of entrapment; some seek captivation, where one maintains the most direct stare, so as to construct a visual hostage; some seek infatuation, where one is shown the unruly price of the charmed, and the lure becomes its own transcendent coffin; and some seek addiction, where the ritual takes its time, cementing the body in a futile, downward spiral. None of these are harmless, but are made of well-crafted fault-lines across which reality disperses and the cosmology of the zero-world assembles its deed.

The authors under scrutiny must track a lethal procession, one that mistreats all literary subjectivities, erecting the future upon a triumvirate of destroyed persons: (1) the destruction of the one who first foresees, conceives, and aspires to the zero-world's inception; (2) the destruction of the one who then initiates the quest, who motions, explores, and discovers the gateway of the zero-world's frontier; (3) the destruction of the first citizen of the zero-world's domain, the one who would be native to its unreality. Several fall to give rise to one, one falls to give rise to several. Nothing less than this, these three valuable disembodiments, can sustain the intensity of its rising populace (nothing quiet).

Principle 1. Sightlessness: Zero-World Consciousness Must Become the Sightless . . .

The pitch black of sightlessness.
The feel of death-generating solitude.

—what time is it? (It crosses your mind.)
what day is it
what month is it
from what year of which century of which history of which planet?

A single cough suddenly
tightening by your side.

Ah, the feel of a release-giving light! —Ahmad Shamlu[1]

Solitude, suddenness, tightening, and illumination: what assortment of misfortunes is this? The first zero-world consciousness brings about a darkening of the creative flare, and always by unnatural means (this was not supposed to happen—there are veteran hands involved). This is not the older story of the abyss, the default of God or the destitution of humanity, this is not the age of midnight and its absolute groundlessness. No, this is the manufactured obscurity of a single becoming, one that is a product of hard labor and trance, the effort of devious inclinations (artificial eclipse). The poet builds this state of impossibility, each line an increment of withering vision, each verse a further step into a cellar air, beneath which the eyes become a lost cause. And so the zero-world is a site of intentional occlusion, its own industry of soft barricades, for which the literary apparatus is met always by the relentless weaving of blindfolds. One improvises a curtain, drapes it across the unsuspecting face, and walks away, leaving things to the triumph of useless sockets (to become oblivious).

What are the technical routes to this dead-end of sight, and how does this basement consolidate its thin walls (to draft the obstruction)? Does one stumble here, cower, grasp, kneel, or even supplicate? Is there any solace in the knowledge that this is only a replicated blindness, the intimation of a radical façade, or is the danger heightened in the wake of a concocted origin? No, it is the very inventedness of the zero-world that is the worst part.

Above all else, one must abandon the search for reasons and instead chase after the delicate effects of this counter-destiny of the writing-act. The question of "why?" is met with silence in the zero-world, but a focus upon "what happens?" succeeds in unlocking excessive answers. We are given this much at the onset, already a major sign—"the feel of a death-generating solitude"—from which one gathers that to read onward is to consent to the annihilation of the one who is most alone (the one who first believed this). Can one die from pure seclusion? What brand of mortality is triggered when one is forlorn, isolated, remote to all that stands? At what point does the lowness of this plane become unbearable?

The key to this initial phase of the zero-world, the extreme sightlessness for which nothing can be recognized, surveyed, or called out toward, is that it marks a self-imposed burden of the poetic imagination.

There is an inconspicuous trade at work here, a steady ratio of suffering and gain, for one can rest assured that someone profits from this situation. More precisely, the complete unraveling of identity in the following verse—"what time is it? (It crosses your mind). / what day is it / what month is it / from what year of which century of which history of which planet?"—leads one to the first critical checkpoint: that the author must perish in the guise of the last creature of reflection. It testifies to the enchantments of the zero-world only so as to banish the practice of testimony thereafter. For this intellectual restlessness, its habit of scrawling, engraving, and foreshadowing, is its own path to overdose/overkill (all idealism ends in blood). And so representation becomes shrouding, shrouding becomes separation, separation becomes uncertainty, and uncertainty becomes a confinement-unto-the-desolated. Stated again, the poetic figure veils itself, conceals its own view from a now-disintegrating spectrum of being, until a certain disorientation takes over, until its own name turns unnoticeable even to itself, and it walks along as the final incarnation of a damned fate. This is a punishing endeavor, no doubt: to be screened, shaded, and cloaked to the extent of asphyxiation—after all, we must remember that "a single cough tighten[s] by your side"—but the emergence of the zero-world hangs upon such hangings. The visor is wound firm across the brow, fixed in its great tension, withstanding long enough for the writer to project itself as the concluding emblem of a near-extinct race (that of the chroniclers). With this, the totality appears to unfold itself, coated in an ambiguous shine—"Ah, the feel of a release-giving light"—causing one to ask further: what radiation is in store, what dim-lit lanterns could be of any use beyond the demise of this rambling entity?

Principle 2. Threshold: Zero-World Consciousness Must Traverse the Threshold . . .

One must stand and descend
at the threshold of a door with no knocker
for if you happen to arrive on time, the doorkeeper is waiting for you and
if your knocking at the door is ill-timed, no response will come.

Low is the door,
behind which you are cast into humility.
The pure mirror had been polished

there
such that the adornment
before emerging
makes you perceive yourself.
However the dissonance at the door
is the offspring of your own desire
not the multitude of guests,
for there
no one is waiting for you
for there
is a movement perhaps,
but the door is immovable. —Ahmad Shamlu[2]

This second poetic figure, having disowned itself as the terminal component of the sightless, is then stationed at a transitional archway: that of the threshold. The injunction is unmistakable—that "one must stand and descend at the threshold of a door with no knocker"—for this is a portal with just two options: to turn back and deny the prospect of admission, or to persist in the realization that one can do no better than to straddle the edge in-between irrelevant spheres. This newcomer, this passenger of the defective journey, like the one before, is not the one to inherit the forthcoming zero-world: the first went blind in pursuit of the idea, the second will forfeit limbs by striking toward it. One is mistaken to assume that the one who finds the door is among the appointed, the chosen, the elect—rather, we learn that "there no one is waiting for you." This one is not ordained to excel, surpass, or even endure the cataclysmic swinging of this latch (less a door than a pincer), but to become its material intermediary. There is no alternative, no exception allowed: whether one arrives on time to greet the waiting doorkeeper (instantaneity), or delays and arrives later than expected (the untimely, the messianic), the implication is the same: that this is no window of chance, for this heavy structure requires a being to pry it open, a mass to stop it from sealing close. Its hinges are immobilized, though a torso is enough to match its insane pressure (to become the wedge, the strait, the conduit). Such is the ultimate "humility" described above: to "perceive oneself" as the "adornment" of this wayfare entrance, to compensate for the rusting crux, to face the all-surrendering frame of the "pure mirror" and hear the subtle cracking of one's own bones as the self-forsaking dissonance of a border.

The words are scarce here, caught amidst a showdown with inevitability. This threshold is its own intimidation; it anticipates, consumes, and leaves anonymous those who even make it this far. Yet this is not judgment, nor martyrdom, but rather the simple gravity of an unfathomable job: that someone must constitute the bridge, the crevice, and the toll through which later things slip through, that someone must sanction themselves as a chasm.

Principle 3. Entanglement: Zero-World Consciousness Must Create the Entangled . . .

In the fetus-filled entanglement with oneself
where your own garment denies you,
in the circle of black fear resembling the uterus
in the darkness from the coarseness of the redness of rancor or contempt.

—release yourself until emerging on the battlefield
even as the specter of the fetus' undiscovered form
Congratulations on your birth, O one of statistical fortune
O, offering of the diminishment of the dead newborn. —Ahmad Shamlu[3]

The color has changed: from the "pitch black of sightlessness" to the "redness of rancor or contempt"—and with it the zero-world marshals a new cartography. In the aftermath of the last genuine character, and the improbable crossing of the threshold, one now becomes entangled in another third self-defeating venture, another far-reaching doom and statement of collapse (many must crash here before anything can be salvaged). If the imperative of the first two sections was to execute the last beings of the real world, then the imperative of this next section will be to execute the first becoming of the zero-world (this is its passcode of strife, loss, and non-bereavement). Herein lies the significance of the "circle of black fear resembling the uterus," for at this instant the poetic voice must play out a different fatal role, no longer the one choking across solitary horizons but now inhabiting the "specter of the fetus' undiscovered form." This is no twisted episode of providence, for the influence is self-targeting and the destination obvious: the eventual "diminishment of the dead newborn." Once more, the foremost particle in the zero-world, its opening presence and earliest manifestation, must be thrown down.

Hence one wonders: what purpose fulfills itself in the wake of this so-called offering? There is no sacrificial boundary installed, no profane limitation, but rather a provision of constant entanglement, such that the innermost quarters are turned outward and into a labyrinthine expanse. The interior grows immense, the anatomical grows geographical, and the ontological grows architectural, as the poetic abdomen strings itself forward as a system of electric currents, halls that extend in incalculable numerologies, corridors that slither, curve, and intertwine. Textuality becomes a prolific trade of maneuvering, passage, and navigation, and consciousness itself nothing less than an ordeal of perpetual fusion and transfusion, combining incidents into channels. This is "the battlefield" of which is spoken above, its successive, reciprocal contests of flesh, organs, and ligature, the zone where all are caught, held, undone, and devoured by birds of prey. Hereafter thought occupies the look of the web, the lattice, and the net, and at their centers rests the one indispensable victim: the one of "statistical fortune," the one whose "own garment denies" them, the one whose tragic outcome was inscribed as a fact of cold necessity.

In retrospect, three casualties alone can forge the passport of the zero-world, all of whom are met with crucial wrath: the one who would first contemplate the land (the seer), the one who would first walk through the land (the traveler), and the one who would first be excavated from the land (the indigenous).

Principle 4. Factionalism 1: Zero-World Consciousness Must Inspire the Factions . . .

No phantoms and no apparitions and no camphorated saints in hand
No incendiary bull-headed demons in the grip
No accusation-covered devil with its horned, tasseled hat
No mixture of hostile lawless absolutes
Only you
There an absolute existence,
A mere existence,
that in the void of self-preservation you find your absence
is the decisive presence of the miracle
your passage from the threshold of the inevitable
is the dripping down of a drop of tar in infinite darkness. —Ahmad Shamlu[4]

These three tales of non-survival do not impoverish the zero-world, but quicken its opportunity (malevolent inspiration). Those who strive are condemned as vital expenditures: to invoke its design, to hound its location, and to settle as its offspring: all of these are tasks of peril, vulnerability, and extinguishing. Their persecutions are inescapable.

These lavish dimensions, though, pale in comparison to the next goal of the zero-world: namely, its epoch of factionalism. For what comes of the three frozen and desensitized levels depicted before this juncture? According to the authors under consideration here, they anchor everything, for they litter the soil as carrion, undeniable temptations to the oncoming deprived; they incite new configurations of hunger, they elicit the roaming, pacing, and hovering of new packs; they are the very justification of desire within the still-developing zero-world. These deteriorated sentinels now taunt and elevate, provoking the salivation of younger hordes; they overflow, beyond even their own depletion, and in the process pave the way for thousands. The ones of sightlessness, thresholds, and entanglement now form the rationale for inexorable proliferation.

And still, there is never enough to feed all sides, giving way to an evolving, distinct criterion of engagement: that of rivalry. One ransacks, another tramples. Here the poetic imagination cannot help but enlist the methods of sectarian violence, and with it all textuality becomes an example of friction, struggle, ambush, secrecy, riot, and combative discourse. Interpretation itself becomes a never-fading cause for attack, mercenary greed, and insurrection, as the divergent cells of the zero-world flaunt their own damaged philosophies. Conquest, raiding, and deviation: such are the chaotic tones of a factionalized universe.

Principle 5. Factionalism 2: Zero-World Consciousness Must Confront the Factions . . .

The zero-world is founded on dishonest routines. Here the project splices into another narrative, tracing the careful outlines of an ominous short-story: "Three Drops of Blood." Whereas the first poetic instinct unearthed itself across varied swamplands, prisons, deserts, mists, and precipices, this author positions his own rare zero-world in the room of an asylum. Such is the backdrop of an irrecoverable literary event.

What do we know (pretend to know) of the one who speaks to us (knowingly delusional) from the first page of this text? For one thing, that he includes some semblances of time: "It was only yesterday that they moved me to a separate room"; "Would I be fully recovered and be released next week?"; "It's been a year."[5] Nevertheless, these stratifications are disingenuous; they compose a near-invisible ruse, for almost immediately we are met by an anti-temporal force: the decree of "three drops of blood." This is a repetition-reflex like no other, untouchable by reason, for this one recurring image has seared itself into the epic circulation of his conspiracy; it shaves across nearly every account, returning us to the same foul degree; in this way, it houses imbalance, the accumulation of a centuries-old curse (what back-breaking eternity reveals itself here?).

Nor is this the only disturbance of time: another figure, who has taken on the status of the asylum's poet and prophet, and who believes that both poetics and prophecy are just matters of self-prompted luck, recites the same verse eight times a day:

What a pity that once more it is night.
From head to toe the world is dark.
For everyone it has become the time of peace.
Except me, whose sorrow and despair are increased.

There is no happiness in the nature of the world,
Except death there is no cure for my sorrow.
But at that corner under the pine tree
Three drops of blood have fallen free. —Sadeq Hedayat[6]

This dire incantation, said over and again, is neither accidental, nonsensical, nor arbitrary; it is neither an echo, a sign, nor a prayer; it is the self-sustaining, rallying drone of the factions, for whom sound, rhythm, and pulsation surpass the weight of comprehension.

From there, we can ascertain that the narrator is under siege, embedded in a nowhere-place filled with detrimental kinds (the lawless sanatorium). At first glance, they appear exotic, primal, bizarre, and unenlightened to him; they are ravenous and ill-tempered, though there is some glamor in their intolerability. Despite his own tiring dissociations, they spin an indefensible matrix; their outcries are infectious, as they contend for his consciousness:

> *It's been a year since I've been living with these weird and peculiar people. There is no common ground between us. I am as different from them as the earth is from the sky. But their moaning, silences, insults, crying and laughter will forever turn my sleep into nightmare.* —Sadeq Hedayat[7]

No doubt, they are legion, vindicating their unstable customs in every corner of this tentacular narrative, fitfully blessed by its author to crystallize at the right hour (always the wrong hour) as agile, ruthless challengers to the throne.

Thus our zero-world figure must negotiate seemingly contrasting interests, disjointed styles of breathing, for all are invited to participate in the misgivings of his consciousness (its wariness, derangement, and breakdown). The mind rotates between chronic orbits of fracture and emanation; it alternates, divides, and revenges (the tactic by which one becomes many, and then too many). But what makes this factionalism and not schizophrenia is the militancy that each possesses; for they do not convince, persuade, align, or barter with one another; instead, they only know one approach: that of war. They are ecstatic in their unrelenting conflict.

> *It was two months ago when they threw a lunatic into that prison at the end of the courtyard. With a broken piece of marble he cut out his own stomach, pulled out his intestines and played with them. They said he was a butcher—he was used to cutting stomachs. But that other one had pulled out his own eyes with his own nails. They tied his hands behind his back. He was screaming and the blood had dried on his eyes. I know that all of this is the supervisor's fault.* —Sadeq Hedayat[8]

Such are the visceral bands in residence, proving that this is no haven, refuge, or sanctuary but rather the warehouse for a post-apocalyptic madness. Consequently, this is beyond the grasp, scope, and versatility of psychoanalysis, for our patient runs circles around every pre-given, corroded diagnosis (instead, we are in the presence of one who fabricates indecipherable symptomatologies). His myriad disorders, complexes, phobias, pathologies, manias, anxieties, fetishisms, compulsions, sublimations, melancholias, and synesthetic relapses are all strategically handed out as symbolic deflections. They are the imperfect demarcations of a perfect front—none lead to the core; all trail helplessly into the vacant hinterlands of a masterful lunacy. Such is an elite ability of the zero-world author: to play ringleader to the factions (this is not to manage, govern, or control but rather to affirm by clearing space for their gamesmanship).

What other clues are given, that one might detect an entrenched consistency? His hatred for the warden is unparalleled, though the specific procedures of his administration are left omitted (power does not tread the same here). For he is less an overseer than a participant, less a superior than an impostor specialist who bottles the delirium of his recruits and turns it toward a zero-world expertise:

> *He is so crazy that he puts the rest of us to shame. With that big nose and those small eyes, like a drug addict, he always walks at the bottom of the garden under the pine tree. Sometimes he bends over and looks under the tree. Anyone who sees him would think what a poor, harmless man to have been caught with all these lunatics. But I know him. I know that there, under the tree, three drops of blood have fallen onto the ground.* —Sadeq Hedayat[9]

This much is transparent, then: that the warden is complicit with the inner workings of this legend, that he assists the many blocs of this dwelling by raising their flag, wearing their robes, and perpetuating their one most severe impression: the three drops of blood. He is an interchangeable element of their confederation—more than implicated, he is enslaved to their anarchic dialogue.

Nor is the business of literature an innocent gesture throughout: instead, it evokes a minimalist cruelty. At first, the writing-act is forbidden—"All this time, no matter how much I pleaded with them to give me pen and paper they never did."[10] But, even when his request is granted, an aesthetic agitation takes hold—"I've been trying hard to write something since yesterday but there is nothing to write about. It is as if someone is holding down my hand or as if my arm has become numb."[11] Notwithstanding, this same domination of the writing-act then converts itself into an all-encasing fright: "When they first brought me here I was obsessively watching my food, fearing that they might poison me . . . At night I would leap awake frightened, imagining that they had come to kill me."[12] This is no standard paranoia, for these sinister notions soon reverse their directionality—no longer aimed at his consciousness, he stretches them outward and against the surrounding zero-world, transported into identical, aggressive impulses: "If I were in his place, one night I would put poison into everyone's supper and give them it to eat."[13] To this end, the zero-world author establishes a profound cyclical relation between its own textual imaginary and an impending existential action, transposing a crew of menacing sugges-tions once wrought against itself into parallel injunctions now wrought against everything else. The map is therefore flagrant: that the swarms, teams, and mobs of the asylum motivated the urgent desire for writing, and that this writ-ing then unfastened its own terror, at first coalesced against its own creative source but then sent reeling into the clouded atmosphere beyond.

Principle 6. First Immortality: Zero-World Consciousness Must Attain Immortality . . .

And there are others still. In another of these contorted short-stories, "Dead End," one finds a man resigned to a futile life in the provinces, awaiting his last days with the most stoic postures. He appears self-discarded, and claims no kinship with the townspeople, anaesthetized to their hollow values: "He was indifferent to everything and, because of this, had fallen behind his col-leagues, a bunch of coarse, clever thieves . . . Even the town, with its parched red earth and ruined buildings seemed to have acquired a sinister, threaten-ing quality."[14] Yet this is no regular immunity, for the protagonist is bound into a tainted intercourse: that long ago he observed a friend's drowning—"The waters rolled over him and the waves slid together"[15]—though it proved only the first round of this spectacle.

There is a literary-existential paradox at stake here, bending across the narrative: that the zero-world figure must secure its own immortalization by extending a plot of infinite subsidence. More clearly, he must submerge another, must ready the scene for a second drowning, leading him to pur-chase a house with a large pool (though he never learned to swim) and thereby swearing an insidious pact with the death-lust of the waters. He is not a witness, but an accomplice; he is not traumatized, but conscripted, as the thread of an adolescent event is laced forward into his old age, encapsulating his subjectiv-ity in a fatalistic ring.

On some day like all the others, a double reaches the town, the supposed only son of the deceased, and heir to the same catastrophic lot, such that his disembarkation throws everything back in order: "Now the double of his friend was seated before him . . . 'Could this be a proof of eternal life?' he thought. 'Perhaps what people call "eternal life" has been derived from this same sort of happening?'"[16] There is no torment over what must happen, only obliga-tion (the clock counts down). Thereafter the young man becomes an appren-tice to the elder friend of his father, an impermanent surface-collaboration of the worst proportions (to orchestrate nothingness). They share a common allegiance to the drama, an increasingly inseparable mindset split between them, a bond achieved over the lifeless torso of yet another drowned compan-ion. Hence the young man is found floating face-down in the pool, a skilled departure through which one is drained, evicted, and resuscitated. And what befalls the old man, who had once feigned a passive charge while in fact commissioned with assassination? He is outcast, becoming more nebulous than before, and vanishes within a storm:

> *The rain had spun a web about him. He was drenched, enclosed in its delicate strands. The raindrops, like slimy creatures, grasped the threads of the web as they fell. He passed like a vagrant shadow through wet deserted streets beneath the rain and disappeared.* —Sadeq Hedayat[17]

This shadow-condition, withdrawing beneath the shower, is what surmounts the ancient dichotomies of life and death, being and non-being, replacing it with the unsettled profile of the undying (textual mummification). This is the more awful face of transformation: impersonal, callous, interminable.

Principle 7. Enchantment: Zero-World Consciousness Must Wield the Illusory . . .

The protocol shifts here, as the zero-world figure begins to evaluate the distinctive facets of a consciousness prone to illusion—that is, to be at once wholly susceptible to the unreal, flung beneath its immeasurable ceilings, and also able to conduct them against others who wander toward this level. The rungs of this ladder are ever-widening, including among them: the nightmare, the mirage, the reflection, the hallucination, the simulation, the memory, the story, the vision, the fantasy, and the dream. Some impersonate the real, others subvert, and still others blockade. Once again, this literary imagination rehearses these many unprotected scaffolds, fluctuating across a commanding range of immersions, inclusions, and absorptions.

Nightmare ("The Whirlpool"). In this story, he depicts the suicide of a man's closest friend, who then meditates upon the source of the former's despair, and finally arriving at the likelihood that he had fathered the child who he had always considered his own daughter (this guilt becomes horrid). The protagonist pounds this one accusation into his mind as an unremitting nightmare (the qualities of which are stalking, terror, and suddenness), until relinquishing his grip on actuality: "These thoughts flashed like lightning before his eyes. His head started to ache and his cheeks flushed. He threw a glance full of hate and fury . . ."[18] His dead counterpart is then costumed as a traitor, and he forsakes his family as a stained, excruciating reminder of the world's duplicity. But the nightmare is amplified further, as a suicide note discloses his now late friend's truth—that there was no transgression—though the daughter has since died from illness, allowing no reconciliation, only decadence and prolonged frenzy. What was most intimate now turns clandestine, and previous alliances become states of nemesis, steering him into a morbid haze: "Then like a madman he turned up his overcoat collar and walked off towards the garage with long high strides. He no longer needed to close his cases. He could go with this evening's coach. The sooner the better."[19] The nightmare leaves the imprint of its malicious eschatologies; he is iced over and staggers off.

Mirage ("The Mirage"). This story treats the artistic troubles of a violinist in search of a valid listener, but who meets only inaccurate recipients. This trivializes his musical productions, and so afterwards he scours for the most banal pleasures to quell his failings (drinking, affairs, nomadic adorations). This is a drastic rift for which each night he falls from his stylistic grace into the back-alleys of base materiality, his talents now distorted and ravaged: "As soon as he closed his violin in its case, he turned into a miserable creature and fell from his demigod's pedestal into the vortex of powerlessness and torment!"[20] His metamorphoses are intermittent, a schism through which he remains half-human, half-conjecture, and therefore recalling these factors: that the mirage springs only from the most tangible, essential need; and that it remains an alchemical trick, able to turn euphoria into instant disappointment.

Reflection ("The Doll Behind the Curtain"). This story provides an investigation of misshapen natures, revolving around a foreign student's slow mesmerization at the hands of a statue. He becomes reclusive, defiant toward social, political, and cultural conventions—in this way, he decodes himself, wipes away his debts, and decides to live as an absurd scholar of the mannequin's features: its stillness, its calming, its muteness, and agelessness. His apartment becomes a shut chamber, though eventually he returns to his homeland, only to bring the object of his fixation with him, into the old world where an arranged marriage awaits him. Upon noticing his carelessness toward all things save one, this intended woman then decides to imitate the doll, only to cross the young man in a state of crazed determination to shatter it once and for all. He caresses her, not perceiving the disguise, and the subterfuge ensues as follows: "Was this real? How could it be? Did he really sense the warmth? He was sure he had. Wasn't this a nightmare? Was he that drunk? He wiped his eyes with his sleeve and threw himself back on the sofa trying to collect his scattering thoughts . . . He put his hand in the pocket of his pants, took out the revolver, and fired three successive shots at the statue."[21] A warning is given here: that in reality's attempt to ventriloquate the unreal, the former is met with a bullet, for the reflection is truly an instrument of merciless reversal, a pretending that drifts, de-certifies, and overturns; she had wanted to become the sculpture, the model, the figurine, and finally the substitute, and instead found herself the effigy.

Hallucination ("The Fire-Worshipper"). Next in the stratum is this story, whereupon a famous archaeologist recounts his travels to the Zoroastrian ruins of the Persian Empire, and therein confesses a paranormal event. According to his version, the night he spent in the ancient fire temple gave rise to a mystical transference like no other—followers of the millennia-old faith appear, ignite flames, pray, and retreat, leaving the Westerner to an occult occasion. The miniature carvings on the imperial walls begin to flicker, dance, and spill from their intricate stoneworks:

> *It was as if the surroundings, the souls of all the dead, and the power of their thought, which was aloft over the crypt and the broken stones, had forced or inspired me, because things were no longer in my hands. I, who had no belief in anything, fell involuntarily to my knees before these ashes from which the blue smoke rose, and worshipped them.* —Sadeq Hedayat[22]

It is an exhilaration, and yet the outcome is irretrievable; nothing remains of the blue smoke, nothing rescued from the enterprise (we know only its martial tracelessness). And so the zero-world author provides insight into the hallucination's mystique: that it ruthlessly cancels its own session, that it coagulates and melts away before an orthodoxy thickens, and that its sublimity, awe, and microscopic victory lies in the fact that it is gone before language makes its claims (leaving no recourse but the flashback).

Simulation ("Dash Akol"). The simulation is not to be underestimated (it is its own serpentine). This story concerns a medieval leader/gangster, one whose thug mannerisms shelter the city from other criminal groups; he is a stalwart presence, charismatic, fierce, admired, and benevolent in the eyes of the people, though this warlord has his tortures too. The cause of his plague is less important here than the disastrous way that it alters him; soon his vigilance atrophies, the once-impenetrable creed of nobility drops casually, he sheathes his weapons and submits to constant intoxication (always among goblets and chalices). From there, he commences a certain monotonous exercise, inviting disgrace, and speaking each night the same jagged words to his parrot before caving into sleep:

> *Worst of all, every evening he looked at his face in the mirror, at the bubbled knife-scars at the corner of his half-closed eyes. At times like these, he would rasp . . . Tears would collect in his eyes, and he would drink glass upon glass of vodka, then with aching head fall asleep where he sat.* —Sadeq Hedayat[23]

This is no incidental night-reverie, for the once-charismatic fighter has turned his drunkenness into an iron simulation; the tavern, the wine-bowl, and the vodka-glass aid in the theater of his mimicries; they scandalize him, for sure, but they also beguile and seize upon the inaccessible (it is a summoning at work). These displays, however sullen, are marked by exceeding precision, such that he repeats the utterance even on the last page, when a cutthroat neighboring villain stabs him in the back with a dagger. What this reveals, then, is that the simulation (against all appearances) is supported by an almost mechanical alertness, but one geared toward the irrational—more than this, it is an application of the unreasonable into existence (closer to sorcery).

Story ("The Benedictions"). From a professional swordsman's estate to a Tower of Silence, the purgatorial region where corpses are deposited on their voyage to the afterlife. It is in this piece that the zero-world migrates to a grotesque field of skulls, jaw-lines, teeth, and splintered ribs—it is a poor, scathing vicinity, saturated with cadaverous half-beings, and there are hauntings throughout the graveyard: "But if one looked carefully into the sanctuary, one could discern a number of white, lifelike shadows sitting on the stairs, or moving and shimmering all about the tower."[24] These are the unaccomplished ones, pseudo-souls of non-belonging, clasped neither by heaven nor hell, and therefore left to trek the scorched middle-country. It is here, though, that they become guardians of the next illusory mode, for the only time-killing occupation available to them is that of permanent storytelling (they hold their own tournaments). They squat in the grayness, among the vultures, spinning outlandish editions of their former lives alongside equally fictive predictions of the next life, as both nostalgia and divination fall apart (into the guessed-at). Rather, the story here is a mark of what has become forever archaic, not immemorial but hideously antiquated, such that all that remains is a bottomless reservoir of hearsay, rumor, and self-deception.

Memory ("The Stray Dog"). And yet even memory is useful here, for this story illustrates another complicated disposition. A lost animal, disconnected from its owner for years, patrols the congested streets, where there is no compassion, no pity, only the sadistic tendencies of the marketplace. Thus the recollection serves as a narrow exit-point from the real, a slit of exodus, though all reminiscences are found disfigured, mercurial, and indefinite: "He prowled about in the alleys helpless and perplexed. Of his past life only a handful of hazy, vague memories and some scents remained. And whenever things were particularly hard for him, he would find a measure of consolation and escape in this lost heaven of his."[25] In this regard, the memory constitutes a self-removal; it allows an elaborate, amorphous relocation of consciousness; and more than this, it is in fact a machinic stimulus. The stray dog becomes a runner, fueled by razor-sharp memories, though culminating as always in downfall:

> *He had gathered all his strength, and his despair forced him to run as fast as he could . . . He had made a mistake . . . His eyes looked glazed over with sickness . . . A cold sweat covered his body. It was a mild, intoxicating coolness. Near dusk three hungry crows flew over [his] head. They had smelled him from afar . . . The three crows had come to tear out his hazel eyes.* —Sadeq Hedayat[26]

These references to a missing, half-amnesic past then contrive and push forward an irrevocable wheel. What one notices is that the sprinting dog and the scavenging crows become a kind of contraption, a proficient, sophisticated equipment, one that slackens, defaces, and manipulates the incarcerating truth of where they are (to the point of their mutual combustion).

Vision ("The Broken Mirror"). In this story, one is tied into a voyeuristic revolution whereby a young man and woman glimpse one another across the facing rooms of adjacent buildings. Thus the vision allows them to trespass beyond their strict self-containments, until the exchange becomes unquenchable: "In this way a mysterious relationship had developed between us. If I didn't see her for one day, it was as if I had lost something. Some days I would look at her so long that she would get up and close her window."[27] This amusement is transitory, though, for soon they dare to take their intrigue into the real, attending a festival together—it is amidst this carnivalesque environment that they misunderstand one another and separate, leading to the bleak omen of a broken mirror (i.e., a severed vision) and three weeks of a standoff across the partitioned windows. The young man vacations elsewhere for a while, only to receive a grim apologetic missive from the girl, who also expresses a feint wish for drowning (upon his return, her room is vacant). What this exhibits, ultimately, is that the vision must be derived of idleness and distraction alone; when it accelerates into the known, when it is handled rather than beheld, when it becomes a record of nearness rather than of vastness, then it is stripped of its most luxurious contour: its bewilderment.

Fantasy ("Laleh"). The next in the illusory sequence, as this story takes the reader across the uncharted wilderness of a hermit who finds himself hypnotized by a young runaway gypsy girl, brings her into his hovel, and plays caretaker. They spend four years together among the cliffs, until the tranquillity is halted by an erotic strain: "On he walked, uphill, downhill, along the side of a valley, through mountains and over plains. He saw no one and was aware of nothing. He did not even notice his fatigue . . . He thought of nothing but [her]."[28] The one who once cradled her is now afflicted, spell-bound; she is no longer safe, unshielded before his longing, and so the guest takes to the valleys again (becoming-untamed). The hermit grows impatient, his mind riveted to this adoptive fantasy, and goes after her: "Everyone he saw on the way looked like demons and dragons to him. The blue and gray mountains half-covered with snow seemed to threaten him. The smell of mint at the side of the stream nearly suffocated him."[29] He visits a fortune-teller, who clarifies that she now belongs to another, one of her own tribe, and has therefore become unobtainable; the man is never seen again, subsumed into the forest—its moisture, heat, and unrest. What is most telling here, though, is the way in which the fantasy exerts an almost meteorological pressure; it floods the senses, turning perception into a jailhouse, and broadcasts the flaws, uproar, and turmoil of nature and man (it is a weather, a climate, and a guarantor of turbulence).

Dream ("Davud the Hunchback"). This is an unwavering axiom: that the dream is not metaphorical. This proposal is self-evident in "Davud the Hunchback," whereby a physically crippled man crouches, sways, and hopes ceaselessly for some attention. One twilight, he thinks he has found a solution to his hardship, a young woman sitting beside a ditch who had once scorned him and now seems open to his companionship: "He planted his stick on the edge of the conduit and crossed to the other side. Without thinking, he walked over the stones and sat down beside the road. Suddenly, he became aware that a veiled woman was sitting nearby. His heartbeat quickened."[30] This is the affective charge of the dream, though soon she mocks him, wresting him back into lameness, ridicule, and humiliation; this is the vile choreography of the dream, one that organizes indecency, abjection, and insincerity. Above all else, as the hunchback scurries away, and in his flight sees a rejected animal lying upon the cobblestones, then placing his head gently against its chest, as a last island of comfort, only to find it dead beneath him, the dream teaches us this: that its main elixir/objective is to sweep all redemptions aside. It does not heal his deformity; it accentuates it and impairs him further (subjugation, wreckage). For everyone emerges from the dream unsaved.

We have partaken of many zero-world constellations thus far, and diagrammed a taxonomy of those most well-suited for its brutality, freedoms, and wild lotteries (half-agony, half-diversion): we have seen the dampened road of one for whom thought becomes an entry-point into the pitch black of evaporated eyes, one stranded at the threshold of an immovable door, one assigned to the devastation of a newborn, we have seen the factions of the miracle and of the three drops of blood, we have seen the immortality of a man turned toward the badlands of his own hysteria, and then ultimately held court with an audience of defectors, gangsters, hermits, gypsies, orphans, archaeologists, fire-worshippers, hunchbacks, starving musicians, stray beasts, and purgatorial spirits. They are all misleading, cannibalizing one another across arid circumstances; they are all injurious and unfavorable, and they must all be dynamically upheld.

1

Threat: Writings of Betrayal

O. Betrayal
(the override)

I.
Machination
(the bracing) (of the stare)

II.
Force
(closeness)

III.
Translucence
(warning) (trained-to-suffering)
(confrontation) (imminence)

IV.
The Accursed
(the irrevocable) (the irreversible)
(the inescapable)

V.
Unrest
(riot)

VI.
Requiem
(infinite finality)

VII.
Sentencing
(the panel)

The Summoned
(provocation)

Plague
(collision) (disgrace)

Execution
(of the stance)

Inquisition
(the turn) (the trial) (the punished)

VIII.
Burial
(of the stones)

IX.
Wrong
(imprint) (the outcast)

X.
Desecration
(the wrested)

XI.
Incarceration
(the underground)

XII.
The Inconsumable
(alchemy) (of the acids)

The writers of Eastern violence show no hesitation in threatening their readers nor the world they knowingly/unknowingly represent, whether by subliminal plays of language or by outright statements of intimidation (the recipients must find their teeth chattering). They itemize the things that shall be run down, daunted, and overawed. And so, to continue here, one has to trust this counterintuitive fact: that, in these regions, like anywhere else, there are tyrants, secret police, mercenaries, assassins, criminals, revolutionaries, martyrs, and fanatics, but none are as frightening creatures as the poets. And they are adored for their violent streaks; the more they threaten reality, the more they are beloved (to resect the paragon).

The literary movements that have perfected this genre of the threat are comprised of those who burn their words before they see light, who summon to the mind what should never have been, that from which all descend undelivered. It asks for nothing. Whatever it does not have, it will take. There is a drift amidst the lacerations of the chest, where rage pours its alcohol into a crossroads between addiction and the desolate. This has arisen before, this temperament of the threat, and with it the authors of damaged veins, who know of acids and of chambers, who wait beneath the walls, for the resurrection of black cloth, whose every thought invokes the nails of a scaffold, those who warn, of the inconsumable, of that which wracks the air and the arms, in service of a stolen infinity. The threat refers to a precise textual becoming, then, on behalf of those who keep watch, who stand guard before the pyres of world, as cruelty and as chain, who train in the ways of outer thirsts, between ecstasy and ruin, fatality and eclipse, those who raid, while in desertion and forgetting, whose outcry is a testament, that all can be turned against itself, whose scream is an imprisoning and whose will is a burial.

Betrayal
(the override)

I was the totality of the dead:
The corpses of singing birds now muted,
The corpses of the most stunning beasts
of land or of water,
and the corpses of humans
noble or evil. —Ahmad Shamlu[1]

. . . betrayal: to conceive of that which is exposed and preyed upon (the banquet), for it must be drawn toward endangerment, this world, and stalked across all dimensions . . . slowly, though inevitable . . . somehow forced to answer for itself, to look upon itself with scared admiration and face its vulnerability (squalor). It must see what can be taken, it must feel that it is hunted, that it is menaced by a foreign presence, something it cannot control, something it cannot own, something that will not bow before anything (it is its own idol). This is where language falls into stillness, into its devastated silence, as a new violence begins its iconography, and something from the outside, something formless, speaks of its own rise to power. The threat is therefore always a writing of betrayal, the commentary upon an existence forsaken, left alone and vanishing, within its universal defenselessness, where the living cannot guard their permanence any longer, and thus allow themselves to be integrated, preventing no aberration, no attribute, to swarm and consume, to drive them toward the cimmerian (negligence). The threat becomes an inquest, it turns within, it stirs in lost steps, it cloaks desire, it decorates everything in smoke and figment (the wraith). Every thought, every movement, must withstand the possibility of being ransomed (nothing is innocent here). And so it circumscribes the amateurs, unraveling its rhythm across the lower back, until terror and exhilaration are one and the same (the armament) . . . it accelerates, through self-made tubes, and the muscles tense before what they know must take place. For the threat will fulfill itself: it keeps its word, at all costs.

To threaten is to commence at the point of inhale, the deep intake of breath, leaving one with two insecure roads of assumption:

1) that something coarse will take place here, such that it signifies an awaiting severity, a conservation of force before the sadness . . .
2) that something has already happened, a trouble once-determined and inscribed, such that it represents a recovery, a disenchanted after-point, the admonition of a now irretrievable past . . .

What is to occur and what has already occurred are now equalized, bound by a disc of certainty, as foreseeability dethrones the appointment, and where a world dies, before its time, before the designated end of time itself, for to threaten is to request extinction in advance, to make things crumble in their preludes. And always petitioned by the dis-contemporaneous one, the one retracted of hours, for to dissolve time is to make everything that persists within time dissolve as well, all that relies and counts upon the preservation of chronology now simultaneously made tasteless (anti-salute).

. . . the override: to conceive of that which is an override, that which observes its own straightening principle above all else, for to threaten is never to defer or delay to another instant, but rather to initiate the process of defeating time by sealing the action in eternity, in torturous longevity, the idea now loading itself in everpresent vials, intruding as an everlasting nuance, installing itself as a reverberating geometry, a virile composite and constellation of the overhanging incident. The threat is that which makes time wretched, subordinated to the map of a dispersed taunting.

*Within the above quotation, one finds the writer who threatens by lodging the totality of the dead inside himself, hurling species together without taxonomy, becoming an embodied treasury of the long-since-gone, and without concern for the gallery within.

(*the drift; black cloth; the intake*)

Machination
(the bracing)(of the stare)

He draws the unseen side of the day, kindles daylight in his footsteps, borrows the shoes of night, and waits for what never comes. He is the physics of things. He knows them and gives them names he never reveals. He is reality and its opposite, life and its other.
—Adonis[2]

. . . machination: to conceive of the machination, that which is valor, though there is no valor left here. The threat enters as a post-heroic phenomenon, where nothing is chosen, and there is no bravery to be shown, where neither the carrier nor the casualty are asked anything, neither for acquiescence nor resistance, since there is only the event that occurs between slender worlds. The instrument, the process, and the mood that follows: these take the forefront. It builds from beyond the realm of decision, as that which imposes, showers upon the world no less than upon the one who brings it toward the world, where all sides are woven together by the inspired persuasion, the elimination of distance, all the while feeling distant (it touches everything, and cares for nothing). Such is the evocation of this war-becoming, of the rally-cry beyond, a critical threat across existence, across being, across the real, across man (whatever has taken propagandized shape).

And still, dimensions must be traversed, some movements started, as the literature of the threat is undertaken, each its own corridor of the broken: a configuration forges itself, as an arsenal of incantations. Nothing survives this writing of death-sentences, its criminal ecstasy and infliction, its will turned fire, the lone consciousness of the world-assassin, wagering with the requiem and the evening of obscurities, the lashings of what must be finalized, across the tightropes of the damned, from within maimed intimations of the end, the solace of the sands, an arcane sojourn beyond the nothing, this ravaged company of thought, assisted through serrated meridians, thresholds of incineration, the vengeance of the south winds , until all is possessed.

*Within the above quotation, one finds the writer who threatens by penetrating the more secluded depths of the world of things, only then to turn them inside-out, a vertical knowledge becoming a horizontal flipping/alighting, willing something other than life.

> *When stone becomes a lake and shadow a city, he comes alive, alive and eludes despair . . . Here he is announcing the lines of peripheries, etching a sign of magic on the brow of our age.* —Adonis[3]

. . . the bracing: to conceive of tightness, what is strangled and narrowed, and the clenching of the musculature, to conceive of that which makes the world give into itself and cave inward, imposing tension (of the insurmountable), for bracing marks only the delusion of safety, as if one could subsist through the impact, as if the containment could enable one to endure the onslaught. And yet this defies the rule of violence itself: it is in fact this withdrawal, this recession, this taking back of expenditure, that leaves one more open to the oncoming count. To press against it only serves to provide the threat with a greater plane on which to impose its damage. One moves into abrasion, not away from it (the lesson of conquest). Fatality is undone by fatality alone—that which would seek to armor itself does no more than to convert itself into an offering. It is this cringing motion that unlocks the radical possibility of the threat, even though it appears to dampen it; it is to compel it into an involuntary surrender, for that which retreats only turns itself back into the wind, into the heart, into disaster. It readies its frame for the fall of disquiet, its reflexive anchoring itself an enunciation and a calling toward the vicious (it makes way for pain). The delusion of flight is since forfeit, for that which runs is that which has already given itself over to being caught (the hostage). The shoulders bow in acquiescence, and the sudden ceasing of breath, a migration of interior strength, silently confesses that its essence no longer belongs to it, that it now pleads with another, the muted admission that it has since relinquished its own holdings (the wealth is gone). For this well-induced bracing reveals the process by which a statement becomes an embedded mannerism, an ingrained posture, a single notion stretched across the ligaments, etched into the contracting spine, its rigidity, its regulatory stiffness, where even the tendons begin to know.

*Within the above quotation, one finds the writer who threatens by supernatural properties, available to him only when things are somehow made other than what they say and mean, signaling his right to become animated and pen his conjurations across the margins of this time.

He fills life and no one sees him. He shapes life into foam and dives. He turns tomorrow into prey and chases desperately after it. His words are chiseled on the compass of loss, loss, loss.

Bewilderment is his country, though he is studded with eyes.

He terrorizes and rejuvenates. —Adonis[4]

. . . of the stare: to conceive of that which stares down existence, what pierces the hollowed eyes of world only to fill with dread (to survey the everything). A reality that maneuvers in concealment, that blankets itself from all sides, cannot endure the thought of being looked upon, leered at for too long, across the supposed depths. And so the threat goes right there, beyond the valances, matching the diffused gaze of power on every axis, across every terrain once hidden, now robbing invisibility (inspections of the curtain). This stare excavates a hole in the other, it crafts a lapse into the façade of Being, that leaves one disrobed, inflexible, and now servile. Its density brings the other's astonishment: thereafter one becomes a pervaded site, crippled by a remote look, one that is no accident but an unavowed calculation; thereafter one is compromised by the fear and pressure of being watched, caught in a mapped physiognomy.

This gulf, this emptied pit, allows the stare to insert an alarming counter-revelation, that which leaves the mind disheveled and entered throughout; it rakes a channel, a mine that gradually drains the other, making it spill itself forward in disconcerted pacings, such that it evolves as the other degenerates, drawn into a vampiric maturation. The stare appears expressionless, though this is no void, no blank feeling, but rather the steady culmination of all affects, the accumulated figure of impulses (disdain, remorse, panic), the complex aggregate that reflects a summit (impassive glarings). Everything is there, every response and conceivable attunement, as identity is displaced by a post-sacrificial conviction, to blend the mutual achings, to entwine sensations of hardship, to feel everything as it groans, clings, and loosens its grip.

*Within the above quotation, one finds the writer who threatens by filling, shaping, diving, chasing, and chiseling, racking up the many losses as he at once perplexes, startles, and resuscitates the life into which he pours himself, swims through, and hunts down.

(*valor; the corridor; the embedded; the lapse; hardship*)

Force
(closeness)

Three o'clock. Daybreak riding on fire. A nightmare coming from the sea. Roosters made of metal. Smoke. Metal preparing a feast for metal the master, and a dawn that flares up in all the senses before it breaks. A roaring that chases me out of bed and throws me into this narrow hallway. —Mahmoud Darwish[5]

. . . force: to conceive of that which pursues only the law of force, the criterion that discards all others, for this alone commands, through its necessity (both exclusive and inclusive), the errant continuity with which it drives itself forward and across, where understanding itself is an enforcement. There is no extension of rights here, there is no sovereignty of beings, no fantasies of autonomy or agency allowed (anti-halcyon), just the determination that sets and bends all to itself, neither as intervention nor rupture (it is an enveloping).

. . . closeness: to conceive of that which nears, which draws ever closer still, that invariably motions towards, closing the rift between itself and existence, that which breathes upon the back, that which hovers and looms, the evocation of an infinite approach (where the middle-ground wanes). This proximity in turn alienates the world to itself, the more it overtakes, the more it decentralizes the customary, and this gradual crossing is tortuous, how it progresses—such that, by the time it takes place, there is almost nothing left to destroy, for the threat itself is nearly enough on its own to disassemble the world.

Seven relationalities of closeness, each directive a torrid enunciation of presence, assigned to this rising greed:

> . . . the threat of being above someone (acumen, the witness)
> . . . the threat of being underneath someone (dispiriting, the gaining floor)
> . . . the threat of being aside someone (mimicry, the parallel)
> . . . the threat of being behind someone (scrutiny, the surprise)
> . . . the threat of being before someone (pre-emption, the antecedent)
> . . . the threat of being outside someone (exoticism, the undiscerned)
> . . . the threat of being inside someone (carrying, the fixture)

*Within the above quotation, one finds the writer who threatens by announcing hyper-sensorial nightmares of smoke and metal, on their way across unknown oceans, and expecting a banquet in their honor wherein they can consume themselves.

(*hovering; evocation*)

Translucence
(warning)
(trained-to-suffering)(confrontation)(imminence)

The flowers of hopelessness wilt, and sorrow rusts. An army of pulverized faces crosses history. An army, like thread, submits and surrenders, an army like the shadows. I gallop in the voice of the victims, alone on the brink of death, like a grave walking in a sphere of light. —Adonis[6]

. . . translucence: to conceive of that which is most wrong, aberrant, and dissuaded, always from the external, and yet engaged in pure day. The threat is itself unthinkable clarity, without the deterrence of metaphor, symbolism, or meaning (to inject meaningless light), this well-lit decree, an unavailing disclosure, that does what it says, in states of irradiation. And still, this does not imply that it is known or even knowable (the silhouette)—that it happens, and that it happens in sheer translucence, does not make it prone to the mind, but rather an illumination without enlightenment, incomprehensible transparency, one that leaves all else as a meek yellow image, one that passes through things so as to show the vanity within. If it reveals, it is only because there is nothing that can be done anyway.

. . . warning: to conceive of that which warns, which extends a premonition, if only to cast beneath the tyranny of the emergent, for to threaten in such ways is to open a temporal stammer wherein the suffering compounds. It allows the task to stay behind awhile, so that, upon its unlikely visitation, it can extract the full currency of the miserable (already claimed, though not yet there). This is how it deploys the imminent, a system of volume where one is made to sense the expectant presence before which one soon kneels. There is no barricade between the intention to strike and the sound of the condemned, the warning that is already the end (stitched together), a piece of counsel turned ripening chant, and worn across the truncated mind. It was done long before this (so it cautions). Here, anticipation becomes torment, a realm left bare for weeping (one laments before one is gone), and its training for the drought (where nothing else can flourish), the poverty of experience, and the creation of an invalid frontier.

*Within the above quotation, one finds the writer who threatens through depictions of shadow-armies (their cause unclear) that leave their mark of foul histories upon the face, and who himself rides on horseback, dashing to set alight the victims' story.

(*irradiation* [*meaningless light*]; *the image*; *the passage through things*; *premonition*; *drought*; *volume*; *weeping*)

The Accursed
(the irrevocable)(the irreversible)(the inescapable)

The corpses of death, laugh together with overlapping limbs
They think that they are alive
The bones glisten everywhere piled upon one another amidst the teeth
Rib upon rib taken in advance
Hollowed eyes, an overturned bowl in the place of empty sockets

Some broken walls
The corpses of death laugh, as they are truly alert. —Nima Yushij[7]

. . . the accursed: to conceive of that which is orphaned, and therefore untaken, since one cannot save life here, where the once-virtuous are made to grovel, where mercy falters and thought scratches at the deathbed of guilt. Nothing is faultless; there is only defect. Old wickedness is met with new wickedness.

. . . the irrevocable, the irreversible, the inescapable: to conceive of that which nests across three levels, and brands the mark of one undone upon the world, stained by the tactics of these altered states:

> . . . the irrevocable—that which cannot be taken off, cannot be shed, that which hounds and remains, which continues onward into a continent of anathema

> . . . the irreversible—that which cannot be taken back, cannot be unburdened, that which makes the return to "what was before" impossible, which robs of the past life

> . . . the inescapable—that which must occur, that for which there is no outgoing path, no redemption allowed (beyond chance).

These three interlacing conditions, this downcast trinity, lock in the matrix of the accursed, granting it a potential for retroactive punishment (assaulted before the sin).

*Within the above quotation, one finds the writer who threatens by leading us into mass graves, where expired bodies commingle too freely, draping arms and sternums across one another, and all of them missing parts (handed over to incompletion), and yet finding their own secret route to consciousness by believing themselves still a part of the life that has discarded them.

(*groveling*; *wickedness*; *assault*)

Unrest
(riot)

Bats on my neighbor's balcony
Bats: some kind of apparatus
Concealed in the walls
Bats just about to kill themselves —Samih al-Qasim[8]

. . . unrest: to conceive of that which is subsumed in tremor, the tremor that bears panic, the panic that bears frenzy, the frenzy that bears itself to the outer checkpoint of fatigue, where weariness overcomes resistance, and this weariness itself, its cowering and its submission, is nothing more than a testament to the victory of unrest.

. . . riot: to conceive of that which, at its kinetic limit, becomes stillness, shaken to the point of immobility, where the unsettled itself becomes a death-masking, where agitation steadies and ices across the form, sculpted into confinement, too violent even for movement. It is a question of duration, this riotousness, having been too long with something, and now ill-disposed, whereupon its strangeness, its base oddity, becomes increasingly apparent, such that the concussive moment is no surprise, not abrupt but so drawn-out, and the threat takes on even the appearance of drunkenness (that which staggers), attracted to lavish speech.

*Within the above quotation, one finds the writer who threatens by allowing multitudes to become machinic configurations (swarms of bats turning into an apparatus), though they maintain themselves in hiding, and forever poised to lay waste to their own assembly.

(*duration*; *drunkenness*)

Requiem
(infinite finality)

When the martyrs go to sleep, I wake to protect them from professional mourners. I say: Have a good morning at home, a home of clouds and trees, a mirage of water. I congratulate them on their safety from injury, and the generosity of the slaughterhouse. I take time so they can take me from time. Are we all martyrs? —Mahmoud Darwish[9]

. . . requiem: to conceive of that which stops at an improper second, and several times, as an unnatural, infinite finality rent across the ground, and the mal-occasioned end, forced to expire either too late or too early: the first prolongs the limit beyond all reason, the second shortens the world before it asks to fall. And always with this last declaration: that we do not die anymore (they die). The requiem that is song, oration, and smoothness, where nothing is upheld, and nothing uplifted, that directs consciousness down the vertical shaft of its own irreconcilability, escorting it beyond the dishonest (where there is no solidarity).

*Within the above quotation, one finds the writer who threatens by forming a covert bond between poetry and martyrdom, against the human mourning-spectacle that parades memory in a grandiose show of grief, and yet who exploits their slaughter as an opportunity to steal moments for composition.

(*song*; *oration*; *the dishonest*)

Sentencing
(the panel)

Drained of all feeling, I moved mechanically . . . I bowed silently to the Committee and headed for the door. I grasped its handle with my right hand and was delighted when it opened easily . . . I knew I would not enjoy a moment's peace, sleeping or waking, until the Committee had issued its final decision in my case. —Sun'allah Ibrahim[10]

. . . sentencing: to conceive of that which sentences existence, calls to the finding, so as to seize control of a future from the vantage of the present, to instantiate the next paces, the next age, the next metamorphic soil, to reach across temporal blockades and insert an absent time into a distinct outline. No right to vindication extended—here the sentencing occurs before the inquisition.

What does this silence ask for, and why is there blood in the wind?
Here is written the secret to the end of all things . . .

The sentencing treats consciousness-as-threatened, experience-as-threatened, desire-as-threatened, all ranks concentrated and influenced by the serious-ness of the one decision, where the voice invades, tearing across borders with aggression, toward the admonishing and bombardment of world (blood-for-blood). There is an unspoken thrill to this charade: the delirium of cataclysms, the fevered interplay of catastrophes, enraptured circles of travesty and sor-row, moving from within occlusion, carving into and across all that rises and remains, a brutality that tests the instincts, an adversarial pose that recom-mences at every turn, to galvanize its chaotic manifestations against all penal-ties, against all machineries of the desolate. No despair in this, no suffering, and no mercy, just an agonic lust from both sides (where soul falls to oblivion). Such is the conflict taken to the extreme of its inconstancy, a masochism of non-essences: that it wants its pangs, commanding cycles of limitless contact, of shackling and retaliation, a mutual conspiracy of the heights, each transpir-ing and receding, ever tempting the opposition to falter. It steals across as a new thirst, eclipsing space in a haze of wounds, elevating the intensity of the challenge, fueling the excitement of this clash, toward the seduction of lethal speeds. Beyond exhaustion.

We have always known what must happen here.

And thus the threat is an exaltation, the traitorous incline, at once an honor-able statement and siren, with no complaint or afterwards in sight. Our visions against its walls, our madness against its reality-cages, now overrun with the intoxicated serenity of dueling quadrants, a mercenary game of prisons and elusion, the endless dance of slit-throats.

And the brothers take what is theirs . . .

What bad shores are discovered, when thought is waged beyond the continuum of what is, as an indefinite threat, arisen from a single grouping of words, an arch-hatred grazed into consciousness itself, inscribed in the ice of being? Once an impasse, now an uncivil method that strays into devouring, amidst currents of invincibility, with scar-drowned eyes, it casts itself across the ropes, to scathe and speak onward, to bleed and draw blood in turn.

. . . the panel: to conceive of the panel, the monitoring, the supervision and supremacy through which it gestates, the chilling sense of completeness, that which convenes and yet offers no shelter, no protective aura, only indomitable halos of nudity, where resentment lingers, before the tribunal, slates without visage . . . and the committee, its rich, cryptic linkage, its innumerable conniving, an unseemly consensus that appears nonsensical to the victim . . . and the room, the thickness and tightening of space, the gradual constriction of the walls, the lessening expanse . . . and the faces, their unfamiliarity, detachment, and hideous dispassion, one that stresses reason and sends the imagination reeling into paranoia, its stark naked militancy . . . and the voice, its complicity, banality, and confidentiality, its austere shielding, ever shifting from one member to another, its incorporation and support . . . and the unity, that it partakes of a collective unbeauty, the tediousness, the labor, the inglorious nature it shares.

*Within the above quotation, one finds the writer who threatens by citing closet-like institutions that leave their candidate pacing through tapered hallways, subordinated by the gloom, melancholy, and nervousness of waiting too long.

(*interplay; vision; supremacy*)

The Summoned
(provocation)

Here
the wake-up call of a rustling
in a thorn bush
will be a compliment to your intelligence
and death,
stinging and fleeing
the eternal companion of your loneliness
abiding in the ferocious spite-poison of snakes. —Esmail Khoi[11]

. . . the summoned: to conceive of that which marks a summoning, that which calls out from the recesses, for it is to know the name of the selected one, though this does nothing but to bring into ruin the one that confers and interprets it (one speaks the name of that which will not hold it for much longer). To threaten like this is to singularize, to draw outward the one, above all others, that will soon decline below all others (the listener is humbled); it is to cast into isolation a lone form, to break it from the crowds, from the other layers, and to make it stand beneath the poor weather of an affair in which it has no part, no voice, no future, except as altar. It is to make suppression impossible (becoming-undeniable), for here the summoned must extend its presence, not because it moves forward when its time draws near but because the world around it draws backward, separates itself from it, now entirely abandoned before the casualty at hand, the offering to a damaged fate. The ramparts and shrouds that once fortified recede from view, leaving one without aid and destitute, in imposed reclusion, and forced to watch the seepage of once loyal worlds.

. . . provocation: to conceive of that which marks a provocation, to stand outstripped, without functional arms, removed from the main caravans and taunted with the obviousness of newfound solitude, its alienation a testament to the lie of what was before, taken beneath the existential forgery of origins and authenticity and the indebtedness of its derivation, until it genuflects, as the threat learns of its audience, and breathes into this weak edifice of identity its own ill intent, a clandestine deal of concession to the other side. With full wisdom of the atrocity, that it has been sold and mis-focused, severed from the past and from the anchors of its metaphysics, no longer worthwhile, the summoned is thus provoked to act on its own behalf, for the sake of that which no longer owns anything, basks in nothing, can store nothing, can abide nothing, not even itself.

And still, something must happen here, whether as a becoming or a bereavement, for this literary action has bathed the name in lifelessness, announcing its defamed status in patient invocations.

*Within the above quotation, one finds the writer who threatens by bidding one into the drudgery of sentience, forcing one into camaraderie with snake-pits (stinging entities).

(*the name*; t*he descent*; *the deal*; *atrocity*)

Plague
(collision)(disgrace)

A dust particle collects its components from different milieus so distant from one another that they can operate for each other only as outsiders. When dust is utilized in creation to compose and concoct, it turns the object, or to be precise, the created composition into

*a fierce operative of horror, with a progressively thickening ominous plot or storyline
. . . The release of these multiplicities disguised as one . . . might be apprehended as an
insider takeover, the rise of a new people.* —Reza Negarestani[12]

. . . plague: to conceive of that which is a plague (the intrepid challenge), for
a knife is laid before this one, told to move either toward transfiguration or
fatality, a rebellion against the old compendium or a swaying toward detriment. Alteration or self-destruction: the first requires a gutting, an extraction
of the lines of delusion that once sustained belief, and a navigation elsewhere;
the second requires a surrender, a revocation of the gasping, now consigned
to pure dissolution. Here one can give out, or one can become an auxiliary
(recruitment).

. . . collision: to conceive of that which brings into collision with itself, and with
the destiny of the disagreement. For what could the receiver speak back to the
threat (and how it smites), what insolence or artifice would not seem garbled,
disgruntled, and rueful, inadvertently lulling into the apoplectic or into thrift?

. . . disgrace: to conceive of that which leaves in disgrace, discredits all it handles, and rams discreetly through the gauntlet, where consciousness must scan
the states of ongoing contempt and the growing displeasure.
*Within the above quotation, one finds the writer who threatens through
civil wars of dust, who convenes an operational theater of powders and grime.

(*the knife; contempt*)

Execution
(of the stance)

*My friend asked me, while the fog was dense over the bridge: Can a thing be known by
its opposite? By dawn, I answered, things will clear up. He said: But there's no time
more dubious than the dawn, just let your imagination flow with the river: It's in the
blue of dawn, in a prison courtyard or near a shrubbery of pine, that a young man
optimist with triumph is executed.* —Mahmoud Darwish[13]

. . . execution: to conceive of that which forbids neutrality, the demeanor that
bans indifference and draws the line across, that occupies and then scores
this necessity upon all it touches. The desert has been internally divided, and
thereafter everything is called to take sides, with an evocation that violates
even the infinitesimal, each particular cluster asked to verify an alignment—to
rest with or against, relegated to either one mythology or the other, for no
breath eludes the obligation of this world-vivisection. All objects and artifacts,
all experiences and events, all images and words, even the nothing itself, are

brought to the front lines of this contest, this charting of allegiances; the walls, the elements, the empire of things, the silences and the metals, the air, deities, and the beasts: all must proclaim themselves before this aspect of the threat. Nothing is irrelevant, nothing left outside the margins of this tournament: it is the supreme exorcism of a position, and they must decide, amidst the bearing of daggered looks, or forfeit the right to both existence and the inexistent.

This is why the execution is also a side-avenue to immanence, for it establishes itself upon the immediacy of a life-and-death relation, a mortal bond through which consciousness can attain the most dangerous proximity; it confiscates and submits the surrounding world, it tests and drives under, it conveys once-antagonistic entities into its fund and hangs its own survival on the destiny of that item, it fights and purges for it without question, as a reflex to endorse its own potential, taking affirmation to its farthest stake, to the extinguishment of self and other if the vow demands it. And then again, if found slinking away in duplicity, there is the swearing of a provisional enemy and the subsequent locking of arms—clawing, gagging, and clenching round—though there is no true difference in either fate, since alliance and disapproval are both sources of entanglement, leaving only the resurrection of the struggle, brought down upon the trachea and wired through perception. All sites are a battleground, all time an execution-hour.

. . . of the stance: to conceive of that which makes possible only two stances (that mask thousands more within), as the once impenetrable veil between the inside and outside now subsides, the territorialism of before now cast away, and an all-encompassing rattle steps forward. The first stance, that of the human, provides the detachment that sustains reality's baselessness; it evades and subverts the execution, it snakes the in-between, fabricating whatever pretexts and concocting yet another enslaving anti-reckless finality from which the disadvantage of its own recurring oaths come: this is the banishment of its own illusion, trading the inheritance of phantom-presence for some concept of authentic being (it cannot accept itself as shadow), ever caught amidst the terror of impending disappearance and thus turning its back in flight. There is another, though, the one of the second stance, that of the authorial figure that threatens, still pervaded of non-actual tales, fables, and parables, that carefully maintains its ties to the emptiness of states, attentive to the plots, mantles, and elaborate layers of untruth; it mirrors the obliterated, the disincarnated, and the foregone, it carries the abyss upon its back (as cipher), circulating the obscene realization, it holds the scales, it talks of the price, the perishing, and the disbelieving. It is fearless (in its counter-tangibility), an immortal substance that cannot recede, close, or give way, it seeks no future for itself or the other, no salvation, no absolute (guided by what lays waste), it incurs demise, attuned to ashen domains that stream and surface amidst the downfall (though undefeated), it turns materiality against mankind, and turns all sayings into a tone of implicit harm.

The misery it elicits is the anthem of the unreal.

*Within the above quotation, one finds the writer who threatens by inverting temporalities, lending the dawn a pallid quality of opposition, dispelling the calm of its azure colors through allusions to a slain idealist.

(*the position*; *tone*; *the anthem*)

Inquisition
(the turn)(the trial)(the punished)

The Prince's head was bowed, resting on his shuddering hands. His forehead was cold . . . The stairs were damp and they had no end . . . Down all those steps he went, down and down all those steps that led to those dank passages and that icy vault and the sheet and the blood and the staring eyes that both were and were not. —Hushang Golshiri[14]

. . . inquisition: to conceive of that which reels against the world in serial interrogations, so as to render existence unjustified, without chance of amnesty (the unacquitted), dedicated only to the rampant wearing-down of the excuse. This is to ordain an inquisition, proving and disproving a certain endurance (to be convicted of everything), that which impales, harrows, and drenches the will in an experience of surveillance (without remission), and which designates the body as the sphere of detection, audition, and assessment (to hold court within), itself an experimental limitlessness of decimating proportions, though the outcome has already been over-determined, seated in unsaid provinces. This inquisition transforms space into a lair of masquerading judgment, with nothing guarded save the affliction itself, its unsteadied interface, its unfixed rounds of massacre (circular futility). Its pulsation leaves all devoid (the pure unforgiven).

. . . the turn: they must not fathom the charge, for the offense was committed by those they do not know (the unacquainted). They would not appreciate the face of their accusers, nor the rationale of the accusation itself (something was done, but against a phantasmatic deviant group).

. . . the trial: they must not outlast the examination (excessive checking), nor the indeterminacy of waiting (slow harshness), the barrier of questions, unanswerable because they emanate from somewhere roundabout (imperceptibility, tentativeness).

. . . the punished: they must not feel the extraction (of the sample); they must not know what was taken and stripped (hypnotic retaliation). They can only know the verdict, not the recourse (this is grueling), just the miniature clue that something crucial was given to the leaders of the prosecution.

*Within the above quotation, one finds the writer who threatens by taking deposed princes into the cellars of being and non-being, forced to find their footing in the dampness, and to walk across evermore dropping planks.

(*detection; the outcome; the unforgiven; tentativeness*)

Burial
(of the stones)

In a glass room
In a museum that squats
in a lost city that crouches
in a deserted land
I live, elevated, confronting the eyes of men,
and paralyzing them. —Mahmoud al-Buraikan[15]

... burial: to conceive of that which accomplishes the grand technique of taking-beneath and into burial, to hunt the last untouched, where there is no turning of keys and there are only low roads left: a subterranean happening in textuality, unrelenting before the fall of writing (the threat eats discourse alive). This is meant to devise the book-as-enclosure, to lure its reader into constraint, into the narrow, where thought creases over and upon itself, mal-formed toward corrugation, until all structures of meaning become sepulchres, and this interment, this firmness of the page-turned-vault, where one digs a mass grave for language, is nothing less than the unearthing of a significatory crypt.

. . . of the stones: to conceive of their extravagance (the ornate stratum), astounding tiers of quantity and matter, for the stones generate a tale beyond even haunting, beyond the power of the undead (legendary eventuality).
*Within the above quotation, one finds the writer who threatens through ancient statues, now seemingly harmless and held behind glass casings, yet still capable of arresting the gaze of onlookers.

(*the untouched; the stratum; legend*)

Desecration
(the wrested)

The hook snagged in my astral jaw
The horns growing behind my ears
My bleeding wounds which never heal

My blood that turns to water dissolves embalms
The children I choke to satisfy their whims
All this makes me Your Lord and God. —Joyce Mansour[16]

. . . desecration: to conceive of that which surpasses impurity, in teachings outdoing the profane, for desecration breeds its own subjects, those who then enact this same process (on barred hereditary terms). Here the rivulet precedes the self, amidst elliptical ties of perpetration: treachery breeds the treacherous, vengeance breeds the vengeful, the curse breeds the accursed, as the occasion defines the agent of the next task, the one who rustles it outward, charged with the identical action for which one was first targeted (and now, to commit once more).

. . . the wrested: to conceive of that which signs the indelicate, the unkind, and the graceless, that which obstructs the refuge, and thus the right to sanctuary . . . to close its doors, to weaken its symbolic structure, to house the threat within (already stationed inside, by the time of arrival), and so to disrespect the supplicant (the refusal).

  *Within the above quotation, one finds the writer who threatens with images of stifled children, and a god-complex through which she becomes a horned, hooked, and embalming form.

(*treachery*; *the occasion*; *disrespect*)

Incarceration
(the underground)

In the cold flurry of moments
your silent barbaric eyes
erect a wall around me.
I flee from you through uncharted roads. —Forugh Farrokhzad[17]

. . . incarceration: to conceive of the realms of sensation now brought toward bondage, as the threat becomes a typhoid, a garb, and a hive, one that leaves subjectivity open to lateral breaches, a tremendous habitat of bestowing and foreclosure, and that inserts its heterodox calling so as to make the other most indignant, worried, and incarcerated within its tenor.

. . . the underground: to conceive of the encapsulation of mind, that now stirs (in desperation), as the idea devolves, bruises, and raps against disinclination.

  *Within the above quotation, one finds the writer who threatens by an escape below, rushing from the embrace of primal looks and thereby graphing unrevealed highways.

(*bondage*; *foreclosure*; *encapsulation*)

Wrong
(imprint)(the outcast)

A hammer was once tested on my body
I was tied with ropes,
dragged along, stretched out on my face,
behind a pair of mules.
Once I guarded a wall
Another time I stood at the gate of a palace
Marched in file in one of the armies,
Was abandoned in the desert,
spread out, to be washed by the gales,
for the hot sandstorms to dry out
my deepest chambers. —Mahmoud al-Buraikan[18]

. . . wrong: to conceive of those with cut hands, who have left their upright tarnish upon the footholds, those of the encasement, of the marring of rock and boundary (what commerce is this?).

. . . imprint: to conceive of the trivial resemblance (misleading similarity), and the never-ending ways in which the messenger subverts the message:

  . . . to leave it unsaid, forever withheld (the undelivered);
  . . . to give it to another, and thus taken astray (the unintended);
  . . . to tell the contents, depriving its privacy (the non-exclusive);
  . . . to alter the meaning, whether by embellishing, omitting, or redesigning the original (the mistranslated);
  . . . to divide it into segments, disbanding the parts (the unwhole).

. . . the outcast: to conceive of the one for whom the village is traded away for continuation, having reached the point where to tread onward one must sell oneself into perpetual misgiving (distrust). The outcast alone can will the dialectic toward reversal, to make polarities unsure, reluctant to dance, wringing the order of things against itself—to trip, rust, and capsize (the upturn)—for the indecency of this skill, the rough inversion of worlds, arises only from the condition of exterior disturbance, from the unharnessed object, brought from the outskirts where each consciousness instructs itself in what is most nefarious, watchful, ascetic, and in the archaic tongue of the unusual and the overseas.

  *Within the above quotation, one finds the writer who threatens by recollections of transitory status, whereby an emblem of worship is quickly thrown into degradation, swept beneath the sands.

(*encasement; the message; the overseas*)

The Inconsumable
(alchemy)(of the acids)

And his ghosts said: his surroundings devour him
his pickaxe uproots him
his hands tear him up
From his ruins walls rose and his palaces stood tall
His shadow split itself in two and both claim to love him
One adores his corpse
the other prefers a silence that resembles it
and his corpse spread as an ether
from which heads and thighs dangle tables
and beds . . .
And his ghosts said: misery, melt him and drip him as the rain of time. —Adonis[19]

. . . the inconsumable: to conceive of the rotation (too fast, too solid), to spin the spectacle onto itself, where it can no longer moderate its own ways (farness), until the cables unfasten of their own accord, eroded beyond recognition . . . self in excess, other in excess, time in excess, space in excess, reality in excess, god and man in excess, language in excess, law in excess . . . agitated and overstrained toward entropy.

. . . alchemy: to conceive of that which cannot be taken in, adjoining its inventions to the unwilling throat (toxicity), and thereby contrives and sells the venomous outsider agent: 1) to visualize that which spreads, proliferates, and disperses itself across things; 2) to practice in the transmutation of substances, making the elements disobey themselves (time of the serum-mixers); 3) to prepare that which the lungs cannot contain, words of the miscreant, of the straits, and of the noise.
. . . of the acids: to conceive of the undisclosed monstrosity, where thought occurs in swarms, the open and the scourge, frequently searching after what is blemished, awakened, contagious in idea, expression, and dream, and which enters always at the eleventh hour (untimely doom).
*Within the above quotation, one finds the writer who threatens through ghostliness, overturned by intimates who now command his trickling into pain.

(*farness; strain; the miscreant; the eleventh hour*)

2

Annihilation: Writings of Cruelty

... Nothingness (of the trembling) ...

TRAJECTORIES OF THE LETHAL
... Corrosion (the decayed), Breaking (the racked),
Disintegration (the faded), Detonation (the erupted),
Corruption (the poisoned) ...

BURNING
... Blindness (the furnace of mind), Transmission (dimension, degree),
Disquiet (speed, dread), Fever (exorcism), Incineration (bareness),
Heat (ignition), Immolation (of the pyres), Arson (obsession),
Ashes (the aftermath) ...

THE UNBEARABLE
... Extremity (the unbound), Torture (the insatiate),
Scream (terminal sound, the oracle, of the throat),
The Scavenger (carrion, the lower race, of the ruins, the outlasted) ...

THE INHUMAN
... Cruelty (the echo), Exile (the unsworn), Instinct (entrenchment) ...
... Prophecy (the ominous, the amorphous), Prey (the following),
Cloaking (stillness), The Unnamed (the rant, of the smoke) ...

This seemingly new strand of Middle Eastern thought has long since developed a taste for the above concept, for annihilation scours across the texts of both the region's literary ancestry and its successors, toward the outmost breaking-point, as a lengthened convulsion at the edge, aligning fever and disintegration in varied schemes of collapse. It eclipses Being in manic strides, at once a reckoning, mutilation, and overcoming . . . for that which can train itself to fall can later train itself to kill.

One must contemplate a strategic terminality: vigilance before the question of the end, of how it occasions itself, the environment and means of humility, and the maximum excision . . .

To handle it as a pale, unnoticed insinuation . . . unrecorded, dimmed . . . the sound, the utterance, the image, the secret, the rhythm, that harbors the still amputation of worlds. To draft the requiem to perfection (as a funeral-march unheard).

Annihilation as concurrent expressions of death, the pathways collected, the spectrum of finality converged: painful death and of the painless, violent death and tranquil death, death while screaming and death in silence, the slow death and the fast death, death by murder and death by suicide, calculated death and death by accident, natural death and unnatural death, martyrological death and death in vain, death in sleep and hyper-conscious death, ecstatic death and tormented death, resolved death and alienated death, defiant death and surrendered death, death by blade and by poison, death by street, field, and by contagion, death in solitude and death surrounded, death by desire, death in terror, and death in rage. This chapter must comb through all such teratical vocabularies, so as to find the stellar within, to sit alongside the boatman in search of coruscation.

Nothingness
(of the trembling)

Once again I emerged into the dreadful night. Once again I sat clinging to the frigid post, listening furtively for the sound of that huge, metal life buoy . . . Here, surrounded on all sides by death's gloom, I might be shot and bleed to death without anyone so much as reaching out to lift me off the ground. I opened the iron gate out of the garden, removing the chain that was wrapped around the lock. The mournful, cold sound of the metal conjured visions in my mind of prisoners on a sinking ship having the shackles removed from their legs. —Ghada Samman[1]

     . . . where all is poverty, and this an archaeology of pain . . .

Dual manifestations of nothingness: the abandoned and the uninhabited, though gradually only the second definition remains, such that all "has never been" (the ditch) . . .

Nothingness as unquestionable/indisputable (non-compromise);
Nothingness as inexplicable (mystery);

Nothingness as heightened perception, making sensorial experience more acute (accentuation);

Nothingness as atmospheric (its density is sensed rather than witnessed directly);

Nothingness as soulless, a relinquishment that trains one to undertake deprivation (to live amidst and as the destitute, and to contend with solitude);

Nothingness as impenetrable mood and illegible haze (dispensing feeling to the unaccustomed);

Nothingness as concentration (thought under pressure, intuition without interiority);

Nothingness as palpitation (that it twitches and generates) . . .

Here one also cultivates a taste for isolated immensities, one learns to transmit void as force, to make the nothing a tactic and implement of war—and so it is the case, to turn a gap into a platform of insubordination . . . for there will be something left unsaid, an excised component that then makes impossible the complete assimilation of this work, such that this omission then becomes the most dominant concern of all, its being-without trampling all else . . . and this exclusion, this elided word, provides an incarnation of trouble—such is the malevolence of the ellipsis, which tells that there is more still, though forever ungiven . . .

. . . of the dire, though never counted, and the first turmoil . . .

Annihilation intensifies terminality beyond comprehension: a man dies, though no one knows the hour, and no one speaks his name. This is its violation and its apotheosis: to nail the earth to sky, and bury God alive; to nail the sky to earth, and bury Man alive. This is its entitlement, won by right, won through steel, to become the lone conjurer of becoming (explosivity) . . . that nothing exists outside these words, though these words smother existence . . . that nothing can be unless executed here, though Being itself undergoes the execution. Rogue performativities in operation throughout.

*In the first description above, the author annihilates herself through overalertness, anticipation, and worsening metaphorical bridges, her back frozen against a pole, pondering a supposed bloodbath in the streets, her thoughts drifting toward the possible snipers looming across rooftops.

Trajectories of the Lethal

And here, where lines are halted, the idea is upheld only insofar as it is lethal, not its truth or untruth, its morality or immorality, but only its ability to pave away, the extent of damage that it commands: there is no other standard, only that of mortal potential. To think only that which might rid the most (inconsolability).

. . . corrosion (the decayed) . . . motion downward
. . . breaking (the racked) . . . motion outward

. . . disintegration (the faded) . . . motion inward
. . . detonation (the erupted) . . . motion upward
. . . corruption (the poisoned) . . . motion outward to inward to outward
. . . these disparate trajectories, distinctive in orientation (how they navigate),
in what they leave behind (what traipses afterwards), and in what they act
upon (the items they clutch, and into which they cut) . . .

Corrosion
(the decayed)

The smell of mold had long penetrated me
In manner civilized and with no personality
Of those with nothing left to say
The walls sweated, humidity rotted the stone. —Metin Celal[2]

. . . the waste encircling (toward depravity) . . .
. . . the insidious contact (becoming-tinged) . . .
. . . corrosion as the proof of borrowed time . . .

*In the second description above, the author annihilates himself through
growing moss, becoming the thicket, a gradual surrender to the quiet violence
of greenness, spoiling, and putrefaction.

Breaking
(the racked)

The night there is pitch black . . . and roses are fewer.
The road will fork even more than before. The valley will split open
and the slope will collapse on us. The wound opens wide. Relatives flee.
Victims kill each other to erase their victims' sight and find relief.
We'll know more than we knew before. One abyss will lead to another. —Mahmoud
Darwish[3]

. . . of that which fails to hold . . .
. . . through methods of dismemberment, to have limbs taken,
appendages stripped, one by one . . .

*In the third description above, the author annihilates himself through split-
ting lanes, valleys, and wounds, creating such giant schisms that even the innocent turn against one another (neutrals contra neutrals), flinging the throngs
from one crossroads to the next.

Disintegration
(the faded)

The city is giving birth to my cerebral death, I feel my head airing out its atoms of the great state, I feel my head airing out its atoms of literary opium, and I expose my bare skull to the healing rain, I expose the skin of my wounded soul to the raindrops of oblivion, every passing hour. —Réda Bensmaia[4]

. . . the absorption of the unsaved . . .
. . . that which avoids its substance, as thought slips into immateriality . . .
. . . that which turns decomposition into an aerial transgression
(fluidity), the frailty of its tide . . .

*In the fourth description above, the author annihilates himself by ripping back mental layers, baring the mind before unfamiliar atmospheres (to start from the head, conflating particle-death with healing).

Detonation
(the erupted)

Follow the cries of my blood and come up one hundred and twelve steps. You'll find the door open, and me on the other side, on fire with anticipation and ready for death standing with you, standing in you till we sit down when a rocket pulls us apart. —Mahmoud Darwish[5]

. . . to worship what splinters (the obelisk, the pillars, the parapets),
for there is such vibrancy in the shortness of its blasts . . .
. . . the violence that slides into notorious attrition (that which is
heard and epitomized, more allusion than obtainable) . . .

*In the fifth description above, the author annihilates himself atop an extended staircase, braced like an outmanned warrior for some oncoming technological mayhem (raining missiles from the skies), and speaking all the while to another who he instructs to join him upon the steps.

Corruption
(the poisoned)

The evil impression which it left has, to a degree that surpasses human understanding, poisoned my life for all time to come. I said "poisoned"; I should have said that I have ever since borne, and will bear forever, the brand-mark of that cautery. —Sadeq Hedayat[6]

. . . from skull to skull, only the pollution remains . . .
. . . One cannot cancel the unclean, its faithless plea and unpardoned patience:
and these, though decapitated, not petrified, these non-desiderata . . .
. . . that which is tainted (discoloration, smearing) and
therefore unacknowledged . . .
. . . Corruption as the recoil, the meticulous process by which
something once loved/wanted now turns into an object of disrepute,
disgust, and incompatibility; now one perceives only the unacceptable, the
inexcusable, some unfounded deviance at the core; to watch to the point of
revulsion, inverted lust, the class of a now unreturnable desire,
as the basis of the infamous . . .

*In the sixth description above, the author annihilates himself through the ingestion of a primordial venom, one that was somehow administered to him from birth and now condemns him to its irrigation (both upon the skin and in the veins).

Burning

I am in a new world, assailed by strange and trivial memories of the life now leaving me. The pangs of death have brought a clear truth, and I am no longer oblivious to anything. My eyesight is sharp. The pangs of death have lit, have magnified many thousands of times, the folds of my life, while the dark corners are as though thousands of angry desert suns were directly blazing on them. —Moussa Wuld Ibno[7]

. . . at night, when bodies burn . . .

The experience of a great burning, cruel and ungrieved (dominion of incandescence), as our discourse turns toward conflagration, torching, and restive sways. It dispatches the emotions, the bane of incendiary tracts, until the calming (unquenched temperatures), amidst the median-point between crimson and blue fire. The thick pyrexia of ash, smoke, and fumes (saturation).
*In the seventh description above, the author annihilates himself through exacerbated surges of clarity, electrocutions of the retina, exhibiting the potency of a sweltering desert landscape.

Blindness
(the furnace of mind)

No one is left in the land who can steal the flame . . .
He bends down, a corpse in the darkness
far from his kin,

submitting to his strangers,
their joints chilled,
their vision stunted. —Kamal Sabti[8]

> ... to seek the double-edged elation found only in the melting
> of vision, kept down low in the evacuated sockets, federation of
> the sightless, for whom the holes cannot be filled ...
> ... to seek the place where thought smolders, at once too far and not far
> enough, and thus the eyes suffer, slung before the oven's meditations ...

*In the eighth description above, the author annihilates himself upon find-
ing a stranger's lifeless body, imagining the distant tribe that no longer claims
this one, and through this receptacle takes upon himself the same plight as the
one over whom he crouches in the dark.

Transmission
(dimension, degree)

Islands made for flame, Asia rising in them, tomorrow rising in them. A sun was
extinguished, we dreamed things that do not occur to the night / My day is measured
by the flame / I cried for help, the voice of the people conquers the cosmos and beguiles.
—Adonis[9]

> ... that it spreads, this scalded faith, upon the feast, upon
> the rays, anti-histories of the sun-scorched ...
> ... to learn the modes of transmission, degree, and dimension
> through which the burning strides beyond itself, its rods,
> its flares, avowed to the hymn of effusion ...

*In the ninth description above, the author annihilates himself amidst a popu-
list overthrow of the universe, instigated by the poet's outcry and by an evening
of charmed thought where some caught sight of something past the human
and the metaphysical.

Disquiet
(speed, dread)

It was still twilight. An oil-lamp was burning on a shelf. There was a bed unrolled in
the corner of the room, but I was awake. My body felt burning hot. There were blood-
stains on my cloak and scarf and my hands were covered with blood. But in spite of
fever and giddiness I experienced a peculiar animation and restlessness . . . Finally,
after some hesitation, I drew the oil-lamp towards me and began as follows. —Sadeq
Hedayat[10]

. . . end of sleep (and onto the hectic) . . .
. . . one witnesses the sinking of the shoulders, now beneath
the heels of dread . . .
. . . to peer within someone, as an impolite vouching,
acquainted with the steepness of the guillotine . . .

*In the tenth description above, the author annihilates himself through linguistic fountains, first talking to himself, then writing to himself, going beyond insomnia, scribbling beneath the oil-lamps.

Fever
(exorcism)

In my unbalanced ship,
In my directionless and pointless words,
there is a fever beyond limit.
In this limitless fever,
a scream emerges from within me.
In the time of death, with death,
Where there is nothing but fear and danger,
Nonsense and weightlessness and clamor,
are errors and nothing more than a detriment. —Nima Yushij[11]

. . . to become elected by one's own hands for induction . . .

One notes the openness to possession, dressed by an imported power of one's own, now wrapped inward, invited to undertake its full coursing. This fever excuses its agent of accountability, it sweeps away all self-awareness, it undermines and transports the subject's voice, it convinces one to act in ways never before tried or dared, and perhaps never again, swelling the confines of possibility for a time, however contracted, though long enough to imperil a world, in the wake of one no longer in control of their hands . . .

Exorcism washes away the existential fever, the night-chills of becoming, by dragging across, then outwards, inhabiting every site in awful extensions, before it exits the condition. Such is the demoniac logic of the purge: that it will leave, but not without having marred the halls, no passage spared . . . the rush, the plea, the eventual departure . . .

*In the eleventh description above, the author annihilates himself through noise, the cacophony of aimless language, screaming, and rocking boats (lachrymose sound).

Incineration
(bareness)

We had begun to arrange our things when I sauntered onto the balcony overlooking the sea, and became lost in its vague horizons, intoxicated by its broken roar and its humid breeze. Suddenly a scream issued from inside the flat. I scurried toward it to find the girl convulsed in terror as flames licked through the top of the door-way. —Naguib Mahfouz[12]

> . . . that one can be made air again, that Being has in
> fact never left the province of winds . . .
> . . . to speak of the evaporated turn, its strictness and
> pathology (the undoused ones) . . .
> . . . no longer an organism (the going of the specimen) . . .

*In the twelfth description above, the author annihilates himself through shocking dreams, moving from the tranquillity of a shoreline terrace to the suddenness of a young woman shrieking (surrounded by fire).

Heat
(ignition)

The city broiled in noon's heat,
the streets burned with sun-fever
my trembling, anxious feet
treaded the mute cobblestones. —Forugh Farrokhzad[13]

> . . . beyond patterns, escalation alone, and the coercion of forms . . .
> . . . for that which ignites itself downgrades the other . . .

*In the thirteenth description above, the author annihilates herself by walking under oppressive suns, as the soaring temperatures of a metropolis leave her consciousness with its own version of heat-stroke.

Immolation
(of the pyres)

The reason for this extra oiliness is that the word phlegein, the etymological source of phlegm, is bursting with a massive incendiary tendency: Phlegein means to burn or

scorch with flame or extensive and destructive fire which glows black as the result of huge
amount of the uncombusted carbon particles. Burning black, phlegein corresponds with
the black flame worshipped by Akht or the black light of Ayn al-Qudat Hamedani. It is
associated with the fire of conflagration which is the fire of holokaustan (holocaust)—an
uncontrollable fire with an autonomous nervous system and a voracious rapacity for
sacrifice: Bonfire (bone-fire), the fire for burning heretics. —Reza Negarestani[14]

. . . of the red insistence, that pours . . .

The awe, the discretion, the hanging of the head, the humility before the
burned, becoming vile and elegant. New definition (of something beyond
mourning): that it fuels the watcher, not with retaliation or resentment, but
with the realization that all is already charring . . . beyond this point, everything drops toward immolation, all events strung up, all experiences fastened
to the wood beams . . . always in subsidence, having slipped from the grasp of
the interval, the aphasia of absolute time, for even time cannot speak amidst
the pyres, has lost its rights . . .

New definition (of something beyond loss): the watcher stands apart, and
then turns away, for this immolation asks that one betray the stove and its
withering ones, it asks for resilience and overlooking, a setting for the discon-
tinuation of memory, and in its place cradles the energy of its fallenness, for
the pyres are their own conduction and exchange. Such is the episode: to weep
not for what is lost, lain across in anguished rows, but for what must be gained
here, of the practice, what must be taken away, its sullen tendency now carried
forward in horrid whispers of the foregoing.

. . . the pyres as the identical (sameness, inter-replication) . . .
. . . the pyres as the commuting of bodies into stacks
(the underestimation of the deceased) . . .

*In the fourteenth description above, the author annihilates himself through
the etymological unlocking of the word oil, chaining himself to a forsaken
sacrificial genealogy of holocausts and bonfires.

Arson
(obsession)

I want to burn the incense
of my days, my songs, my book,
my ink and my inkwell.
I want to pray
to gods that never heard of prayer. —Adonis[15]

. . . this is the new arson, drawn through the anatomy of Man . . .

This method is a beckoning, installation, and meeting of seared routes, one that discloses desire as a form of diabolicism—to wish upon flames as vitalism and devotion. . .

. . . to set the last fire—the implications of the final glare, that occurs out of sight, out of sound and mind, far enough to remain unseen, quiet enough to remain inaudible, at an hour when the rest bow to sleep, not watching the distance, and with no trail to mark the way—the mangled experience of the one who enkindles the last ember, in full view of the forfeiture (an elapsed profession), as the abdication of longing, though once addicted . . . alone, and in revulsion . . .

Obsession: its enormous subduing, the horrendous subordination of the universal to the singular, through which an existence is captured and thrown beneath the tracks, now slave to the minorized desire, and its whirlpool-effect, whereby the particular becomes the immeasurable, fluctuating center.*In the fifteenth description above, the author annihilates himself through the destruction of his creative instinct, ridding the products of his inkwell and turning to unacculturated gods.

Ashes
(the aftermath)

The first box burns with an ease that makes me shiver with delight, look how they burn so high, look how they crackle, the pages, the pages, that were so hard to engender, so easy to annihilate, so lovely to conceive, so ugly to conserve! At least they'll have warmed my body! —Réda Bensmaia[16]

. . . of that which cannot be left behind (some make
careers of the aftermath) . . .
. . . to pass down a scholarship of ashes . . .

*In the sixteenth description above, the author annihilates himself amidst the orange light of burning manuscripts, guided by an aesthetic theory of anti-preservation (no need to keep them).

The Unbearable

*He pounds the onerous wave with his weary hand,
his mouth gaping, eyes flung wide open in terror,
he has viewed your shadows at a distance,*

and has swallowed water in the indigo deep,
in every moment he grows more impatient. —Nima Yushij[17]

. . . when pain asks for more, though there is no more . . .

To cross the ledge at which everything gives in, to wrack the spirit across an impossible, shattered scene of debilitation: this is its hell, its total captivity, reign, and darkening. It lays hands upon unexpected contortions, those that crucify the deeper sectors (so as to play the game again), it dialogues with the emergence of restlessness, and the return of thirst (age of the unslaked).[18]

*In the seventeenth description above, the author annihilates himself through submersion, caught beneath the surf, his mouth full of sapphire water.

Extremity
(the unbound)

May my prison be no enclosure
Other than the skin over my bones . . .
. . . such that whenever I sit with my solitude in the emptiness,
seven gates will slam shut
upon the longing and belonging of one's existence.
May they be shut,
Yes may they be shut
And may they stay shut
And upon every gate
seven heavy iron-locks. —Ahmad Shamlu[19]

Descended extremity (its own concept of the infinite): that which scrapes the bottom, the emptied contents, toward depletion, to speak of what has been drained. There is no celebration where there is perplexity (only discomfort).

*In the eighteenth description above, the author annihilates himself through an imprisonment-becoming-seven, matching his own rage against the thunderous clanking of shut doors, biting down upon bolted archways and hallowed by the multiplying gates that have become bridges.

Torture
(the insatiate)

One moonlit night,
the moon appears in sleep

and carries me to prison
like a moth that devastates itself
It takes one there . . .
We are drunk and sober, martyrs of the city . . .
We are asleep and awake, martyrs of the city . . . —Ahmad Shamlu[20]

> . . . to write the torture-chamber, to speak the torture-chamber,
> to become an agent of its strange passion . . .

To create that which torments oneself, torments the other, and which torments together as a kind of kinship . . .

One tortures to extort the hidden, to disentomb that information which remains unspoken; one tortures so as to derive the confession, to force the encounter with what has been done, to wrench the utterance; one tortures so as to attain revenge, to draw the admission of lowliness from the mouth of the one who now suffers, the agony pointless beyond its own service (agony itself the reason).

There is an immediate promise born of this relation, a barter led by the striking of one against the other, such uncommon intimacy between the one who pleads for no more and the one who knows only that more is on the way (the switch, the replacement). There is a barren tide in such cellars, filling and tipping flasks of misery for the suffocated and the wailing. All is reduced, denuded . . .

There are dual positions and transfigurations of the torturer:

> . . . one either turns lifeless, a devout, stoic functionary of the act, conveyor without expression . . .
> . . . or one turns intoxicated, attracted to the tremulous reactions, owned by the allure of the process and the deliberation of gazes . . .

The one who is tortured, though, has further inroads at its service:

> . . . beyond coldness (indifference, despair) or pleasure (pain-lust, self-flagellation), there is fury (to concentrate energy in the jaw, in the chipped pieces, through enmity, becoming-incensed) and estrangement (to become convinced that it happens to another, someone from before or after this).

And then, at long last, two basic procedures behind this ritual:

> . . . the first is to reveal what has been disguised, an untold, grisly unit of experience now made apparent, manifest before the eyes, the vulgarity of what

was once kept fast within now shown without possibility of recovery or denial. To make the unseen available, at all costs, even if still untenable to consider, to parade the image of a most quarantined secrecy through the mind (to face the resuscitation of a once-caged world).

. . . the second is to fabricate another narrative, a false serpentine, and to make the tortured suppose that it embodies the unconscious zone, to make one stare into the horror of that which one actually is not and has never been but is made to fathom that it runs in some inner place, to construct a phantom cauldron and to call it inborn, to convince one of the authenticity of an inferno beneath the surface and to enslave one to its bottle-shaped depth. Spectral webs, an artifice of caves.

. . . and then, to go even further, to inject this pseudo-impulse into the fragile veins of that now believing other, to insert into the sinews of thought this syringe of another configuration, and with it to infuse and release a host of concocted drives, lurid and carnivalesque, such that even in its fiction it remains hooked in the system of being. The first act constitutes a looking-glass, the second an indescribable distorting influence and intrusion (the triumph of the interspersal), the cunning of an illusion turned into pure defect, the total internalization of the lie.

*In the nineteenth description above, the author annihilates himself by moon-light, thrust into jail-cells and forced to call upon martyrs caught between opposing states of mind.

Scream
(terminal sound, oracle, of the throat)

I am vaster than that faded desire
Such that I rise within the searching of a stray scream. —Ahmad Shamlu[21]

One damaged intonation left to rain transience upon sheer life—half-slang, half-apocryphal (the simplicity of a self-slaying doctrine)—this maimed resonance, within the convolution of fangs and sound (as repetition begets a tirade). This scream wrongs the air (its own cautery, its own martial waves), this scream is the derangement (of the famished), where the word races toward prolonged incomprehension, truth thrown down, into rifts, and expression aspires to barbarism (of the chest), the listening that chokes itself (of the quiver).

. . . The scream as oracle, at once esoteric and writhing, mean emanation of the chosen, always belonging to the language of another clan, of different codes (the otherwise), through which one develops the temper (only animosity is enigmatic) and finds the vessel, endowed with partial impressions (to be written upon), outlined in glimpses.

*In the twentieth description above, the author annihilates himself through the throat, commenting on that expansive realm of the larynx out of which he makes an errant ascension.

The Scavenger
(carrion, the lower race, of the ruins, the outlasted)

And as for the winds, they brought me nothing but shrieks of perdition and the mournful, wintry scent of destruction mingled with smoke and the stench of rotting cadavers that blanketed the pavement. —Ghada Samman[22]

. . . Studies of the scavenger: one whose survival is based on the others' non-survival, to loiter and consume the dissipating, or to feed from another's kill (the after-violence); the lower race—those of the dregs, of the bottom, of the abject rungs, who eat from the ground, as the mouth becomes the lowest organ (where need bends, becoming-hunched); of the weeping, of the watchers and the listeners, whose sight and hearing only enhance the destitution, the nexus of decadence and nihilism; that which gathers relics, toward a new theory of the object, the forsaken thing, the valueless and the cast-aside (lameness), of the attics and of the wayside, of the underpass and the swamplands; of the ruins—to become a late dweller, the one entity that knows such structures are slowly being overtaken, caught in a test of continuance that they are failing, their starkness, their sunkenness, leveled by existence—and still, these ruins are a space of liberated air, that whips itself across the boulders, through open passages, filled crevices, and speaks through murmurs, howls, and screeches; the outlasted—space that has outshone its own time, willingness,, and architects, beyond the generations . . .

The scavenger must become a kind of third god: where to think it is to die from the thought (becoming-unsown) . . .

1. That which disowns the connection to man . . .
2. That which has forgotten the connection to man . . .
3. That which was never connected to man . . .
4. That which played no part in the creation of man, but will acquire him . . .

And thus, the one for whom the soaring view brings only disparagement, spurn, detachment, or puzzle (the irrelevant) . . .

. . . This evicted divinity, of murderous neutrality, exists in the narrow, the one that stayed out of the business of the origin, and who does not compete for the present of the world, but rather waits to inherit the outcome, and thus remains temporarily in sleep and rested, for it knows something, knows that only the time ahead matters, the time beyond the end (obsolescence) . . .

*In the twenty-first description above, the author annihilates herself through the stench of gangrenous bodies that litter her war-torn streets, betrayed by the wind and smoke that lift this reeking world to her balcony.

The Inhuman

. . . such storms as this, fanaticism without equal (against the brow) . . .

Cruelty
(the echo)

This language that suckles me betrays me / I shall bear witness to this and live on the edge of a time that has died. I walk along the edge of a time that has not come . . . Except that I am not alone. —Adonis[23]

. . . to fall in place, surviving just long enough to die . . .
. . . beneath the myth, within cruelty (what legacy is this?) . . .

Cruelty concerns itself with the edge, though not for reasons of the drop, nor the expanse, the vertical and horizontal breadth lain before, but rather the echo (and the controversy therein). For the echo crosses space, defies materiality and carries itself, though still an incommunicative entity, where something is said with no intent of being heard, calls for no other . . . a note flung out, heedless, yet that now escapes and runs toward unwanted destinations. Thus it signals, though unsolicited.

And even more, the echo allows the crier to confront itself in the prolific role of stranger, to circumscribe itself within its own rebounding accent, and therefore to perceive the inside saying as an outsider indictment, now returned badly, ominously late, brought back (from poor country), and in diminution, this time more vague, indistinct, and waning ever still. And yet, this miscarriage is its own critical revolt, for the original has also accumulated new debris in its travel . . . it gathers alternate movements as it circles, it introduces innovated forms as it returns, embodying a capacity for transportation within annihilation . . . that once sent out, no thought remains as it once was, no impulse, no desire, no utterance, nothing entitled to retain itself, that all axioms are enjoined to fusion with the outer, and the dawning of non-contrition. Thus it cycles, though twisted.

The echo transmits the articulation in parts, carrying only fragments of the initial pronouncement, only the hammering remnant of its tail (the fractured archetype). In this way, it also proves the needlessness of a speaker; the text scrawls itself (in ambient streaks), maneuvers its own arc (careening), without a controlling center, without a knower, and thus could come from anyone (though now anonymous).

> . . . the dead are not missed here . . .

*In the twenty-second description above, the author annihilates himself through untimeliness, forming alliances with either archaic or unrealized temporalities (and with some faceless others), and which charges him to see his mother-tongue as a traitorous force.

Exile
(the unsworn)

I have existed with a name not of my own
I have wept from a pain not of my own
I have derived life from a pleasure not of my own
I have entrusted life to a death not of my own. —Ahmad Shamlu[24]

. . . the disorientation, the being-torn-away . . .
The unsworn as a flooding, cartographies of the nowhere (vortex) . . .
. . . becoming-lost, while making others stranded (inundation) . . .
. . . into drifting, aimlessness (tragic sails) . . .
. . . of the beneath, the beings underwater, and the
undertow (thoughts that resemble ocean floors) . . .
. . . the absurd, the clientele, the race . . .

. . . The exilic imagination is enlivened by a sequence of moods: as striations, without clear motive or closure, which drape themselves in multiple curiosities (of the peculiar)—volatile, simultaneous, disjointed—showcasing their attempts, failures, and transitions, spread out in concurrent arrays, and highlighting the effect prior to the cause (that one senses something wrong, before it happens, before the foundations, aims, or purposes are relayed) . . .

*In the twenty-third description above, the author annihilates himself through self-impoverishment, throwing away the inheritance of sensations in which he has basked until this point, renouncing even his death at the moment that it comes for him.

Instinct
(entrenchment)

I desire no further journey.
I desire no further embarkation of a voyage.
The passing train
That ruptures the silence of my town every night
No longer illuminates my infinite sky.
And the path
In the aftermath of the bridge
No longer feels like a gateway to new realms. —Ahmad Shamlu[25]

. . . this hyper-location, brought forth by the dislocated . . .

. . . Countless overtures arise from the unrooted instinct, and thus made more versatile, since it can entrench itself in every context, across every site, ultra-insertion, for it belongs to nothing, remains nowhere and unhinged, given to constant self-extrication, amusement, and re-incursion.

*In the twenty-fourth description above, the author annihilates himself through stasis, voiding the prospect of the discovery and exploration, and shutting out the wanderlust with which he once departed for new plateaus.

Prophecy
(the ominous, the amorphous)

At night when the cloud of vodka rains
and the drill of your gaze
becomes sharper,
more pointed, more focused, more precise
than the sharpness of that wholesome liquid
and you see
from the height of intuition
more naked than revelation
that being good
is the cheapest of goods. —Esmail Khoi[26]

> . . . for those who shun their eyes, so as to see the ominous . . .
>
> . . . the amorphous tokens of the seer (the picture, the flow, the trait) . . .
>
> . . . the rise of a strenuous laughter, the thrill and hilarity
>
> that overcome self and overturn the personal . . .
>
> . . . light covered over, swathed in prophetic mist . . .

*In the twenty-fifth description above, the author annihilates himself through drunkenness, beseeching the hospitality of tavern-keepers, and allowing the uninhibited gaze to privilege nudity over morality.

Prey
(the following)

They would love to see me dead, to say: He belongs to us, he is ours.
For twenty years I have heard their footsteps on the walls of the night.
They open no door, yet here they are now. I see three of them:
a poet, a killer, and a reader of books. —Mahmoud Darwish[27]

> . . . preying as the emblem of the new animality, its subtle hazards,
> of that which attacks, consumes, and balances (leaves only bones) . . .

. . . One turns to the shades and inquires, for there are only two entities that would spend so long dangling from another's back, equipped to lurk and prowl behind: the slave and the murderer. Thus one finds the eternal stalker, and soon the rival, for to accept the following is to allow oneself to become the misguided . . .

*In the twenty-sixth description above, the author annihilates himself through a decades-long vendetta, a warrant drafted by himself against himself, and which has called forward three bounty hunters in search of his prized head.

Cloaking
(stillness)

Your skinny little body in its satin sheets
Your pink room wrapped in silence
Your eyes rolling among rich furnishings
Banging in the dark against dead rats against pillows
And we who wait for your final throes
To tear your testament to shreds. —Joyce Mansour[28]

. . . cloaking as the opaque pretense, utilized by practitioners of harm . . .
. . . to conceal something, or to conceal nothing . . .
. . . to screen is to leave what lies beneath in stillness, in
false calm, sheltered, stationary, and disdaining the visible . . .

*In the twenty-seventh description above, the author annihilates herself
through lust, opulence, and indulgences that then turn verminous, making
one soft and susceptible before a waiting enemy camp.

The Unnamed
(the rant) (of the smoke)

—*Why are you waking the world from its slumber?*
—*What you hear is not my voice. It's the sound of my corpse hitting the ground.*
—*Why don't you die quietly then?*
—*Because a quiet death is a degrading life.*
—*And a loud death?*
—*It is to stand firm.*
—*Did you come to announce my presence?*
—*No, I came to announce my absence.*
—*Why do you kill, then?*
—*I don't kill anything except killing. I kill only the crime.* —Mahmoud Darwish[29]

We are in the jurisdiction of that which inhales its void, which offers itself
before the disappearance of fortune, the exposure of the larynx. One wonders
after its solitude, its cosmology of pale volition; one wonders after their feeding
customs, whether they dine alone or share their kill. Here one does not throw
away the rancid.

. . . What thought exists now, what sensation of bareness might still be salvaged? This cannot hope for acceptance, this thing between the temples.

And then the eyes . . . less eyes than covered wounds, less covered than sewn
together against the will, and coated over with the nothing, where nothingness
means the sealing-shut of all remaining openings (except the mouth). They
say one closes the eyes for many reasons: in terror, in surrender and in sleep,
whether to deny the world or to maximize the intake of its slow, undeserving
pleasure. And what if blindness is just extreme dilation, where the organs swell
beyond impossibility? One searches for the holes in vain, unable to resurrect
such fallen sockets.

An image is enough, an image that carries a sign, a sign that carries an ailment, an ailment that carries the sutured flesh of difference. If only there were bodies still, for had they survived, persisted the steep immersion of the face, perhaps then this kind could have regained its equivalence.

. . . No, these eyes are the artifacts of a price well paid, the hint of a violence once duplicated. All proto-animations dwell in persecution.

. . . And still they stare, as if they see something, something that has no place being written.

These are the unreflected . . . which is not only to no longer recognize oneself but to lose one's likeness, the evidence and projected sign of having been somewhere, the image and the mark, to exist neither in the world of forms nor of appearances, the mirror left cavernous, unlicensed, without a semblance or representation (where one is no longer something).

The one who is gouged, rises to walk or stumble away, and leaves everything upon the ground . . . as if eviscerated, but in awful, measured fashion, such that each step, each mistaken pace, causes one to leak, to bleed out, until nothing remains of the interior realm, and even the emulation subsides (the failing of the original and the impostor).

Their rants evince continuity, as the expression writes itself, into hysteria, as thought turns toward automation, the strings held elsewhere, subservient to the pulse of the inflicted work.

*In the twenty-eighth description above, the author annihilates himself against annihilation itself, so as to make the announcement: that there is nobility in firm death.

Chapter 3

Sharpening: Writings of Evil

I. Mystification (rhythm)

II. Control (strike-intent)

III. The Unspoken (calm)

IV. Ritual (wrath)

V. Inexorability (of the carving)

VI. Chasm (irrelevance, of the walls)

VII. Vengeance (cipher, totality)

VIII. Disappearance (dead-end)

IX. Drive (the sealed gaze)

X. The Envisioned (the chronicle)

XI. Culmination (self-destructive height)

XII. Evil
Immersion (the half-surface)
Mastery (configuration, tactic)
Chain (extortion, enslavement, disavowal)
The Desolate (spiral)
Ascent (the exalted, of the blade)
Serration (of the scathed)

The Middle East is where wounds become unrest, and unrest becomes the sharpening . . .

An image nears, of terrorizing potential, converging as a vise, a jaw of insane retribution . . . this lone figure, back toward the everything, shifting in place, cryptic even before itself, sentinel of the sharpening (to leave timorous). The dread that emerges from sight of this action pours down with incomparable density, for it is possessed of domains, diffused with a power derived from still-unpronounced vantages.

Middle Eastern literature, upon close scrutiny, is littered with iconographic diagrams of sharpening, sketching the years of those who assimilate varying elements of brutality, who struggle for pure ascension over the nothing (expiring sensations), and who eventuate the work of filing, grinding, and honing these right-revoking implements. They are disturbing instances (and yet they are deposited all over), unwed to the rest of life, and forever staying within their own holographic capsules (until the designated flash). For once caught here, consciousness finds itself compelled to abandon its former existential allegiances and to instead meet exclusively with pace, with breath, with currents, itself an act of swaying before the low immediacy of drums. Watch the arms, watch the chest, watch the slow beating of limbs . . . but never the words. Here movement supersedes truth.

And what becomes of the text-under-sharpening? It is a doubtless conversion, relinquishment of self, relinquishment of world, turned toward fury, transition from the chasm to the dead-end, from endurance to escalation, from the immanence of the nothing to the imminence of warfare, from within the cold dominion of solitude, across straits of deprivation, a restlessness, from within territories of the unprotected, grave dissolutions of enclosure, all-surrounding, born of entropy and exorcism, all breath an incantation of these same ruins, from within the proliferation of untruth, the will to compulsion arises, it circles, from within the extinction of being, from within the reign of suffocation, a profound swinging, overcast, angers itself, the unbearable temptation to movement, a fugitive race drawn across the forgotten, stolen world, it rains its disquiet, frailty hardened into insistence, piercing air, excising strength from within the incarceration of the fallen, evocations of the barren, this nothingness asks for something, the sharpening, supremacy of outcast motion, it unlocks itself, as a summoning, faint yet hostile, an unraveling across the eroded, a quickening across deteriorated space, it circles and scars the abandoned, enveloping existence in desert shades, resurrections of disaster, all-descending, it circles, stalking, as a thirst concentrated, and then accelerates, this unhurried excruciation, wresting its dissent across the void, aggravating the confines of its surrender, and then excelling into the exhausted, an altered return, caught fast in the haze of emergence, where even illusions must draw themselves to extreme dying, overtaken by the instinct to suffer, an awakening to pained entrancement, it wrongs the twice-collapsed, surviving to rule the desolate, a premonition of darkness and effusion, dimensions under siege, defenseless before the convolution of becoming, until the departure into chaos, it circles, hastening its nightmare pace, ominous and unbending, convening the legacy of annihilation toward resurgence, maimed riots of the demand, the formlessness of ignition, a prophecy to end the reign of prophecies, engraved in smoke, it preys upon the wearied, hunting down the damaged earth, and then unfastening the origins of its violence, a razored expectancy driven outwards and against, from within such arid lairs, a sudden partnership, the convergence of esoteric brandings into an offensive, an action and ill-destined gathering of convulsions, the manipulation of desire as foul momentum, it rakes its offering across the disintegrated, riding hard against the clearances, without arrest, attaining an unspoken degree of severity, the culmination of an impact, as its talent floods the open. It circles like no other. There never was an age for this, the sharpening.

Such is the poetic horizon at stake, where all language encounters abrasion, the relationship of thought to world mirroring that of blade to stone, at once a meditation, embodiment, and singular act of carving. Thus the sharpening transforms text into an impermanent knife, now caught amidst the precision of wounds, a carefully attained hurt, at once cold and tempered, committed from within the writing of iron, such that all consciousness enters into alliance with blood, and all perception becomes a roaming arena of the torn.

Mystification
(rhythm)

The knife sharpener appears
In the kingdom of rusty things
Like a prophecy
We have forgotten. —Sargon Boulus[1]

An image nears, shaped of *mystification*, state of diluted wisdoms, engagement of the immaculate rhythm, rhythm of metal, of the crescent, of the gyration, where the pupils roll inward, drowned inward, detached from all else, to the extent that it constitutes an unbroken compulsion, the subordination of thought to movement, a movement-becoming-cruelty, and beyond this: the transformation of will, imagination, and body into an available mechanism, unceasing against fatigue (this one has been charged), irreversible against the tide of what lies ahead . . . that it leans (forecasting) without ambiguous steps . . . continuity turned savage, recurrence of the ill-omened, back and again, return without merciful pause, without silken exception, training-ground for ruin . . . these fatality rings, where consciousness runs and loops itself (voltage, levitation).

How is this procession maintained, this perverse logic of the ever-forward (clearing-way)? Moreover, how does this image of the sharpener become a poetic ethos (how does one write such dangerous obscurity)? Some attain this effect through subtraction, taking out details, building holes, gaps, crevices in their narratives, unexplained parts, always a game of withdrawal, retreat, and dissimulation, and thus they vanish from the chasing grasp of their watcher, becoming faceless, by virtue of excavating these unsurpassable gulfs. It is its own beautiful game: for one knows them better in the third movement than in the tenth (unrecognizable), growing increasingly distant by means of self-rescinding reports, slipping away into the horizon of the lessened, the alleviated, and the unsaid. But this one, this sharpener, checks out another proclamation: it takes on the challenge of excessive telling, effusion, outpouring, that then piles concept upon concept within an unknowable oceanic sphere. Here one tries not to build abysses but mazes—too many stultifying turns, too many achromatic possibilities in circulation, such that the eyes go blind before the overdose of illuminations—that is why there is an almost metallic, architectonic nature to such projects, a more subtle yet impressive circus . . . episode after episode, hallway upon hallway, underpass upon underpass, swamplands that subdue only to become wondrous, smooth lines that twist further than should be allowed, elegant in their super-completion (too far), each clause a detrimental safe's code, rendering layer onto layer, stratum onto stratum, where clearness becomes its own traveling set of complications, sinuous and lattice-like, where entanglement becomes the criterion of the worst enlightenment, as increments of hyper-meaning accumulate, in upward mounds, and cause sinking, amidst an elaborate network of wells, rivulets, catacombs, and spinal columns, until the surrender of mind (submersive futility).

*As for the passage, one wonders: from where does the knife-sharpener emerge (where has he been) such that he now wields the unsettling power of appearance (can he leave just as easily), and was he expected (does every region have its own sharpener, lurking in the surrounding hills, breeding the hermetic one who will give them a way out)? Even more, whose monarchy is this (did he once rule here), though it remains with vacated throne, and what major development has happened in the meantime (are the people ashamed at their refracted condition, and fear his judgment)? Why has rust overtaken all things (what decadence nurtures itself in his absence)? Has he arrived in the old age of this place, to announce decline, incurability, and funereal calm? Why does his coming forge a prophetic kinship (was he once sacred), and what false clergy has demanded the forgetting of his deeds (whose power-structure trembles at the mention of him)? Has he since cut out his otherworldly tongue, or is he still a great blesser/curser of cities (why is his sheer physicality its own downstairs metaphysics)?

Control
(strike-intent)

Cut to pieces, slashed through the limbs, hacked into still unharmed members, amputated, scratched, furrowed by nails, incised with teeth, jagged with sharp edges of broken bones, cut unevenly along the lips, carving out the cheeks, shaving off all elevations on the body. —Reza Negarestani[2]

An image nears, shaped of *control*, the anticipation of a shredded life, this one motive vowed within the thorax, seared into the hands, and with it the inner acceptance of the line . . . that it has long since envisioned this scabrous outcome, has performed the downfall, the determined aspect fast approaching (it lights the match) . . . and this pending formula: that there is no other avenue (without misgiving), that it is always far too late, that this one will not turn away, nor against itself, that once crystallized there can be no decomposition of purpose, no screening garments allowed, only the rabid self-witnessing, the fanaticism of the sharpener's gaze, this one that watches, that sees the razor, marvels, and traces its consequences . . . such is the startling outside of its conviction, its towering crux and stockade (triangulation).

This strike-intent is saturated with risk (to think this through is to become colorless). It is the birthplace of lateral extensions: first the internal struggle, then the superimposition. It sees the way it happens, it studies the domino-links, how it equalizes (the scrupulous plan), it discovers the impact, the pyramidal sensation, the flourishing loss involved, what will be taken away, and forces itself to stay within the idea (straining the retina), until it has fully internalized the surgical wrath of its instruction. It knows only too well what will come of this, what it asks for and what it must give back (this is no question of faith) . . . for the eyes never close here (anti-ignorance).

*As for the passage, one wonders: why does the sharpener convene this self-performed autopsy (chronic dissection)? What beastliness thrives within the open wounds (native soil of the feral)? Why the incessant Eastern calling to incision, amputation, decapitation (are these the passageways of some counter-intelligence)? What are the familial ties generated through cutting (to compartmentalize, dispense, and remove the unfit pieces)? Where does one take the useless portions (where do these liminal sections accumulate, loaded upon one another in morbid heaps)? Why must the sharpener, opposed to blunt tools, adapt all vertical edifices into horizontal masses (is this the key to formulating a bastard unity), and is there a subtle geometry to these death-allotments?

The Unspoken
(calm)

He appears
Without warning
With his hard face at
The mouth of the alley. —Sargon Boulus[3]

An image nears, shaped of *the unspoken*, where language is overthrown by the impenetrable script of the event, where all is consigned to an arcane bottle (nothing is forthcoming), the serum of introversion, and with it a pestilence beyond the grasp of meaning (nothing is flaunted) . . . for what must occur will occur, at all costs . . . this quiet born of inevitability, of vile assurance, and the speed of the near-damned. This calmness is its own rooted mark of discipline, of the one who has devoted all attention, at disreputable expense, in order to turn thought into an embankment, pipeline, and aqueduct, and for whom no conceivable statement can parallel the immediacy of the sharpening itself (neo-scholasticism). There is no practical need for the speech-act, its parallel chasing of the moment, its superfluous broadcasts, its irrelevant decibels, for one will hear soon enough what is to take place here (corporal proclamation). The sharpener's silence is nothing more than the frightening maturation of the reason, as the facial expression translates its manifesto.

*As for the passage, one wonders: What monolithic doctrine is so confident that it requires no announcement of its ways, no textual settlement, or is the sharpener himself the walking emblem of this transaction, his own body the slate upon which misfortunes are written (the foreigner's war-paint)? And why would he ever warn them, thus jeopardizing their susceptibility (anti-fairness)? Is his toughened face not the telltale sign of the emissary, the one whose pockets are laced with cyanide (the right amounts)? Is there an inverse correlation between the open mouth of the alley (into which all are gradually fed) and the temporarily unused mouth of the sharpener (from which no emission is permitted)? When he turns this strict corner, what new galaxial arrangement takes hold, for is he not the executor of something altogether "not-this" (another entirety)?

Ritual
(wrath)

But
He is a specter of his place of origin
A mutant hungry for the taste of iron
Nourished by the sun. —Sargon Boulus[4]

An image nears, shaped of *ritual*, of automated wrath, for it is this anti-illustrious ceremony, this improper custom, that paralyzes above all else . . . the unflinching module, without prayer or consent . . . the coagulation of a scraping procedure, amidst the steeling of a look that shows nothing, gives nothing away, and balances the most jarring equation: that the imagination must ice itself. This frozen rage, captive to its own misting, coated in glass sheets, takes one beyond even passion, since it exists for the sake of nothing save the stringent play of its carousel . . . it requires nothing, and therefore cannot supplicate, cannot fall to its knees and beg, neither for mercy nor for desire (to venerate frost). The composure of this unnatural elocution: ritual without deity, soothsayer, or cleric (no weakened derivations), but rather guided by the sovereignty of the frigid place (its poor climate) . . . this is what guarantees the affair, nailed down upon the slab, amidst the worthlessness of shivering.

There is a certain formality here, an inward officiation, where one waives the comfort of the individual name for the unmentionable glory of the title ("the one who will . . ."). And this convention works: for each brush-stroke purges awkwardness, bans anxiety, makes psychology grueling, turning one a servant to oneself (transfixion), one of cancerous humility, supervising the different phases of application (the scalpel), swallowing all tendencies in the wake of pictorial lowliness.[5]

*As for the passage, one wonders: At one point did he begin to disparage the clan, the nation, the superstitions of homeland, the cowardice of all origins—no programmatic trust, just the epithet of his own ensuing delegation? What is the connection here between spectrality and durability (does it stem from remorselessness)? What mutation grants one the preference for such sour affinities (the alkaline tongue), and how does one savor this displeasure? What embittered mother allows a child to be nursed by solar rays, or was this the priming for some alternative knighthood (acerbic chivalry)?

Inexorability
(of the carving)

This gap in my memory
When I follow a shadow
Takes me
Across the seasons
And I listen
To a semi-buried melody
That repeats. —Sargon Boulus[6]

An image nears, shaped of *inexorability*, where time throws its widest net, wrought into an impeccable fraud, into the unwavering, the resolution of a giant wheel, and the perfect symmetry of instincts (there is no anachronism). These are not gentle vectors, but rather carvings, the amalgamation of unsound properties: repetition, destiny, concentration, resurrection, deviation, and tracelessness (such are the inserted categories). Thus it improves . . .

This transference is a becoming-inexorable, capitalizing upon the indefinite . . . it is not transitory, this acrimony, for the damage could prove unending (the will does not break down). The inexhaustibility of this traffic (unwinding), arm against mountain, ligature against instrument, is a contact that wears away one so as to enhance the other (the reckoning of a war-criminal). It takes the usual restless energy of the body, the habits and physical ticks that string themselves toward waste, the rapid blinking or dangling of limbs, and combines them into a secured halo (no boredom here)—all nervous syndromes are bolted in a new leaden modulation—this is not conservation, but rather channeling, and the more it squanders, the more it swells (no frustration here). It tightens the endemic slackness of physicality, forbids relaxation, and contrives its own sensorial bloc. More than this, the traveling radius of the sharpener, slamming back and forth, leads to improvisation . . . for automaticity creates a learned agility before the accident (there will never be another emergency)—this clenching, this locking-down, is the beginning of propulsion.

   *As for the passage, one wonders: What amnesic lapse has found its way into the consciousness of this world-severing author (did he burrow inward and excise his own memory banks)? What place does the shadow, as a specimen of pure ethereality, have in the muscular universe of the sharpening (what is its devious contribution)? What are the acoustic registers of this flexing (what is the importance of listening here, when audition brings nothing but an inquisitor's tune)? How does one graze the seasons, using antiquated hymns to create an oblique path to the interminable?

Chasm
(irrelevance, of the walls)

Now, in the mute dark,
forbidding walls grow tall again,
border walls rise like plants
to become the sentries of my love's grove. —Forugh Farrokhzad[7]

   . . . one cannot exonerate what takes place in the dunes, nor the glare that
      follows those who hail there (half-recluse, half-profiteer) . . .

An image nears, shaped of the *chasm*, where consciousness asserts itself as a tilted base, the proposal of a non-state (to accent the lingering decline of being), a zero-stillness where the pulse of violence trembles. The derangement of a voyage through this other nowhere, without country, mistreated and sunken, amidst the suppressive turnings of an absence-labyrinth (where thought wrings itself). Here rest the inlays, the reliefs, and the veneers, unmourned intimations, damned to walk in circles, chests perforated by empty space, overrun by the density of gray air, each stirring a confession of five erasures, a pale coursing toward dead-ends, mirroring the self-cursed vacancy within. No madness, no evil (not yet) . . . only the succession of dried-out winds. Condemned: remnants of the nihilistic travel, sacrifices without altars, unsworn to all but the dissipating piece (withering below), the caressing vengeance of the wasteland, imprisoned by the futility of breath and the power of suspension, the immanence of this underside nothing, caught fast in a silent canvass (of the forsaken), the lost steps (of the buried alive), an existence borne in runaway traces and effaced chains (of the scarce). This is its own immortal mortality: vagrants of force, sentenced to the eternal destitution of the median, collapsed movements striking collapsed space, the impossibility of going-against . . . forgotten and ailing cadres (no longer empyreal), though treading still. No opening, no closing—where there are no walls, no echoes of resistance can survive.

There is a spatial paradox within the sharpening (whatever bottom this represents), one that interactively melds the experiences of con-traction and oblivion. On the one side, it must form a chamber (within itself)—it must commit itself to entrenchment, to isles of clear contain-ment (to become confined), the concentration of a lone cell, ceremony of separation and narrowing. On the other side, it must form a clearance (around itself)—it must sit amidst sweeping exposures and unfilled atmos-pheres (in the wings). This is how the sharpener at once encloses itself in the most decorative action, a will to caving, ceaselessly obligated to itself, inconceivable pressure, that it stays, crouching in strangled spots, that it tyrannizes its own becoming, its sulking position, as an anti-fever born within four mythological walls . . . while the field around it remains infinite, unbound, and evacuated (to constrict within vastness). This out-stretched ravine, deprived of light, windswept, space lain bare, where the body kneels against earth, handing itself over to the regime of this new undertaking (accommodation). There are no elements left, not in this impoverishment, only the watchman's candle, and a tightness drenched in arid glades. Thus it disembarks, finds its supreme rim, and shores itself toward the eradication of the inside and the outside, where one joins the instrument, becomes the condition and the setting, becomes the desert, becomes the jungle, and the scythe.

*As for the passage, one wonders: Why is this darkened courtyard no longer a place of frivolity, and what words uttered in this once-cheerful garden have had to be choked back? Who are the snaking vines meant to keep out (partition), and who is being kept in (precaution)? In this tale, is the sharpener a figure of fortification, prohibition, or plunder? Does he support or puncture this oasis, and how is the sharpening significant for the poetic reference to love (what romanticism could withstand this)?

Vengeance
(cipher, totality)

Dervishes come
who lived for some time in caves
with scorpions and serpents, dogs
follow
the cars of
a wedding procession . . .
The departed arrives
and the arrival departs:
the accused
the witness
and the judge. —Sargon Boulus[8]

An image nears, shaped of *vengeance,* for this alone can manage the abnormal synthesis of flexibility and constraint: vengeance can be sought across endless axes—to disquiet the mind, the body, the soul—and with a thousand tactics, each more scathing than the last (the jackal); even if one strategy of sabotage fails, strays, or misfires, another is advertised immediately in its place . . . and so the vengeful consciousness returns instantaneously to the outset-degree, to the oily beginning, and devises an alternative fashion. Where and how are variable, interchangeable, the means overshadowed by the end, such that the intricacies of the pursuit, the way in which it unfolds, is secondary to the fulfillment itself (this is its flexibility, the cipher that can always be revised). And still, the target remains fixed, unshaken, rigid beyond all else . . . the eyes perceive only one (this is its constraint, the obsessive totality of the one who deserves what is done).

This pertains to its temporal plot as well, for there is a heightened urgency, a tireless need to exercise retaliation, an agonizing speed of experience. No rest. Until over, the rush of its absolute necessity will plague. And still, vengeance is willing to work patiently, to exert itself over prolonged spans, to prey over eternal time, for the pain of the long interval is superseded by the wish to finish it right. All that matters is that it is done, whenever the hour. We have until the last exhale to bring it down.

Beyond this, vengeance has no life except at its ecstatic height, when the wounds finally bring satiation. There is no aftermath, there is no beyond, no life to which one can return, no life to follow. One does not walk away and grow old in the following years of vengeance (no peace); one annihilates both sides once it occurs. It ends itself when it ends the other, for no existence can be fathomed afterwards (no sons, no daughters). It would be wrong to con-tinue; no, it must pay the price of such unspoiled devotion, it must prove the level and plunge with the event . . . that it has drowned in this venture beyond all rescue, that it has known the penalty all along and accepts it without exception, that it must fall alongside the fallen (this has always been the bet). So it ends well, at the point of outright consummation, at the threshold of its own extreme success (there is no salvaging this womb). It destroys itself right at the instant of release, at the instant of the first and last smile. It is done, and the one behind it as well, washed away with the rest. There can be nothing else, nothing more (just these short gratifications). This is the terror of its nobility . . . without graciousness, without sentiment . . . the decorum of immanent vengeance (we must redefine pride).

To speak of a vengeful textuality is to seek a literature of well-set encryption, to bury text within sneaking text, message over message, mapping sense and nonsense, and to interpret only what is embedded (the unnoticed mosaic). This is not a mere palimpsest, for such a book would do far more: it would prove a beacon, inspiration, and arrow to the next session . . . as there are those beyond the gates who know the capital is a fake, and that it bathes itself in the artificial light of lanterns, all the while the ragged make their way nearer by the stars.

*As for the passage, one wonders: Who are the mystics, these ones of symptomatic focus, who dwell among legendary germinations and maladies of paranormal abilities? What vehicles are these that dare to rejoice over unions while the sharpener (so close by) polishes the instruments of bifurcation? Why is everyone in a migrant state, collectively causing an age of inversion (they flee in the wrong direction)? And finally, who is this unholy triumvirate that somehow feigns the right to judgment, when all that matters anymore is the unlit torch of the sharpener?

Disappearance
(dead-end)

The world is an opening
guarded by
shards of a mirror
on a ballast of mud
through which pass
various
forms
of creation:
Everyone comes
to saunter
toward this alley. —Sargon Boulus[9]

An image nears, shaped of *disappearance*, where one distills the apocryphal feature of being blown away, where the discontented slope, infest, and resolve themselves in erasure . . . amidst the sophistication of the dead-end. This is its own grim factor, for the disappearing ones are not to be mistaken for a principle of avoidance; they are their own scourge, those of spontaneous deceasing, who leave murals and banners attesting to the inheritance of a certain derision (the barrage), those of lunar turmoil who detest the ones who would hang on too long. And so, some part of the sharpening, for all its remarkable solidity, is predicated upon another self-ventilating standard, one of wafting (the gust) and surfing (the crest), a floating aeration of identity (while others merit only the dirt).[10]

*As for the passage, one wonders: What is the function, prestige, and gravitational pull of this alley (where all traverse yet none are welcome?)? Do they grovel here (as the creation becomes the creature)? Is it a theater of recovery, dispute, or altercation? What villainous monument do they embrace, in search of what vindication?

Drive
(sealed gaze)

On his back
The hone of skin and stone
And on his eyes
The dark spectacles of the blind, a man. —Sargon Boulus[11]

An image nears, shaped of *drive*, where the unlikely beats itself into likelihood (the maiden), deems itself worthy and ossifies (the clause), and gives rise to a new prototype of the hostage (the command). Thus the sharpening is a kind of attachment, a choreographic persuasion (though they do not dance in this cold place) . . . they only rock, in convincing arcs (they are so thorough), so as to produce an unyielding revelation, self-fossilizing scraps of bias, and the sealed gaze of amazement (they become spectacular).

*As for the passage, one wonders: Who is this apparent man, some former luminary or one who dabbled in providence and was crippled for it (reprimanded by gods), and why must we pay attention to his skin? What is the meaning of his sojourn, and must one pay charity? Did he look too far into things, eclipsing himself, and who has he advised before us (a thinker of orifices)?

The Envisioned
(the chronicle)

When the world rusts
And the ones fasting in the houses
Dream
Of who knows what feast
In what festival. —Sargon Boulus[12]

An image nears, shaped of *the envisioned* . . . for what does one make of this antedating, this transitional kingdom of idle hands, where one constantly practices (for how it will happen), where one speculates (on how it will feel), to picture the sliding topography of action over and again? This is its own optical signal: that of the chronicle, where one is compelled to record the event beforehand, for the pre-representation makes it unretractable (reality always follows this sort of text). It gives justified arrogance—the more it is said, the more it is planned, the more it is theoretically suggested, over-pondered, and mimetically induced, the more it gains in sureness, for it brings to mind a brilliant self-reliance.

*As for the passage, one wonders: What festival is staged (why does no one know what feast this is), and what deprivation (why do they starve themselves)? Is the sharpening its own celebrated task or are these housed ones scratching out a last farewell? Is there anger here, has he come for them because they have allowed his precious trinkets to rust, that they did not care for his blades, is their fast a preparation for his return (from the wayward)? What purpose does the dream serve here (to kill time), is it just a faint gesture toward paradise, allowing their scared imaginations to skip the retribution that must take place in-between? It seems his envisioning (unsightly) has motivated their vision (idyllic), with just one difference: theirs is fanciful (never to accomplish materiality), whereas his is guided by the expert fingers of requirement (it has been stipulated).

Culmination
(self-destructive height)

But we stiffened up, full of defiance, to wander again, with panting breath, lost and ravished, among the craters! —Réda Bensmaïa[13]

. . . where the air thins, and the vertigo lives . . .

An image nears, shaped of *culmination*, as the sharpener perfects incensement . . . where contempt finds its maximal level, hits upon exasperation, and with frustrated sinews then jolts upward, becomes an installation of gasping intolerance (the zealot), whispers its fanaticism (no more of this), and demands the fall of self or world (there is no in-between). Beyond this self-destructive height, there are no dynasties, no crowns . . . as thought is rendered solemn, repellent, and minatory.

*As for the passage, one wonders: Against what does this defiance turn (what opposition), why is there panting (what exertion), why the ravished sensibility (what eroticism), and what does one make of the spatiality of the craters (a deposed astrology)?

Evil

The walls are painted black to halfway up. It's about nine o'clock at night; the light is feeble. People look overwhelmed by it all; their expressions are grim, evil. —Yusuf Idris[14]

An image nears, shaped of *evil*, as that which presents an unknowable lucidity . . . obvious, flagrant, violently manifest, and yet incomprehensible (the formula of awe) . . . as that which permits treachery, the highest treason of openness, the ripping-apart of the bureau, and the intimacy therein (one can only truly betray what one knows well, having seen the inside, hiked within, though no longer belonging). And there is more that distresses us about the sharpening, its superfluous packing and irrelevance, its wasteful and unproductive standard, that it joins itself to an action that signifies nothing, that its intensity appears misplaced, and yet it remains insistent, devoted to this slight execution that happens nowhere, as if a cosmos exists between hands and steel, as if a world lives and dies by this shifting of forms. And it does. Above all else, this is an exercise in the wrongness of thought: to be so invested in a chore that stands beyond the borders of the real, a single tainted emanation. Nothing more pious than the silent numerologies of this nothingness-becoming-something, as it bites into itself, and what it foretells amidst the rest.

And so the sharpening manufactures its coupling with evil, though here it assumes an inconvenient redefinition, for it requires its own daunting mathematics and epistemology of vice . . .

13 Axioms

1. Evil is watchful (it is awakened), though also the enemy of consciousness (it puts others to sleep)
2. Evil upholds a kind of sorcery (a matter of inflection, invocation, and counter-sacred power)

3. Evil acts in both passion and indifference (necessity dictates the oncoming mood)
4. Evil remains unacknowledged (it moves across the seas, through imperceptible ripples, covered tides, and the invisibility of vapors)
5. Evil knows of the hidden (it does not recognize anything private, immune to layers, veils, mediations, and thus soaking itself in the supposed recesses—nothing can be diverted from its gaze)
6. Evil brings the paralytic tongue (the dialect of impossible belief, the word-in-arrest—it draws forward the unspeakable, for the verses of evil, whether poetic or profane, base or enchanted, reflect the deathliness of language itself, and thus the living death of men)
7. Evil threatens exposure (it plays upon this one unsaid fact . . . that existence has long since fallen . . . and manipulates the scales in order to wrest the delusion outward, for it will give itself over, relinquishing its own hold, in order to deracinate this universal denial; it will go down with the others, as long as it can vanquish the assurance that this is anything more than a phantom-life . . . now warped, worn through, and unraveling)
8. Evil practices in complex modifications, using rapidity and slowness, grandiose and minimalist infusions (it conceives an involved process, and halts the world through subtlety or glaring interruption)
9. Evil perpetuates itself through self-subversion (it frays and thrashes itself toward disassemblage)
10. Evil practices in closeness (it is a style of intrusion, as that which approaches, rides into, and strides across)
11. Evil imposes only that which it has also undergone, if not more viciously (it tests its reasoning on itself first, assaulting its own thought-streams, disowning its own flesh, before reaching for the other)
12. Evil is a state of exception (it is an alternative grace, and can be combated only by being copied)
13. Evil is generative (it gives way to aberrant, unanticipated entities, and then leaves them undefended)

*As for the passage, one wonders: Why do the crowds always throng to the gallows (what vicarious expenditure), and who is being hanged today (have they been told)? Is the sharpener himself a martyr (first or last), or the one who martyrs (delivers them to their tribute), or the one who makes martyrdom forever unattainable? Why did someone stop painting the walls (has idleness taken over this town), why the reference to the clock (does specificity matter here), and why hold this killing-occasion so late at night (why not in the light of day)? Is evil nothing less than the feeling of being completely overwhelmed, and does it not signify its conquest of the soul within the helpless expressions of those whom it takes (placing its own mask upon the onlookers)?

Immersion
(the half-surface)

In a place far removed
From myself . . .
This white eternity
That swims in my head
This crow that
Comes
To invade its whiteness. —Sargon Boulus[15]

An image nears, shaped of *immersion* (to reside in impassibility), those of the borrowed half-surface (quicksand phenomenon), where one cannot see but only feel what happens below (whirlpool phenomenon), those of the split environment whose lower or higher parts are submerged, cupped within the depths, and who soak themselves in nether-materials so as to ruin all others they later touch (this is its own excellence). There are many legends of figures encased beneath or above the waist, half in marble, half in smoke, half in vases, or half in granite, and they are often portrayed as either cheated or redressed beings, scolding themselves and begging for antidotes and remedies, rather than seeing their equatorial conflict (where the hemispheres contradict) as another sanction. This one knows better . . .

Those of the sharpening become stuck in just such ways (unthawed poses), where entire sections are closeted or flung into cisterns, planted as temporary and covert receptacles. How do they handle being beneath the rains, or beneath the noon-time sun, before exorbitant amounts of wetness and heat? How do they consult with those limbs of theirs that have been grafted elsewhere?

*As for the passage, one wonders: Is eternity always the prize of the one who has dared self-removal? Does the fact of its swimming, with the head still above the foam, tell us that the underneath is a liquid zone? Why does the crow, as an unclean striation (black-feathered), crawl across the whiteness of this haven? Can the sharpening leave no room for the pristine?

Mastery
(configuration, tactic)

I was playing, I saw, a losing game.
I'll begin with magic incantations (from my lifeless body). It's high time to confront
my infirmity. I'll kindle a fire upon my mountain. It's time to make peace between
confinement and the enchanting rose. —Samih al-Qasim[16]

An image nears, shaped of *mastery*, where consciousness becomes an adaman-
tine device, a gentle noise and mechanism of the corrupted, where thought
turns skeletal and specialized (the scion), with an indurate skull that seeks
favor, adoration, and burden. The sharpening thereby attains the status of a
configuration, at once organized and suspect, constructing itself as a stratagem, tactic, and pulsating contraption. To see only one frame, but to know
there are many particles here . . .

    *As for the passage, one wonders: What is the nature of this gamble with
invention (the making of . . .)? Why is divination the point of beginning (aiming from a necro-vantage)? What sickness must be validated in order to win
(does one ambush through submission)? What is the connection between the
sharpening and magic—is it a concept of healing, autosuggestion, or gnosis?
What are its paths of induction (hydromancy, pyromancy, cheiromancy, aero-
mancy, geomancy)? Can it ever secure peace, and if so what kind of tranquillity
is in store (utopia-becoming-dystopia, dystopia-becoming-utopia)?

Chain
(extortion, enslavement, disavowal)

Skilled at slipping adversity's collar? What sort of profession is this?. . .
Ah . . . now I see!
I have no choice but to keep on running
As branches and boughs are winding themselves
And closing in around me.
"Satan's grove,"
I curse and run—
But where?
There's no one to show me the way ahead
and there is no turning back. —Samih al-Qasim[17]

An image nears, shaped of *chain*, where thought binds itself, and the surrounding, a manacle (beyond gold or copper) consisted of tenets of engagement, reciprocity, immediacy, and tension . . . that which holds together at the
expense of great pain. Thus the sharpening forms its own necklace, turning
consciousness into a full object, laden with the observant power of the artifact,
the talisman that weighs down with a preestablished, withheld meaning, to
carry the far-off charm, allure, and guile of that which is crowded by an eccentric will. It is an extortion: to find the chance for bribery, to make things bow
in exchange for a promised release (forced supplication).

    The chain exerts itself as a fluctuating spectrum of nearness and distance,
joining the target only after having flung it both high and low, and therein using
two methodologies: (1) to elevate the other (the pedestal), and then self-exalt

in order to reach it; (2) to lessen the other (the gutter), and then self-diminish in order to reach it. This is its clinical mode of enslavement and disavowal (to become the analogue), somewhere between technocracy and paganism.

*As for the passage, one wonders: What professions employ the chain (the machinist, the hunter, the jeweler), and what are the contrasts in their use of tautness? Why is it that, twice now in this section, we have heard reference to the grove, and what devil do the branches serve there? Is the sharpener (and by extension the writer) an escape artist, the one who always hides the pin in the sleeve so as to undo whatever shackles are lain across the wrists? Is the sharpening not voluntary?

The Desolate
(spiral)

My early life was spent among the shepherds and horse-breeders who, seeking pasture, travel to faraway lands to set up tent, at night gathering around fire on mountain-tops for hours on end. Of all the years of my childhood I remember nothing but savage fights and other adventures characteristic of a nomadic people's simple pleasures through unchanging life cycles lived in blind oblivion to the outside world. —Nima Yushij[18]

An image nears, shaped of *the desolate*, where blackmail becomes the justification for pilgrimage, anointing, and tribute, a torsional sanatorium that is its own library (of unwritten vendettas), where insults are taken down in journals, letters, tomes, and encyclopedia (unreliable inventories). This is not a monotonous space, but a swirling, cyclonic anti-tropic, forming castles without imitation, with their own tonics inside, and their own warrants, and where one certifies the conversation between weeds, brass, and membrane.

The sharpening commandeers this spiral, it seals itself into nothingness and uses it as the rock across which it composes and concentrates itself. Nothingness as the basement of its gathering (it gives appetite); nothingness as the crib of accentuated presence (it abrades so as to escalate). All movement, all sound, is elevated in its midst, and with it the one who sharpens develops the most acute awareness of every whisking, every impulse, every breath or want (among the pebbles). Even the most fragile expressions appear invasive, a violation, an irrevocable crack in the continuum. It does not eradicate but aggravates the staleness, makes hard and ferocious what might have been overlooked; it leaves experience deafening, a perforation of the air, racked and rent by agony. For this reason, it must be understood that the desolate asks to be wronged, asks to be assaulted (it wants to be widowed). It establishes itself in expectation of the approach of the traitor, the fugitive entity that will assert its arrival, that will taint the void with the undertone of war (it seeks its anathema). Nothingness itself, the way it hisses, is an enjoinment to access and then to treason, for it knows that only a rogue would set its encampment in a wasteland (it craves demolition).

*As for the passage, one wonders: Who is this consortium of shepherds, horse-breeders, and nomads? Is this the lost race of the sharpener, descended from those whose bodies are interchangeable with the animal carcasses they carry across the valleys? What do they do there, within this adventurous hermeticism, what is their idea of recreation (those who fight for amusement), trouncing one another throughout the gorges? What kind of poetics would replicate their ways (anomalous joy), placing them in the tar of language?

Ascent
(the exalted, of the blade)

I see myself only upon the margin of history, on a blade-edge. —Adonis[19]

An image nears, shaped of the *ascent*, what comes after the province of unspeakable pain, and goes away having already assured the performance (for here all destinies rest at the threshold of a blade). Ascension is a will to chaos: the hilt as chaotic possibility, and the hand that envelops it, that grips it, as the coalescence and ownership of such anarchic toil. To grasp it, and to make it work for this. And when it emerges, the one of the sharpening, the one who has engaged and lived within the captivity of stiletto and mineral, is already itself a devastating ridge. At this moment, there is no need for initiation, for provocation, since all contact evokes this spliced den. No exertion, no expenditure . . . its composure alone is enough to shave across all it touches. It does its work, as all falls sway to being probed, stuck, pricked, and gouged.

For when it stands, and begins to walk (across the rope-bridge) . . . this is the zenith at which the image attains its terror-presence. It carries its allegiance outward, enfolds existence back into its emptiness, its ultimate marshland, and keeps count as they descend. This proto-assassin consciousness will watch the fall-out; it remains until it is over, it advances itself against their sanctity, to lay bare the cavity within, and to expand it again, to allow it to strain and submerge, and then to take it, to scavenge the caves and feed off the ashes, to abduct the power that springs from the annihilation of man, the annihilation of the real, the annihilation of being (to drink from the rejected). From the catastrophe of such spectral walls, an offensive deepens.

They will never survive, though this was never for them. The challenge is to arrive at a windowsill where mercy becomes impossible, restraint becomes unthinkable, and seizure the last imperative (barbed imagination). Something affirmative is taken from these condemned states, a fresh thirst derived from the nightmare, these deprived remnants of the nothing's vengeance, as this other one grasps their dissolution as a reservoir for its own speed. This now destitute mass, exorcised of nominations, faces the sharpener toward its over-hanging empire.

This is the true look of exaltation: to be chosen, selected for honor, victim-hood, pain, differentiated from the rest, and to be granted invincibility over everything that has passed through the void and fallen. This allows one a cer-tain preference (of the brandished, the dented, the spiked), for to drag some-thing across open flesh is to encounter the tremors of vulnerability without hope of release, to endure risk at its fiercest (somatic malevolence). It seeks the transformation of the body into a pick and shovel, such that all physical move-ment possesses within itself an intrinsic violence, the coal miner's precision of a slicing-across, as that which forever navigates the materialization of pain. Here it develops the instinct for tangibility, envisioning itself as a scaffold for the world, and the body its willing executioner (individual militarism). And just as the blade, while falling through air, unveils for itself a multiplicity of angles from which to strike, so must the body disclose amidst each swaying yet another vantage for punishment. Each motion conceives the very means and space of its impending incision, each stride capable of scouring everything, such that in each instance it becomes the reflexive intimation of its quest. It withholds noth-ing, not even nothingness itself, slowly avowing the complexity of its delirium, as it masters the unbearable art of the gash. From pure immobility to the most untamed spraining, from the calculated to the erratic, the bones tighten (the awaited), so as to return to every venture with tactile, knife-like prescience.

Consciousness acts as the woeful shining of this blade, forever invoking the limitless fear of either side, deplorable notions running across an infinite sur-face (with the grain), and then its point . . . a chronic temptation to piercing, the seemingly effortless invasion of all hiding-places. Here it attains its fatal duality: the curved edge that without time-lapse can then re-conjoin itself as a line (the horror of its straightening), plunging forward, into, and beneath, and therein stabbing at the border between interiority and exteriority. This unex-pected contortion, yet somehow always expectant, from the slash to the lunge, from coercion to penetration, is what circulates and inflates its shock. For the entirety of the blade is suspect, each segment representing its own sovereignty within the steel plateau, even as they follow one another in smooth progres-sion, descending further and further. Nowhere along its trajectory is safe, as the weapon itself defies the brittle constraint of a totality, functioning instead as an elite synchronicity of punctures, each able to flash outward when called upon, to rattle the breastplate, now wounding, now scarring, now sliding into unknown depths, into what is most guarded. And it is this—the immensity of its flowing torment, the refined desecration of barriers between inner and outer, the elegance of its entrance and exit of forms—that maintains the form-lessness of its own becoming. Its marked passage dissolves the illusion of the unadulterated (it severs the essence), loaning hurt to each occasion (it reveals what can be tipped), through the climax of a wail, the swordmaker's one satis-faction, an affirmation brought only by the expenditure of a crying-out.

*As for the passage, one wonders: Does it also list its disposals, within some personal-impersonal archive, and why would anyone sell oneself to such irra-tional rationality?

Serration
(of the all-scathed)

Crushing between his hands
The stone
Screaming to the sleepers that he has come
He has come
To sharpen the knives. —Sargon Boulus[20]

. . . to become thorn, the generation of thorn . . .

An image nears, shaped of *serration*, within the shedding of organs, and the disemboweled frame . . .

*As for the passage, one wonders: Why does he so despise the sleepers (the people), why must he, upon his cross arrival, rouse them from their slumber, only then to cut them (through the fabric), and why is there no anesthesia allowed? Why is it that now, after all this smoothness, we find him crushing? Why is it that now, after all this silence, we find him screaming?

Chapter 4

Deception: Writings of Midnight

...Midnight...
Tyranny (the eventual) ...
        Standstill (the slot) ...
                Struggle (the obsidian) ...
                        Vanishing (the epoch) ...
                                Suspension (the stranded) ...
                                        ...Abduction...
Dispossession (the infinite stolen) ...
                Violation (the stalked) ...
                        Seizure (of the arms) ...
                                Second Immortality (ransom) ...
                                        Elusion (of the fugitive) ...
                                                Endangerment (phantom-chance) ...
                                                        Collapse (the unguarded) ...
                                        Criminality (rogue thought) ...
                                Stealth (the mask, the veil) ...
                                        ...Illusion...
                                        Manifestation (the arsenal) ...
                                                Convolution (the lie) ...
                        Distraction (the component)
                        Fall-Out (sacrifice, occultation) ...
                                Scarring (the axial wound) ...
                                        The Inexistent (the unforeseen) ...
                                                The Unforgiving (trespass) ...
                                The Tearing (incision) ...
                                        The Starved (asphyxiation) ...
                                The Opiate (temptation) ...
        Legion (fragmentation, of the code, of the valences) ...
                The Shards (architectonics) ...
                Reflex (traversal, the ancient) ...
                Damage (occlusion) ...
                        Intimation (the mercenary) ...

The contemporary constellations of Middle Eastern writing have restored a medieval treaty with deception (the mystics know of this). There is no skeptical compromise, just the integral cooling and cheating of thoughts that generate their own ecological forum, their own global dungeon and unnoticed artillery (the hidden items on the coroner's shelf). Such bisecting texts thrive upon the power of untruth, relinquishing their seemingly angelic margins to conjuration, haze, and obscurity (they leave one wading). This is the newest ascension of the unreal, the gilded realm of distorting stimulation, where sorceries of discord, fierce yet spectral, produce their halos of creation and destruction, and the chaos of the lie (they leave one groping). No authentic situation has ever survived the touch of this (they leave one trying): to risk everything to become a particular kind of illusoriness, that which allows for the most rarefied transversal, to use the semblance toward martial ends, to entangle hallucination-streams and revenge oneself through cunning vices, with a laughter that desolates, a desolation that laughs. Deception as axe: at once a challenge and a perishing (ours is the hour of a virtual midnight, and in it we remain unformed).

The Middle Eastern author must build camp from an outlandish vantage, reconstituting subjectivity as a phantom "I" with no recourse to the resurgence of a reality-principle, a dreamscape with no recourse to waking, no way out from the regime of fabrication. To derive intensity from the conception of oneself as a spectral god, a smoke-born entity, the highest apparition of an imagined world, each haunted motion a mirror of the fantasia. It goes beyond even the sovereignty of mirage, beyond the nihilistic outcry that nothing "is," for it means something else entirely to entomb the world in trance, where masks become armor, and to will the throes of deceit, to sanction manifestation, adulteration, and decay in the same stride (fearless swaying).

We summon ourselves to the hour of deceptive executions, to the insincere darkening of mind and world . . . where all thought is fractured, all being crucified . . . having come here to incite consciousness toward the threshold of its own false extremity (superficial bleeding). To become the violation of all that walks and breathes in older faiths, that which draws the knife across the aspiring body of existence, what steals and preys, allied with disquiet and inquisition of the trusting. We are the manifestation of an armageddon-whim, the anticipation of four counts of made-up rage. We preserve nothing, we grieve for nothing, we stalk ourselves across the far-fetched walls, trained in the perfection of unlikely betrayal . . . to turn the earth improbable, bizarre unto itself again. We move in blindness, across the uneven (synthetic excess), without the mercy of awakening . . . unsworn to all, we scar and condemn, we take back what was never ours, as the incantation tells us. Thus we call ourselves to the warfare of misapprehension. This deception is what binds us, its ecstasy, its evil, a fatality-temptation, at once twirling and distraught: that all must go the way of brilliant eccentricity, and by our hands. It is no less than the teasing abduction of existence (taken beyond its mirrors), that which punishes the convention, that which commands the mistaken toward the repetition of a theft unforgiven. For it is here, from within the great affliction of a pretext, that the deceptive will has convened us: our presence, our arms, our relentless speed, cruel and unfathomed, as sight becomes tantalized before the stratagem and the curious return. This Middle Eastern imaginary breaks itself open through uncertified evocations, borne only in the silence of our striking, in the sacrifice of our eyes, demanding that we endure, beyond madness, beyond the last rows of the profane, in defiance of satiation, possessed of impossibility alone. It is an imperative to the joker's delirium, to the inexhaustibility of foolish infiltration, to the vengeance of the starved, an exorcism of irresponsible compulsion, where restlessness carves itself into world. This deception raids the myth of permanence, at once inexorable and fragmented, wresting all toward the prism of the exaggerated and the alleged, through vanishing and collapsed parcels (though still unsurrendered). And we, the carriers of its phantom-will . . . we stand across its edge, ourselves aligned with unreality, our conviction that of shadows and hyperbolic readers, aware that nothing is left unscathed, that nothing outlasts the endangerment of this lie, this single impulse to misinform. It is an intimation of our virulence, of our severity and our forgetting, our pain and our innocence, of the icing of veins and the coalescence of desire as stone (to control the asinine). We suspend ourselves in reckless and invented confrontation, in this deep hardening of a conjecture-becoming-instinct, between storm and burning, exaltation and contempt, until all is driven under. It lives and dies by the enforcement of our most faking or shallow words, itself a trial and secrecy of senseless ruin (the seizure of time, the abrasion of space), and of exposure before lacerating speculation. We speak with the carelessness of unwise invaders, where the balance of experience is angered, and where all elements must descend toward feigned chaos, toward the final tearing of what cannot happen (or so one guesses).

Midnight

The breaking-open of a deceptive consciousness implies midnight, for it is the epoch of discovery of a cadaverous space (the closet), blocking the depths, suffusing the nothing, and requesting an inhuman entourage to disembark. It is the envisioning of time as a nonsequential stream of detonations (though cold), each instant its own apocalyptic flaring (though dim), a self-contained blast into falsehearted infinity (one after another). These heatless presents, damned to an arctic fate upon arrival, allow no impending rise or fall, all intimations of possibility sealed fast within their own boundless undetectable catastrophe . . . nothing imminent, nothing to come (one has been robbed without feeling it). This is an impalpable deprivation, the peaceful effacement of illumination, amidst near-immaculate evacuations of breath, where thought is vanquished, stranded, achromatic (without iridescence), an unspoken temptation to treachery (the most sinister), to the exultation of travesty (the most ominous), the moment of all-banishing serenity.[1]

Tyranny
(the eventual)

Until the time when night falls once again, until the moment when the dark night returns, not a trace of my blind readings, not a trace of my blind wanderings, not a trace of my blindest memory, not a trace of my tracks left blindly behind me, not a trace of my blind larceny, of my fears, of my falls, not a trace of my oblivion, not a trace of the blood of the blindman within me, nothing remains but the black night. —Réda Bensmaia[2]

Midnight makes use of a tyrannical eventuality (what will happen), shifting between concealment and transparency (what did happen), the subtle cyclicality of exposure and dissolution, relentless transience, unveiling only what is already faceless (what cannot have happened). It is an unannounced occasion, falling across existence through the serrations of a nightmare, a tirade of downcast skies, compelling the pupils beneath the canopies, the maze of the unseen, the rampant flooding of a faded world, an instance of submergence, immersion, and subdued mindsets, where all light is enshrouded, consigned to ceaseless dusk. The Eastern front is despotic with its itinerary, hammering out the most elaborate atemporalities, the collusion of being and non-being into a force of the abandoned period (all-eclipsing, all-extinguished), damned to the unclear and to the hunger for occlusion.

*According to the above selection, we are faced with a self-persecuting figure searching after the corner where one can act with assurances of pure tracelessness, where one entertains a dictatorial wish to have one's own history swallowed, the autocratic will to be stamped out of the picture (unrecognized).

Standstill
(the slot)

Under siege, time becomes place
Petrified for an eternity.
And place becomes time
Lagging far behind its juncture. —Mahmoud Darwish[3]

The midnight-seeking writers also realize the authority of the standstill (of what keeps the object in place). It is to bring language into the slot of the twelfth hour, where the instant no longer holds expectation but somehow continues to induce trembling, for timeless fear is more commanding than dread (nothing to wait for), the breath of inaudible brutalities (nothing to long for). Such standstills are paralytic junctures, turning an instant into an era (gruesome calm), one of ghoulish, macabre, and regret-laden sentiment (there is no confidence).

*According to the above selection, we are faced with a mind snowed-in from all sides, for the affective output of such experiments (the setting of all suns) is one of siege and petrifaction: to become-enshrined (without dignity). Consciousness is found lagging, perpetually catching up to the forever (and so what if it did?), and unable to solve the conundric transposition of time and place that has perched it upon the rocks.

Struggle
(the obsidian)

My eyes two dim corridors,
my cheeks chilled marble,
sleep shall snatch me suddenly,
drain my sighs of pain . . .

Suddenly my dark life's curtains part,
eyes of intruders
creep and slither
on all my papers, on all my notes. —Forugh Farrokhzad[4]

It is within the blanket-experience of midnight that one begins to struggle, with no unified purpose other than to skewer the obsidian (the righteous dismantled, split through the crucible). For here a disenfranchised consciousness must steel itself, must obtain some credit and attempt a seismic shift, whether by pushing back (against the void), flailing across (into the air), or lashing out (toward some semblance of a window). Nevertheless, soon enough one is made the victim of a bitter joke of viscosity, for to panic is to drop further into its basin, to drill oneself into setback and reiteration.

*According to the above selection, we are faced with a condemned sleeper, one who blinks, tightens, and then shuts her eyes in naïve hopes of escaping these granular dunes of non-time. Nor does interiority offer solace, for the more she presses her lids in refusal, pulling back into the once-safe den of self, the more the night-intruders follow her, taking up residence in her thoughts and writings (as sighs turn to moans).

Vanishing
(the epoch)

For the sake of an anthem, for the sake of a story told on the coldest of nights, the dark-
est of nights . . . —Ahmad Shamlu[5]

It is not quite long before such authors are met by the great suction of these post-
temporal rings, for a poetic midnight sustains the pure circularity of violence:
from the first threat to the second annihilation, from the eighth sharpening
to the fourteenth rage to the thousandth assassination. Such is the undeterred
recurrence of the wager, risking consciousness to hacked orbits of action
. . . being-as-circle, time-as-circle, necessarily unravels both being and time,
now casualties to a chaotic spiral. This rotation, turning ardently in its field,
advances alongside the following overlays of individual experience (now a table
of contents): that there was once a subject that distanced itself from all existential embankments, threatening its own makeup, and yet the more stern this
withdrawal, the more it begged the gentle nexus of annihilation (to burn alive)
. . . from here, in the aftermath of this delicate trial, what particles remained of
consciousness then conveyed themselves forward, into the true desperation of a
sharpener, as an inclination unhooked itself across the barrenness, at first scattered yet then hardened and incessant, as the acceleration of a precursor will . . .
and then the rage came, one that summoned itself to rasp, that would cast its
devastating gaze against man, against the real, with an assassin's posture. Such
was the exportation of a war . . . and then again, over and again, fulfilling the
dimensions of this whorl once more through coarse repetition.

    And still, it is the implication of this circularity that proves the most strik-
ing, prompted by an inauspicious detail: that all of this, without beginning or
end, has been the bailing-forward of the violent imagination itself—this was
not in fact the doing of an oppressive existence, against which some reacted,
but rather each portion has been directed into emergence by the poetic figures who now seek so-called retribution. One should not read the chapters
as a progression, but rather as the execution of simultaneous presents able
to bend backwards and set the stage for their own promotion before they
actually appear to undergo their respective becomings. They are at once the
architects of their movement, their instantiation, and their attainment. An
instinct not from beyond but from an alternative concurrent unreality that
then defines the immediate shudder, reaching across to determine and compel the vision's manifestation, eliciting itself seemingly before its own arrival.
And yet the vibration is in fact always present, always creating its own creation,
as the guardian of each initiative. It wills that which would will *it*. It anticipates
itself, backs and resurrects itself, all in one war-tremor, the guarantor of a
deceptive meridian.

And existence as well, the designated enemy-formation, that which supposedly curses and plagues the textual becoming throughout its excursion, is nothing but another conjuring of this same violent imagination, the outcome of its enthusiastic call to self-opposition. The poetic front wanted this reality to come about (it is their own gastric doing), if only to disfigure it before the end; they take credit for bringing it all to pass, if only then to stretch against it with grand prejudice. For an inflictive thought, what might be conceived as the height or depth of this unfolding by virtue of its relative voracity, alone could create existence; it alone could possess the roar to bring "the world" into play, and only so as to carry out the categorical game of conflict. Nothing escapes it, and yet there is no ultimate unity, just the reflex of its paradox, the instantaneous rise and fall of a vanishing eternal. Becoming as the elliptical compulsion of an outworld: that this had to happen (though there is no veracity to it). Neither a finality nor a destination, rather it is the full incarnation of a drive, the culmination of its difficulty, though still irresolute and displeased in its wanting for both reverberation and collapse, still ensuring its own transience and multiplicity by bridging all aspects, from the preface to the epilogue, into a contrasting alignment of strands, a self-reinforcing circuitry without essence, without center, and without termination. Disoriented inter-alliances, tributaries that flood into/across/against one another, exposing the impossibility of differentiation (resurgent cords) . . . that aesthetic warfare shatters the matrix which leads into its own actualization, overturning any absolute formulation of stages. Here all factors must be played out, induced and carried through, concomitantly and without stratification, as a storm of cyclical fusions. For it is the sheer imbalance of its rounding, the mania of its nonprogression, with all facets occurring at once and in indiscriminate rows, beyond logic and seasons, that allows it access to regeneration. This becoming has no past, no future . . . just the inexhaustible return of a blood-imperative.

*According to the above selection, we are faced with a competitive story-teller, one who seeks the best/worst conditions to weave a midnight narrative, waiting until the harshest evening of the year, with poor weather and visibility, before he lights a match in the lantern and begins his hymn (for he requires militancy, and the climate will weed out those incapable of fanatical disbelief). He needs those who would suffer immeasurably just to hear a well-crafted fable sung across the cemetery.

Suspension
(the stranded)

Thick death for whom the air in the room became laden with clouds, and the air became heavier, and the light became like isolated strangulated threads. —Yusuf Idris[6]

One must circumnavigate another disk amidst the encounter with a midnight consciousness: namely, the experience of suspension (to be stranded between the voids). This is not the weak notion of the interstice, but rather the more austere destiny of the vise, an aluminum jowl that nonetheless renders an archway, though to pass through such portals is to endure the exceptional narrowing of thought. All ideas compress, as if caught within the slimmest aperture, within pinpoint confinement, fitting through nothing (antithesis of the skeleton key), until crashing through the dam (the barrage).

*According to the above selection, we are faced with a choking form, one for whom even the semi-tangible phenomena of light and air become roadblocks, slender and tenuous strings squeezed across the now-consenting neck.

Abduction

Deception shares an overlapping vicinity with abduction, some isle of pick-pocketed essences, where each movement disguises an imperceptible trespass and a gang-vowed imagination finds itself incessantly caught between infiltration and escape, eyes cast upon the outlets (everything can be made cavalier). One must become fraudulent here, one must teach oneself to steal, to steal everything, to steal breath itself from all that dares respire (everything can be denigrated). One must grant oneself the right to take, to creep within the unventilated warehouses of the sacred and capture what never belonged to it (everything can be mocked). One must rob even time itself, to embezzle from past, present, and future until each surrenders its wealth (everything is cargo). To practice abduction is to become a fugitive element, a master-criminal of thought and experience, where one masks and turns stranger to everything, where one alters one's position in each second and learns to tread in ambiguity, where elusive forms of stealth allow one to study the existential underground, for one must become subterranean in order to possess the unknown. There is no sleep in abduction, no time to dream, only the constant interplay of piracies: the eyes are always untraceable here, though set upon the chosen target, waiting to seize hold, to attain that instant of effective proximity when things can be wrenched from themselves. No, the one who would break the world must first know how to thieve the world, to risk everything to take everything, and to will secrecy as a weapon (everything can become a throw-away).

We are no longer interested in the stagnant identities of pure writers, artists, intellectuals, or philosophers; we are only interested in madmen who write aphorisms, liars who paint, arsonists who compose music, and contract-killers who quote philosophy from time to time. In the Eastern poetic imagination, this anti-conservatism is a given condition and is applied to the textual realm without hesitation, for there is much that the writing-act can gain from the lessons of abduction: the relocation of the organs (the centrality of hands); the gauging of points of vulnerability (to sense the unseen weakness in all sites); the immediacy with the thing as singular focus (the revolution of the surrounding world around the object); the waiting (drunken-unto-stillness, masterful boredom); the alleyway (hidden body, hidden space); the wager (risk-exhilaration, the fluidity of constant exchange of the stolen item); failure-temptation (to attempt what causes the most potential damage, the collapsibility of the endeavor); the varying modes of acquisition (taking, lifting, swiping, misappropriating); the revocation of rights (non-sovereignty); the disorientation of the order of things (divestment); the dislocation of context (wresting-beyond); antisocial alliance (the thief-code, mortal intimacies of divulgence, guided by the whisper, the extreme closeness of the mutual lie); the storytelling-race (competitive density of legends, accounts, false testimonies); the survival-bond (proximity based on action, expenditure, the speed-rush of the collective escape, and the ever-present possibility of betrayal); the elusion (stealing-away, departure, flight-movement, gaze to the periphery); the crouching technique (of the lockpicker, supplication gestures of kneeling turned against themselves, against the sanctified idols); the perfect disappearance (the one who was never there).

Dispossession
(the infinite stolen)

I cut my lower lip shaving and I was by the gates of the Black City, a city made of black marble, a black city made of marble in the middle of the desert, the closest mine of marble hundreds of miles away. Strange city. Strange marble city far away from any oasis. Black City my soul called home. —Leonardo Alishan[7]

One advocates borrowing some of the characteristics of reprehensible actions, the graceful outlooks they enable, in order to administer this euthanasia to the law (to rock the thrones). One is gratified by the disgrace that this brings to the edifices of domination, prompted by a decadent view of the origin: that all things have already been taken so far from their rightful owners that it does not matter whether they are unanchored yet again. This is the mantra of dispossession, motivated by a concept of the infinite stolen; the source is forsaken, no longer derived from a definite foundation, and thus opening the way for more illegitimate modes of confiscation.

*According to the above selection, we are faced with a man shaving his own face like marble, though it is more a ritual transportation, where the smallest deviation can fling open the gates to a forbidden metropolis (to lurk through the anti-edenic).

Violation
(the stalked)

My fields lie dry, and all my schemes
have come to nothing
the enemy has found my hideout
                with his cunning eyes . . .
. . . woe! he's preparing for my breast
                an array of arms. —Nima Yushij[8]

There is an abducting-mode of consciousness for which the first thing one looks is the entrance, or the several entrances, since the height of violation is to make the other choose that which has no right to occur, that which it does not want any part of, and yet comes to want it as it happens . . . the profane turn, a sudden disposition toward that with which one should never have allowed, though now becoming undeniable. It converges upon them, wins them over slowly (a serpent searching out precious stones), giving new connotations to the experience of the stalked.

Stalking as the substitution of knowing with watching . . .

– The watcher looks from twisted angles, often through reflections, with an indirect stare
– The watcher gains an attachment to the untouchable, that then becomes mutual dependency (though the other does not know it)
– The watcher remains imperceptible, save in the pressure of the over-attentive gaze that is somehow sensed
– The watcher develops an infatuation with the facial expression, often an unreadable twinge
– The watcher is drawn to a state of exception in the object, its subtle difference from the rest (not radically altered, but slightly divergent, a minimal deviation in the performativity of the one gesture)
– The watcher seeks perfect repetition, ensuring the future encounter (not wanting conciliation, or some teleological closing of the gulf, but wishing that this inspired separateness would go on evermore)
– The watcher cultivates a nameless intimacy (the unofficial bond)

It is through these careful orchestrations that stalking insists upon yet another triumph of the imaginary: this is not the unattainable but rather a tangible craft . . . there is no scrounging, no contemplation, when the object is not present, and no need to possess or claim it through further interactions of touch. This play of hidden, disconnected looks is itself a cleft beyond reality and fantasy, as one endeavors to reimagine what is already happening in full grasp (defiance).

*According to the above selection, we are faced with a mischievous poet awaiting an enemy, one who sits across the bend (in far-off spots) and unleashes turmoil upon the chests below.

Seizure
(of the arms)

I shall come, I shall come, I shall come
With my hair: diffusing smells of the underworld
With my eye: intense experiences of the dark
With shrubs I have picked in the meadows beyond the wall. —Forugh Farrokhzad[9]

Deceptive transformations, though they ultimately cast open the boundaries of possibility, must first gain their strongholds through stringent acts of seizure, for to tie oneself to an enterprise that would leave sites changed is to require the fixity of the arms. There are ways through which a single proposition can embrace and then clench an entire reality, predicated always upon a bastard synergy of the idea, the spoken, the written, and the action. And so, the abductor must incorporate within its wing-span, for no sublimity is internalized unless the upper limbs are engaged, towing the rooted thing into its clinch, and thereby resembling the osmotic power of the alley: for, most of the time, nothing happens there, but when it does, it is always the most upsetting event (the moment of unsafe inhabitance).

*According to the above selection, we are faced with a since-deranged picker of greenery, a woman of the meadows whose hair and eyes betray the fact of her going-under, and who reiterates like a children's rhyme the fertile prophecy that she is coming for us.

Second Immortality
(ransom)

If the storm does not pass, I'll act surreptitiously; without in the least dying, I'll make out as if I were dead so that the family <?> and my friends <?> will bury me. When they wrap a shroud around me, I'll secretly conceal my waiting inside of me. No one will

*want to know a thing about it! Otherwise they would make sure they weren't burying a
man who was still living.* —Réda Bensmaia[10]

The simplicity of one underhanded idea is sufficient to invalidate all else (only
the deception is immortal) . . . and so any great treachery requires a great
intimacy, to memorize the inside of the other's reverie, if only later to forget
it, a bond then shattered, the implicit knowing of the other now undercut, a
proximity now revealed as distance and estrangement through an expert disclosure . . . to conceal the absence of nearness, the gap, the lapse, to conceal
what is not there between sides . . . and then to bring about the inexplicable
opposite, compassion disowned, with motives still unclear, discarded to the
rift. This is how one achieves the existential hostage-taking that is the focus
of this section, for becoming is itself a process of continual ransom: that the
horizon of the next phase abducts the current phase, setting a price, withhold-
ing the return until one enacts the turn, and thereby forcing one to exceed
what was harnessed, to excise the lifted present and strike onward, such that,
by the time one is given back what was taken, one will no longer have any use
for it (the consequence of the beyond is obsolescence). On the other side of
this sequestering, one will not even want the restoration (such is the key to
becoming adamant).

*According to the above selection, we are faced with a man who will fake his
own death, maintain patience as he is wrapped and buried, and then resume
the world of the living unexpected and indomitable.

Elusion
(fugitive)

*. . . in waters of disaster
in waters of dread:
water of a thousand hair locks,
water of a thousand eyelids,
water of a thousand incidents in remote straits.
water of closed chambers—
in the privacy of petrified birds.
Labyrinths
that conceal
crimes and offences
in the deeps.* —Yadollah Royai[11]

Some work tirelessly to improve their agility within webs, where thought seeks
varied sheets of expulsion, eliding, and avoidance. To become elusive, living

as the perpetual fugitive, is to realize when one must start running, elevating the rapidity of heart-rates and using swiftness, tempo, and haste to dodge the oncoming rounds. More than this, though, it is to gather oneself to a certain dryness when the moment of voyage arrives, to repudiate and leave behind the host of subjects and objects with whom one has grown acquainted, and without farewell (one can study the methods of monks, mystics, sailors, soldiers, traveling salesmen, and runaways).

*According to the above selection, we are faced with the enclosure of deep waters that have claimed thousands before, collecting body parts as their own amulets, though soon we learn that these are less closed spaces than labyrinths set in motion to absorb our sight away from other wrongdoings (one misdeed covers the other).

Endangerment
(phantom-chance)

Thus he had written: "Man's own thoughts are the most hazardous things." His student replied: "So thought must be a thing," and requested that his book be laid alongside him in his tomb. "Have them carve a minor rivulet in the open space of this stone . . . for we rotate upon the axis of danger." —Yadollah Royai[12]

There are plans that rest in the ditches of northern cities, those that are always composed with a hint of endangerment, for this is the gamesmanship of abduction, its foul playfulness: to keep score with existence, to estimate the relative injuries and track the winning and losing of pieces, all the while injecting a phantom-chance for its own defeat (the perfect strategy builds an imperfection into itself). Hence, the desire for an abduction-exploit must entail the presence of a flaw, if even a miniscule probability of being undone, ceaselessly preparing all the while constructing the trap-door through which one might also slip.

*According to the above selection, we are faced with a sage and his disciple, meditating upon the tomb and the phenomenological magic of books and tablets, aware that all thoughts of exploration also harbor within themselves the chance of sailing off the edge of the world.

Collapse
(the unguarded)

Concerned at my side, the dawn stands
Morning wants me
to make the announcement of its vital breath to this life-forfeited lot.

In my liver, alas, a thorn
breaks me from the road of my travel . . .

I grope around
to open a door
I wait in vain
that someone might appear
a clutter of walls and doors
breaks down upon my head. —Nima Yushij[13]

To operate with an abduction-mentality is not only to constantly locate what has been left ajar and gaping, but to understand that one exists within a collapsible universe. Having thus been left unguarded, one seeks to multiply the avenues by which things might fall apart (to craft the malfunction), for there is unparalleled elegance in demolition. The manor, the courthouse, the village square: these are not reliable shelters; each are just terraces overlooking the cliffs into which all built-up monoliths skid downward, becoming a juxtaposition of split boards.

*According to the above selection, we are faced with a traveler who delivers messages on behalf of the dawn, yet who soon finds a curious thorn embedded in his side, itself a bad omen that all doors lead into rickety domiciles, where one is showered beneath wooden beams.

Criminality
(rogue thought)

Clearly there can't be a real crime without the evidence of a piece of bone! Now there, maybe that's the master's secret: he has created a sentence without blood, a simple sentence that kills all pretension! A criminal sentence! —Réda Bensmaia[14]

The abductor must bring thought itself into isolation, away from torches, banquets, and sirens, so as to live among rogues and in suspicion (within the layers of the suspect). It is in this reclusive zone that one starts keeping diaries, those of the highwaymen, of noxious acts introduced into the ethical plane, writing that can imitate the filaments of criminal charges:

> Theft (writing that captures something of value, penetrating the interior
> space while the proprietors are fast asleep)
> Extortion (writing that exploits the fear of revelation,
> having found the one unprofessed detail)
> Arson (writing that brings a standing structure down,
> rendering ashen worlds)

Fraud (writing that employs counterfeit identities, encouraging misimpression)
Loitering (writing that makes words linger, hovering too
long in the doorways of consciousness)
Assault (writing that bolts across an otherwise shuttered physicality)
Vagrancy (writing that feigns abjection and courts
sympathy for ulterior motives)
Perjury (writing that bears false witness, confusing plausible retellings)
Intimidation (writing that compels action through
anticipation, alluding to the follow-through)
Prostitution (writing that solicits, seducing the mind
through the transaction of soiled bodies)
Trafficking (writing that slips tainted materials across the
borders, placing banned goods in freights and crevices)
Indecency (writing that exposes, showing its misconduct)
Forgery (writing that perfects the false signature, utilizing
the system's ability to be copied)
Homicide (writing that kills the other, proving that life is not sacred)
Suicide (writing that kills itself, proving that life is not sacred)
Harassment (writing that violates the imagination,
asking for something too many times)
Intoxication (writing that funnels the reader into addiction,
making available certain substances)
Treason (writing that counteracts the State, often
through collusion with the rival)
Espionage (writing that slinks, listening to private dialogues)
Hacking (writing that decodes, fueling a subculture of stolen files)
Corruption (writing that abuses power, selecting its
investigations based on bribery)
Heresy (writing that forwards an outsider orthodoxy,
modifying the dogmatic creed)
Trespassing (writing that disregards the land, trampling the fenced)
Desertion (writing that defects, keeping no company
above the option of leaving)
Hit and Run (writing that collides surprisingly, flees the
scene of suddenness, and does not identify itself)
Inciting a Riot (writing that sparks civil disorder, arming
secessionist impulses and taking to the streets)
Vandalism (writing that breaks glass, mars the walls, and
posts un-beauty across the most venerated)
Conspiracy (writing that agrees to future infraction,
coordinating diverse abilities)
Endangerment (writing that is reckless, disregarding
the impact on the other)

*According to the above selection, we are faced with a criminal author who leaves no evidence behind, no bludgeoning, blood-trail, or spattering, and yet pretends to be nothing other than criminal.

Stealth
(the mask, the veil)

There was the garden and the vale, a moonlit sight.
Substances the size of their shadows.
Staring at horizons and the night's beloved mysteries.
My eye was awake and a world's eye asleep.
No sound but the sound of the night's secrets. —Mehdi Akhavan-Saless[15]

Among the most indispensable of qualities in a deceptive literature is stealth, for it is through this notion alone that one turns the masks and veils of others into forces of revelation, to reverse their purpose, no longer screening but shooting forward, and to use one's own transparency as a kind of undetectability and deflection, the opening that closes, that takes away relation and renders inaccessibility.

The mask leaves the eyes visible, amidst the confidence and freedom of the masquerade, though one can make the visor obsolete through marking, the flaw that reveals and distinguishes, that tells the story of the one now hidden. The mask is also a double-energy: for it is through the erasure of identity that it produces the freeing temptation to come closer, to act without consequence, under the protective cover of anonymity. Finally, the mask is a scary utopian image of a world held in place: the sealed, unchanging expression, the encasement of the false smile, and the soundless laugh (such is the peril of the vacuous).

The veil hangs so as to shield from contour, disassociating its wearer from a particular context or emotion, but also distancing the viewers, depriving reaction and the ability to read the other. Its worth is therefore defused only when the sentiment it conceals is forced to spill to other parts, provoked or magnified to the extent of surpassing the covered area: the despair now revealed in the chest, the hate now concentrated in the fists, the terror now relocated to the stomach, the frustration now ripping through the voice (such is the peril of blankness).

*According to the above selection, we are faced with an eavesdropper, a skilled listener of nightly conversations, prying throughout orchards and valleys to hear an excluded euphonics, aware that shadows reveal more than so-called truths about the mysteries of a sleeping existence.

Illusion

Deception and illusion are not such synonymous terms upon second glance, for they intersect in a curious association, nor does one unconditionally serve the other (both are loyal to themselves, above all else, and not even that). And still, it is when their agitated plaits can bow into one another that an all-saturating, vicious caliber is achieved (overflowing unreality), one of such vexations, where the literal goes foraging in vain, and with it the new symbiosis: fatal deception (to kill by lying), or deceptive fatality (to lie by killing).

Manifestation
(the arsenal)

Myths refuse to adjust their plots.
They might mesh, for just a moment, with a certain flaw.
Ships might drift towards land, towards a bewildered land,
and the imaginary might afflict the real. —Mahmoud Darwish[16]

A dual-edged theory of manifestation is at stake here, first asking how to infuse, bond, or solder an illusion into the real, and then asking how to transfer, debase, or persuade a reality into illusion (to organize an arms-race between straight and crooked stances). This is how one compiles an arsenal of blasphemous forms, axioms of belief turned inside-out, where once-sure entities bend into impossible undertones, though in either manifestation scenario it is the illusory that prevails, for both sides have been brought into trickery. Furthermore, while an illusion loses little by flaunting itself as something solid, a reality forfeits everything if it confesses its doubt for even a second (thus the inborn advantage of the artifice).

*According to the above selection, we are faced with mal-adjusted mythologies and shipwrecked vessels, where the lighthouses beckon seafarers to crash against the shore, the waters now run by madmen.

Convolution
(the lie)

Find my body without delay, pray for me and have me buried. Above all, find my murderer! For even if you bury me in the most magnificent of tombs, so long as that wretch remains free, I'll writhe restlessly in my grave, waiting and infecting you all with faithlessness. —Orhan Pamuk[17]

Willed convolution outshines other paradigms in which a subject equivocates out of necessity (pathology), dreams out of necessity (biology), or fantasizes out of necessity (sublimation). This deliberative kind of lying, on the other hand, is not indebted to the unconscious, and in fact sends all remnants of psychological submission reeling into exteriority (active imposition). Once repressed underpasses now become deviant wildernesses sprawling around the real: for this is something brusque (from which canyon?), nothing like sarcasm's kerosene but rather an under-syntax that can lounge, bellow, or peel (from which creek?), planning trysts that scuff against the hypostasis, until the reification of the straitjacket.

*According to the above selection, we are faced with a slain narrator, mistreated even in the afterlife, left in a well to dissolve somewhere without justice, and ready to turn his paranoia into faithless infestations if the demands are unmet.

Distraction
(the component)

Behind this dune we have an oasis. Leave me alone. Leave me to rinse myself off in a bit of its mirage. I'm tired of running after myself to catch myself before I die. —Samih al-Qasim[18]

To channel the outer storm toward an inner distraction, for survival and diversion are often one and the same; to create a sub-reality, stage the counter-misgiving, and derail the gaze. And still, all interferences require the formulation of a component, an attractive item that leaves man panting, thus compelling one to search after the artifacts that populate a world, the miniaturism of its charismatic details, if only to use them against it. To find the trivialities they worship, staging them at attainable distances, so as to commit the other more pivotal assignment.

*According to the above selection, we are faced with an oasis where one can cleanse themselves in apparitional waters, washed free of the memory of self (and its chasing).

Fall-Out
(sacrifice, occultation)

. . . living luminously between two eternities of darkness . . .
. . . dead, but I have not been buried, and therefore my soul has not completely left my body . . . I do feel the deep torment of my soul struggling desperately to escape its mortal coil. —Orhan Pamuk[19]

To become enthralled in the pronunciation of one's own deceit, sunken into the gradual construction, its beckoning extensions and refinement, to the point of a fall-out (of awe); to become astounded in the face of one's own accumulating deception, as it touches upon existence. This is a new morphology of sacrifice: to knowingly give oneself over to hollow causes and word-plays, for no other reason than that one likes the sound of them (aesthetic devotion). For to be caught within a self-enchantment is the most efficient form of occultation (a larger shape passing over a smaller one); one is no longer an impostor, no longer obvious, for the woven spell has taken hold of its announcer.

*According to the above selection, we are faced with an entity struggling to negotiate the transition between body and soul, physical and metaphysical belonging, such that an unfinished mortality leads to an undesired immortality.

Scarring
(the axial wound)

Ahriman continues to butcher his body as every day new meat and tissues flow into the wounds abnormally, as they shut the wounds closed and forms scars—excessive scarring. —Reza Negarestani[20]

It is the illusion that scars worst of all, barbaric in its depth, leaving axial wounds that then turn into fascinating connective tissues, though these fibrous areas subsequently point the way to those who have been chosen to be recognized. One can no longer hide from view or retreat from the staring crowds; for the line follows everywhere, leaves one ascertained by everyone, constantly spotted as someone with a perhaps maligned history and therefore at once watched and left alone (others look and separate). The illusion, though, does even more than this, for it implants the injury within one's very composure, not a stroke upon the flesh but upon the demeanor, the expression, the nature with which one walks (to seem forever stung by something). There is little chance of healing from this, except through further deceptive mutilation, becoming nothing but a lattice of engrossing stripes.[21]

*According to the above selection, we are faced with self-deifying types who consummate abnormal genetic rites, basing unholy theologies upon ripped hides.

The Inexistent
(the unforeseen)

Without noticing you slide toward the madness of dreams.
Without noticing your eyes close down on life.
Your huge pupils drown in the white ocean.

Your mouth falls open while spilling the excess
Of your unmoored brain
Of your paralyzed tongue.
The room the whole room tenses up waiting
For what you see when you're seeing things. —Joyce Mansour[22]

They say it never was. They say it fell apart. They say it is forgotten. They say it left its mark. They say the others came for it. Thus the inexistent can only be viewed by its effects, as an extraneous figuration, three steps outside of creation, as that which does not consent to exist, does not seek or want to exist, shows no origin within this existence, bears no right to existence, gradually perceives a rift between itself and the existent world, threatens the existence of all things, and finally sacrifices itself to the one that then sacrifices existence as a whole (universal intrusion). When these varying conditions are met, then one might look for the arrival of the unforeseen—auspicious for some, unfavorable for most (a kind of ghastliness).

*According to the above selection, we are faced with a sliding consciousness, and the room where strange things are surveyed (leaving the jaw dropped).

The Unforgiving
(trespass)

Like a sworn enemy indifference follows me
grows like grass
settles like dust
strangles like a shell
I transform into a sickle;
Change into a brush;
Make myself into a cough

But had it not been so short
It would have reached its hand
Around my narrow throat and
Choked me long ago.

And while it continues to train its hand
I continue to try to grow taller. —Paruyr Sevak[23]

To eradicate forgiveness is to keep the players in a state of embryonic conspiracy (to set things in advance), whether to release or to disarm, giving rise to a foreboding trespass. This latent calculation most often comes from a desire to keep the injustice seasoned, to savor the distasteful and leave the terms of infraction undecided, pulsating, and fresh (nothing is recanted). They settle their tents in the inchoate; they glean, wallow, and enrich its grooves, and cobble together misconceptions that block all soteriologies. For there is some sweet residue in the maturation of one's being-wronged, a harsh yet enlivening flavor upon the tongue (it ages well), as one bitter event becomes an eternal justification.

*According to the above selection, we are faced with those who show no compassion toward the searching grip of indifference, who desecrate their own wombs, lengthen their necks, and stay up late outreaching narcotization in order to remain invested.

The Tearing
(incision)

Epidemic openness devours and butchers with such voracity that openness loses all its signifying and qualitative aspects . . . it means to be devoured-open. Laceration, being torn to shreds, cracked and laid open all suggest a strategic participation, a communion, or active communication with a ritualistic butchery—openness. —Reza Negarestani[24]

Some learn to develop a strict infatuation with the tiny violence of needles, advocates of freakishness and exhibitionism who want nothing more than to turn their own outer layers into a smuggler's border, a porous two-way threshold whereby some things ooze out and others seep in. They dream of infinite semi-illusory slits, they turn their own bodies into an acupuncturist's doll, riddled with microscopic pinpoints, going beneath whatever devices of tearing and incision are available, so as to leave themselves tattered, gaping, littered with holes, and ripe for the next.

*According to the above selection, we are faced with the butcher's obsessive interest in rending, wondering how one could exercise such precision with a hacking instrument, only to discover that it comes from prior visualization (he dreams of hewing down).

The Starved
(asphyxiation)

Our dear martyr's body
is left unburied
left upon our hands, left upon our hearts

like the dumb gaze of disbelief,
our chieftain he was, this noble warrior
crusader of our cause, leader of our host. —Mehdi Akhavan-Saless[25]

Phantasmatic experiences have a way of leaving their participants starved, amidst a thinning of the air that then becomes a thinning of the herd, as the breath-taken fall before the magnetism of an event horizon. And what does one look like who has been emaciated by illusions, or a city depopulated by malnourishment of the unreal? These are questions that should be answered, for they hold the correlation whereby theory's decrying of the lack can be made obsolete, the subject no longer wanting, by virtue of a counter-theoretical promotion of the imaginary—many have resorted to feeding their stomachs with apparitions, becoming leaner, asphyxiated, and even skeletal, and come away stronger for it.

*According to the above selection, we are faced with the unburied body of a rebel, left by some monarch to decompose in the thoroughfare, to make what was once heroic now sensorially offensive, forcing the passersby to cover their mouths and fast indefinitely from repulsion.

The Opiate
(temptation)

I smoked my whole stock of opium, in the hope that the wonder-working drug would resolve the problems that vexed me, draw aside the curtain that hung before the eye of my mind and dispel my accumulation of distant, ashy memories . . . My thoughts acquired the subtlety and grandeur which only opium can confer and I sank into a condition between sleep and coma. —Sadeq Hedayat[26]

There are times when one seeks existential anesthesia, the temptation of the going-under, for which the opiate then presents its consciousness-bursting avenues: there is timidity, then imbalance, then talent in the wake of its fumes. One stoops above the grill in sordid dens, searching for the breach into numbness, growing steadily pitiless toward the waking race: there are long tables in these places where men and women collapse, their bodies strewn across one another in haphazard adjacencies, the ugly commingling of the sedated (deadening unity). And yet there is some power in this slow-breathing configuration, something incredible communicated by their oblivion, daze, and taking-leave of the accepted world.

*According to the above selection, we are faced with a drowsy subject, one who is fully transfixed by the miracle of the drug, and who trades his stockpile of alienating memories for the unknown euphoric circumstance offered by the harvested plant.

Legion
(fragmentation, of the code, of the valences)

My magic and madness belong to wisdom,
my blood is the gurgle of deaths among graves
the screech at night of the door
the wind's howl in a skull
fleeing slaughter into slaughter.
Come! Look at me now—
gaze at my charms and clamor,
amazed at what you see. —Samih al-Qasim[27]

Through illusory legions, one coalesces smashed things into a paradigm of aggression (to align the fragmented), harmonizing resilient droves, chimerical troops, a ravenous dissension of non-souls (so many spawned), aiming their complication against the totalities of Being, a torrential succession of the undone . . . disquieted, traceless, the inexorable surfacing and clouding of whatever will not bend before oneness, but rather snaking the immateriality of the twice-faded world. This leaves the code—that which keeps its word, though the wrong word, not the dominant message but the anti-promise; and the valences—that which rotates, thought slung in decrepit orbits.

*According to the above selection, we are faced with trans-masochistic clairvoyants that colonize through the folklore of porphyria, those who congregate to sleights of hand and special charms.

The Shards
(architectonics)

Only when he goes to bed at dawn does he twist and turn with fury in his head, for a long while. He too, like so many others, had a horrible nightmare . . . what must have been especially horrifying was what he knew all along, but he still threw himself into the trap, again and again, because there was a trap in the dream. —Réda Bensmaia[28]

The architect's nightmarish wish: to turn knowing into an act of construction, the synchronization of thought and hands (ironwork), flattening and linking, to build the frayed and irregular arcade which always resides at the perimeter of its own prospective razing, fragile yet rugged (glasswork), an emblem speaking this: "that everything will be taken down." This is how a deceptive consciousness becomes an assault of the shards, that which continually splits and withstands fracturing, breaks and is broken in turn, sustaining discontinuity from all angles. An instinctive un-building that elicits a vicious dance of reflections, imperfect rings cast forward as wreckage from within (the atomizing semblance). Cruelty embedded in the material, torment inserted in the failing compound, a shelter turned against itself (exodus to ruin).

*According to the above selection, we are faced with a restless sleeper, the one who harangues his own mind with brutalizing visions, and turns them into a creaking prism of floorboards.

Reflex
(traversal, the ancient)

Some sniper had fired a shot at the rope and in so doing had demonstrated his prowess for everyone in the neighborhood to see. He'd said to us all: I'm capable of hitting any target, however tiny or delicate it may be. Every one of your hearts is within my range. I could put bullet holes through your arteries one by one. I could aim inside the very pupils of your eyes without missing the mark. —Ghada Samman[29]

When illusion turns into a reflexive action, it combines the practiced and the emergent (instantaneous custom), becoming the way through which a lone fugitive sensation can assume ultimate dominance over existence, a mild predilection enough to override all else, supremacy of the minor, the infinitesimal, by which the most irrelevant holds hostage the continuum of experience. This is a second primalism intrinsic to the impulse, a neo-savagery that simulates the torn instance before the first human, and that allows one to activate an absurd traversal, where one can overcome distances and oppositions, the spectrum thrown into admixture, so as to devise the unknown through the ancient. It is through the daring of an outdated inquest that one approaches the unattained affect (backwards can be forwards).

*According to the above selection, we are faced with the marksman who has turned a technique into a lightning response, reaching across space with near instantaneity while in the same breath ascribing an immemorial quality to the sharpshooter.

Damage
(occlusion)

Raging and drunk and mad it is,
Raising the dust like a dark trembling tent,
Ruining soon what it had made.
Like a cogent magic the wind can do as it wants.
Drunk and mad,
It raids the heavens and earth. —Mehdi Akhavan-Saless[30]

When sanctity falls to lunacy, and madness climbs the walls, we find ourselves
in the province of a damaged consciousness, one that is a disaster-unto-itself,
blockaded to what lies beyond, one that speaks only to itself, in a language
undetermined, a derangement that cannot see or hear the outside, embedded
in an alternate existence that obstructs the understanding of and engagement
with the real. This is the logic of occlusion under which the first phase of imagination operates, but then some light tampering takes place, an almost unnoticeable readjustment (the inaudible shift), through which this illusion-stricken
mind begins to project unfounded guilt upon everything that surrounds it (the
paranoiac streak). It becomes more expansive in its range and yet more narrow
in its perception, as all beings dwindle before the same reigning idea.

*According to the above selection, we are faced with tenacious breezes that
have somehow attained intoxication and psychotic leniency.

Intimation
(the mercenary)

An expiring voice exists between East and West;
occasionally, it does say something:
I am scared before the shooting comet,
and how it signals a divine infliction.
Let us begin the prayer of ghastliness.
The prayer of ghastliness. —Mohammad Reza Shafi'i Kadkani[31]

A manipulative agent, at its most effective, is able to funnel the illusory world
into a more subtle form of intimation: where the real can be disturbed by
an allusion, a vague suggestion, something remote now able to possess grave
impact, an intuition attentive to what is not yet there and a susceptibility before
the thing that is waiting-to-come. It coaxes a deep experiential imbalance
(rampant disorientation) . . . to make sway across the ropes, to mistrust where
one stands.

This is why radical deception must be categorized as a mercenary endeavor, for it integrates the most pressing skills of the former: that it attacks with suddenness; that it enlists asymmetricality in its tactics; that it sabotages and ambushes; that it is always outnumbered (under siege); that it moves from the inside to rise up against its own atmosphere (internal rebellion); that it ties itself to outside forces (no concept of the foreigner and the native); that it serves no cause beyond war for the sake of war; that it rushes forward in waves, and organizes itself in cells; that it shows the willingness to sell what is most intimate; that it will fight with any camp for a certain price (the sedition of purchased limbs); that it perfects the impersonal; and the anonymous kill (to take just another one).

*According to the above selection, we are faced with a moment of horrid intervention, this god's dark side, that sends meteoric punishments hurtling down and through space.

Chapter 5

Rage: Writings of Overthrow

O. Overthrow
(vicious disposition)

I. Initiation
(the trigger, the enemy)

II. Hardness
(hyper-withstanding)

III. Exhalation
(of the breath)

IV. Deceleration
(the arrested)

V. Blackout
(diffusion)

VI. Ecstasy
(of the drums)

VII. Thirst
(the devoured)

VIII. Instability
(the strayed)

IX. Overwrought
(the elder)

X. Hate
(the across)

XI. Hostility
(the uneven)

XII. The Interlace
(manipulation)

XIII. The Undone
(reign)

XIV. Immanence
(of the blood)

XV. Prism
(atrophic space)

Middle Eastern literature has perfected the chemistry of rage (growling), summoning its morphologies of textual anger in waves of a permanent striking. This rage is the moment of poetic imbalance, a hate that moves across the real, not against it, descending in night-raids; it forms a quadratic enclosure, it forms wrathful instinct (the fangs). This rage wills itself as pain and creation, and it grants no amnesty, no escape, fusing the qualities of excess, nothingness, defiance, and interruption in a single motion of words. Here everything is driven into abrasive fits, everything is made to tear at the walls, everything is invaded and broken. Rage is a new regime, one born of riot and convulsion (it trains the mind and body to rasp). It is the alliance of force and speed, and it inflicts itself upon existence without mercy (the mission). Its emanations make contact and cross great distances, wresting each site across the borderlines of a becoming-decimated (the unsheathed ones). Nothing evades rage, at once omnipresent and seemingly erratic. It is an insatiate action, one that commits treason against whatever crosses the path, one that sentences itself to heightened confrontations (the outcry). For rage is the holding tank of a world-aspiring aggression, a heathen's pendulum, and it never disappoints, as it uncovers every potential excuse to complement its own incandescence.

Overthrow
(vicious disposition)

From now on my occupation is to uproot hell so that, hell having revolted against me, pounded upon me, driven me to despair, felt itself alive, wanted to discuss, believed I had been forgotten, combined mixtures, different things, sought to be rid of me by crushing me, replacing me, it's the battle, I can't forget it, I can't be the victim. —Réda Bensmaia[1]

One seeks the color of a vicious disposition, and with it an iconography of rancor. Rage liberates the dwindling experience (the anti-pillar, the anti-vintage), taking one outside the domain of victimhood by calling upon the poetic imagination to overthrow even the limits of the demonic itself (one must learn how to do this). There are countless examples of this gesture, those of a daring outer consciousness who boast that they shame even the underworld to insignificance, for they have outmeasured rebellion, have matched vitriol at the nadir of things and undone the dialectic (supra-stricture), crafting their own light-sensitive inflammation.[2]

*The lines reveal: that the enraged are irresistible trophies for other unpleasant formations, that still more unfavorable types feel themselves alive when marshaled against them.

Narrative 0: Gathering (the Prison-Players) . . .

Some poets tell of those who take advantage of their hell . . . without justice, without injustice.

One witnesses the transversal of crooked, affluent narratives: they all came, seated at stained tables, those who had been electrocuted, the ones who had been burned, the ones who had been drowned, branded or cut open, those without eyes or nails, tongues and even minds; and now here, this carnivalesque gathering, of the grotesque and the seductive, not a space of the silent/the muted but of competing eloquences, at once barbaric and elaborate, of figures distorted and disproportionate, limbs elongated or incomplete; they are the residue not of an overdetermined psychological history but rather of an amorphous event, not codified but provocative and intricate; we must learn from these catastrophic archetypes, from their errant tactics of entrancement and survival, no longer the casualties of bare life, of a raw and organic past, but rather as the progenitors of a still-unfolding style, a style that comes from their former experiences of evil, but only so as to allow them to become something even more evil, for style is always evil (because it diverges). These were not heroic figures, no incarnations of tragic downfall, but a pack, both of wolves and cards, now humorous, versatile, enlivened, monstrous, embodying a vile rank of affirmation. There was no repression, beyond weeping now, only a new morphology of laughter; the wretched had taken on the ill-fated speed of the storyteller, a constellation of anti-identities, anonymous, nameless, post-ideological, post-subjective and post-political, without trauma, community, or memory, but rather visceral manifestations of a radical illusion; they were not real, but rather abstract, cosmetic, performative, evidence of a concocted materiality, a subtle conspiracy of the undead (they had willed their own unnatural extinction). Rather, they had turned their recollections of martyrdom into emergent signs of complexity, where coldness becomes impassioned, leaving an affective mine-field, an unappetizing crew that had found one another again, on the outside, changing the passcodes of despair and futility into an unrighteous right to immediacy. One is mistaken to mourn here; few know what must take place in order for there to be an aftermath. It was as if the total negativities of what once happened, the levels of isolation, torment, expulsion, condemnation, displacement, abandonment, these zero-degrees of pain, were now recast as delirium, toward a rare, formless inscription of rapture. This leads to just one conclusion: that the poetics of the torture-chamber is its own kind of play.

Initiation
(the trigger, the enemy)

He's still among us
   Fill his empty cup
Repeat the songs he raised
In chanting to the sky,
Recall how wine and grief
Could never weaken him
Hand firm on the trigger. —Mamdouh 'Udwan[3]

It is in rage alone that all is equalized, that all are equalized (though pitted against one another), for everything becomes collateral. What makes it such an unpredictable force is its process of initiation, for one never knows what starts the outfit rolling, what cranks the lever that then leads to thunderous circumstances. Almost anything can fashion a reason to become volcanic, can serve as the trigger by which irate trends ensue, such that everything then soars into bile and fulmination. Fighters in states of rage cannot be trusted to discern their proper foe; even supposed allies take three steps back when a certain look flashes through the eyes, for they know that anything within the line of sight can be battered and flung down. In this sense, rage constructs the basis for a universal enemy, sours all countenances with the same enmity, and aims across whatever comes close. And this arises from the enraged figure's own sense of peerlessness (that he is like no other), willing to plunge all else into acrimony for the sake of one's own exceptionalism. One moves better than the rest, shrieks louder, and therefore deserves to be the only thing left standing.

*The lines reveal: that the enraged will remain, amidst toasts raised in honor of iron-clad reputations, as nightly remembrances of their counterparts left behind.

Narrative I: Body-Experimentation (the Pioneer) . . .

Some poets tell of the torture-chamber, describing the countless means through which power harmonizes its wretched melody, parading their methods as a kind of artistic atrocity. There is no fetishism, exoticism, heroism, romanticism, glamorization, or moralizing in the recounting of these agonic tales, nor is there an underlying premise of responsibility or engagement— they simply happen, and thereby allow us to advance a new theory of poetic rage. The most telling examples occur far beyond the borders of utility, where there is no longer any viable information to extract from the prisoner, no reason to continue digging this well, nothing functional about the misery, and so it evolves into gamesmanship (torture for its own sake). The following are some of the prominent modes with which the Eastern poetic imagination contends at each turn.

Sometimes the guards use heat, scorching the flesh down many layers, noting how the oscillations of high temperature will make the body writhe, coiling in all directions, as if running from itself, seeking deliverance from what blazes (only to learn that everything blazes). In some instances, the prisoner is laid across a scalding metal table, warmed to the point of whiteness, which achieves the desired effect of making them turn frantically from side to side (if there are straps, they are kept loose so as to allow thrashing), continually sacrificing one part for the next, making ultra-fast deductions as to which sector can be given over, and for how long, before shifting once again (a choreography of avoidance and substitution). Then there is also the introduction of boiling liquid (sometimes oil), whether by being plunged into a bath, soaking in a tank of infernal proportions, or having it poured from above, with one bucket after another creating a torrid waterfall. There is a hemispheric distinction: in the first case, the lower body is inescapably immersed, and one keeps the head above the surface, just safe enough to evoke its instinctive howling; in the second case, the face meets the searing fluids before all else, grimacing as it takes the central burden (the skull swells and throbs), only then for it to trickle down the spine and beyond, such that one flails the legs to spare them a similar penalty. This two-pronged method creates a civil war between northern and southern appendages, and soon one begins to ruminate on their individual preference, deciding which branches matter more, and which portions they wish would withstand the greater share. Finally, there is outright burning, whether by torches, rods, candles, or smoking implements, which enables a compartmentalization of the body into enkindled patches (becoming-embers); that way, unlike the totality of the table or the bath, one can later sit in the cell and marvel at the particular wedges that have been divided from the rest (sporadic partitions), that stand out in discoloration and sensitivity, split from the whole as negative exceptions. They no longer look like the majority, these ragged insignia, either redder, bluer, or greener than the remaining normality, but not the same anymore.

On the other side of the spectrum, there is coldness, whether imposed or natural, extreme or gradual, through over-exposure to ice, snow, and wind. This is a low-maintenance tactic, since the guards can simply allow the long winters to do their work, letting the incarcerated sleep on the chilling slab of the cell, without blankets or covers of any kind, shivering throughout the entire night (forming an ever-shrinking human ball). The imprisoned become a chorus of clattering teeth, and the prison itself a hypothermic silo, as the tortured are confronted with yet further decisions in their effort to manage pneumonic discomfort: when the walls and floors freeze over, should one take off garments and place them beneath? And to make things worse, the guards can always break windows, allowing unfriendly gusts to rush in, or reduce the prisoner to nudity, accelerating the formal progress of frostbite, or more than this, sometimes wet coats and robes are thrown in the cell, tempting the prisoner to an unreasonable, short-term solution (are they desperate enough to fall for it?). This is a seasonal maneuver, of course, since the same can be achieved with sweltering once the summer arrives. But, then again, there is always the possibility of sub-zero waters, and there are poetic retellings of a consortium of pools, wells, and ponds dug into the dirt of the prison grounds precisely for this purpose: not only is there the typical glacial impact, but an added dimension of muddiness, rankness, and filth (as if a swampland clings to the frame).

Electrocution is another of the most salient procedures at constant disposal, testament to the false glory of science and the underbelly of technological knowledge, favored policy of the asylum, administering jolts from one edge to the other, reveling in the efficient circuitousness of nerves. The sting in one region carries to another, careens against the brain, and is shot elsewhere again, as one reels at the over-connectedness of their own anatomy, rocking furiously in the chair (gripping the arms), cursing the labyrinthine flow from organ to organ, vein to vein, and the apparent facility with which man stole the secrets of lightning. For the most part, it is an interior damage (thus most squint as the conductions go through), leaving no tangible outer traces, and is of special interest for its manipulation of intermittence: there are periods of subsidence between currents, where one winces amidst the few aftershocks, unclenches the jaw, sighs perhaps, and then braces again for the next chapter. The poetics of rage often comes close to this snaking outworld of voltages, having seen the live-wires at their best, and leaving one to wonder: what a strange sight it must be, to watch as fumes seep from one's own body (the vengeance of energy).

Sleep deprivation has no substitute in the inner circles of the prison-poet's world, as the guards work tirelessly to irritate the already-tired, upsetting circadian rhythms and rendering expected patterns impossible. In some cases, they never allow the full shutting of eyes (chronic half-closure), not even a split-second drifting before the disturbance comes crashing forward, and in other cases wait just long enough for the dream to commence, then dispelling its onset, most often through a tyrannical deployment of noise (the clanging of bells, the rattling of the bars, the mean shouts of the guards). They enlist a barrage of quintessential distractions against the one longed-after retreat (one wishes for a deafened universe), overturning even the ancient codes of battle for which the enemies would agree upon times of respite, worship, and truce before resuming the trade of horror. Here, though, no convalescence is ever extended: for just as fire, water, and electricity were supposed to hold affirmative meanings, yet another pure connotation is reversed, as "awakening" is similarly stripped of its ideal-type and made into a nastier process, feasting upon the well-being of its holder. There is only serial rousing, dilation, restlessness, rehearsals of the unsoothed spirit, whatever form of application takes shape: some speak of being made to stand against a wall for prolonged sessions, beaten each time the body slouches, submitting itself to the need for darkness. The irony is transparent: for daring to raise consciousness, these writers will be kept conscious; for daring to bring life, they will be resurrected inexorably.

Soon enough, both muscle and bone are invited to the foray, often joined together through starvation, traversing the outmost hunger-barrier (where atrophy and emaciation become irrefutable), or through other orthodoxies. In some cases, the poetic figures tell of having weights suspended from their extremities (the fingers, the heels, the lips, the ears, or even from the neck), forming boughs and branches, converted into clownish trees from which any number of items hang (including other people). The imperviousness of knots becomes apparent, their flawless elaborations of soreness, straining, and tension, as the prisoner hunches over to compensate for the immense pressure at stake (sometimes things sever). One stoops to counteract gravity, seeking lowness as a remedy to the swaying, but this offsets little (the talisman wins): before long, whatever swings might tear straight through (leaving irreparable holes). Or, across other fronts, there is the breaking of bones, both small and major; things do not dangle here but rather fracture, crack, and snap (anti-softness). The poets tell of those left crippled, those who were subjected to the clockwise ratcheting of the rack, and who limped or hobbled away years later (with malformed ankles and ribs), still prone to aching and jutting, for they never set right.

Whipping and stabbing rely upon the permeability of the skin like nothing else, together attacking the surface and the depth, with particular attention to the instruments. Flagellation is nothing so novel to the history of civilization, and so there are limitless stories to convey images of flaying, verses that speak of the absorption of the lash, where cords flash across the instep, leaving one unable to stand or walk for weeks. And still, this reinstates an old yet worthwhile debate over the intricate relationship between pain and repetition, for the foreknowledge of its recurrence (that there are always more strokes to follow) both exacerbates and tempers the marathon: one is belted once, with a hundred more determined, and is thereby forced to stare uphill at the remaining levels of scourge (does counting along make it better or worse?). Nor is the piercing of skin a less infamous commerce in this place; stabbing has its own notoriety, evident in miniscule puncture wounds, pockets of imperial arrogance, caused by an array of utensils or half-shattered bottles, the hallmark of porosity, where pointed canes first scrape and then dive under.

One must add drowning, suffocation, and strangulation to the admixture of poetic revelations. Some are collared or submerged for a while, brought to a three-quarters cessation and then pulled back from the ledge (as the lungs fill, grate, and cave). Resuscitation is a matter of expert timing (when to unfasten the cinch). But there is a more cunning articulation of this experience, applied through entrapment, the sequestering of the prisoner in a confined space (the tiniest rooms): closets that look more like boxes, where the floor and ceiling nearly touch, where one crowds oneself, unable to stretch, and claustropho-bia pales in comparison to sheer rigidity. These most spellbinding writers, who delight in their capacity to mesmerize, rivet, and transfix their readers (to clutch through enchantment), some of them perhaps learned this talent from having been crushed, gripped, and pinned down themselves (to clutch through disenchantment).

Extraction brings us close to the tail-end of this non-exhaustive archive, for the guards have a keen eye for superfluity: first they decide that whatever comes in pairs can afford the loss of one (some self-amputating madmen arrive at the same conclusion). Beyond this halving of symmetrical parts, they also take into serious consideration the things of which one has many, bothered by the abundance and wanting to restore austerity through cutting (one needs only so much of something, and the rest is opulence). And there is a third cri-terion: the excision of things that will grow back (they enjoin resurgence). The removal of nails is among the most popular example, particularly elegant for their fragility and crystalline nature (some guards were said to make decora-tions of them).

Finally, there is the exploitation of sound (as weapon), amidst recordings of screams played in constant loops, forging a conglomeration of sonic harm. The frequencies of these simulated cries, however artificial, sow their uproar into the mind of the captive, confirming the immutability of the prison (audio-haunting). Nor are the utterances of the guards any more tasteful—false reports, vulgar jokes, ill-mannered threats—engulfing the residents with profane speech-acts and words of inconsolability. One cannot help but listen to these tirades, the ebbing of their same lava, though a special poetics is born out of this growing revulsion toward language.

With all of this established, the intent of such narratives is to show the way to that rare one who would steal the reins of this catastrophic landscape: namely, the contrarian prisoner who aids the imagination of the guards in devising superior schemes. He will show them better ways of reaching within and tak-ing away. What does this require: to transfer oneself from the role of target, to then start dabbling amateurishly in one's own suffering, to then becoming a true disciple of disciplinary effects, to then gaining mastery over the wheel? This is not mind over matter, but rather the mind's fascination with matter, supernatural coordinations of ligature, as the prisoner observes, adopts, and controls the sphere of anguish. He stays up through the night, entranced by the complexity of such routines, transcribing in his mind the past successes and failures, taking an analytical distance complemented by sensorial infatu-ation (to experiment on oneself). Soon he requests pen and paper in order to draft new schematics, and begins the eerie custom of scrawling, toiling over the technique, juxtaposing complicated diagrams, pictographic representations, and stick-figure drawings of himself with areas of vulnerability pointed out (the finest spots). He becomes dialogic, a respected architect, conversationalist, and educator, encouraging the guards to improve their versatility, accentuate their skills, and attempt his more original illustrations; he becomes a visionary and seer, creating stratagems of eventuality; he offers involved rhetorical explanations about the segments not yet worked upon (waiting to be trashed), widening their arsenal and organizing their untried potential (embellishment); he anticipates the next testing-ground, leaves himself naked and ravenous to reenter the laboratory, and shows signs of jealousy when others are carted into the interior rooms (impetuousness), all so as to discover the summit of what this place can accomplish (paramount affliction).

Hardness
(hyper-withstanding)

Light the fire so I can see in the mirror of the flames
The courtyard, the bridge
And the golden meadows.
Light the fire so I can see my tears
On the night of the massacre,
So I can see your sister's corpse . . . —Samih al-Qasim[4]

Rage is often associated with hardness, vigor, and remorseless adrenaline, but in fact should be viewed as a motion toward advanced sensitivity, toward the most gentle tolerance (to undertake without the anesthesia of Being). It is not to become hollowed but rather unconditionally responsive, and to crave the reaction, the impact, the tearing-inward, marked by an idiosyncratic desire to withstand. It is to become formidable, to wield enormity and turn consciousness into its own dynamite, though only through gigantic trials of endurance.

*The lines reveal: that the enraged ask to be taken to the most crumbled spots, so that they can internalize the full range of images of massacre; the more corpses looked over and tears stored in vials, the more durable the ethos.

Narrative II: The Mock Execution (Understated Laughter) . . .

Some poets tell of the mock executions that are rampant in the prison, and the radical variations that the guards engineer in their boredom (idleness is a source of such genius), each a specific kind of torment that positions psyche against body in some glaring way. We first confront the poet in the cell, then, as he is given some forewarning of the event to take place later in the square. It matters what time of the day this announcement is made, whether it is delivered in the early morning hours or noon or at dusk, for the temporal shifting throughout the remainder of the day then becomes drenched in a certain atmosphere. After all, if one is told at dusk that the following dawn will mark the hour of execution, then the midnight takes on a quality like no other (the blackness of that time resembles death itself). It also robs sleep from the proprietor of this information, as he tosses throughout the late hours, adding an insomniac twist to the occasion (they will show up the next day wired and frenetic, a gifted trait of their sleeplessness). It also turns one into an ironic enemy of the light, as the first shafts that break through the cell window only serve to exude a fatal glow (there is something so wrong about being shot while bathed in light). On the other hand, if one is told in the morning, then they gradually keep count of the sun's descent, they keep their eyes bound to the increased dwindling of illuminations, the strength of shadows upon walls and ground, until the last flickers expire and night takes uncontested hold of the world. This creates a desperate attachment to radiance, as the sparks embody nothing less than survival itself, and one anxiously charts the vertical slope from shining to glistening, from glimmering to mere gleaming (the miniscule differences between these words matter so much in the prison-space).

It also matters greatly how long the interval proves between the notification and the execution itself, so as to let the mind wind itself to maximum alertness, terror, or conviction. If one is told that it takes place within an hour, then they must combat the suddenness of the confrontation, since they are given a compressed amount of seconds with which to assess, evaluate, or overcome their condition; they are brought flush into the matrix of this brief happening, without the necessary allotment of time to contemplate an action or a feeling. It is not long enough to enumerate all the things that must be registered before one makes departure; it is not sufficient for memory or mourning, one can barely include anything of substance within an hour's span, and so nostalgic reflection is callously disbanded. One can recall or meditate upon only a few select things, and without the wherewithal or composure to choose correctly, to isolate the most significant items or figures within one's personal hierarchy, which results often in a flooding of both useless and precious recollections, an undifferentiated surge of experiences. One lacks the ability to cut through the irrelevant images, lacks the strength to focus and elevate some above the broad flashing continuum of the entire life, and so exists in the cell (until the designated moment) under the pressure and havoc of a cacophonous stream of ideas, associations, and pictures. These ones are said to often sway their heads in disbelief, thrown from side to side in an indiscriminate storm of possible inquests, for the imposed urgency of the execution leaves them open to a true spurting of the mind, an unwanted masochistic exercise of consciousness whereby thought goes into overdrive and swamps its disoriented listener. By the time the guards arrive, he has been relegated to complete passivity, rendered helpless, stunned, and bewildered by the outpouring of his own interiority upon him, for this is the awful look of the knowing subject gone too far: here we meet the one who is forced to know too much, in too small a period, and therefore inundates himself with deliberations. If the philosopher is the one who takes time within the world, pausing for a while in order to figure, analyze, conjecture, then this one is brought before one of the most philosophical junctures imaginable without the right to take time; being executed demands the seriousness and inspiration granted only by longevity, but here all speculation is rushed, all notions half-formed. Such is the power of the one-hour decree: to uproot epistemology itself.

Then again, there is always the other approach: that one is informed of one's destiny a full day or more beforehand, and is therefore left to ponder the concept in excruciating lengths of an otherwise empty period. There are stages that often take place here as well, an incremental downfall that has much to do with speed, for often this individual will take the vast remaining time in order to exhaust oneself: they pace for a while in rabid steps, then fall back upon the mat, they punch the walls for a while and make the knuckles bleed, then fall back upon the mat, they curse god and man for a while, and then fall back upon the mat. Beyond neurosis, and into dissemblance.

These animations, though, only seal their detriment further: thrashing against the gray bars, roving across the concrete floor, hurling shrill insults to the guards, does nothing but to drain their already condemned form in a choreography of useless expenditure. One moves a great deal when so much time is given, half-athletic, half-epileptic; one speaks a great deal as well (in high-pitched tones), half-lyrical, half-gutteral, as if trying to fill the void through frenzied motion and auditory bursts; but this is a disingenuous attempt: what comes will come, and each prolonged hour proves this with even further certainty (it calcifies around the room, forming a second skin, the prisoner's final shell). By the time the guards arrive, they find this one haggard, self-beaten, having spent all energy on the waiting-game generated by a simple elongation of the gap, somehow defeated not by the execution but by the intermission itself, where a single interlude can rip apart an entire consciousness, where the slowness of a single recess can wrench one into exasperated spasms. Thus we see the worst face of duration, one that yields lethal impatience and brings to pass yet another ontological blood-letting (always spilling too much).

And we are not done yet (not even close), for there are still other instrumental details that the guards regulate in order to heighten the stakes of the execution: namely, the delay or the early arrival. This is a seemingly minor disjuncture, but one that further interrupts an already interrupted temporality of anticipation; it adds another problematic layer, as if the original quandary were not enough to invite instantaneous madness. But no, it is never enough there (power always seeks to paint further coats), and so they invent this grueling arithmetical adjustment. In the first instance (the delay), one must battle with addition, afforded the extra sliver that is at once a gift and a curse, since it was not requested (there is no luxury of appealing) but thrown upon the prisoner as a kind of unbeautiful procrastination. A strange illogic even surfaces at this point whereby one grows paranoid at the executioner's deferral, as if there could be anything worse than what they already know, and begin having qualms about the motives and implications of this temporary suspension. They start asking questions (the horrid underside of wonderment), guessing at double meanings and examining what might be hidden up the sleeves of the rulers of this place. Rather than use these supplementary minutes well, appreciating the unplanned reward, they become participants in its trickery, as an unspeakable doubt takes hold. In this respect, it is an endowment that spoils itself, that leads into tightening, compaction, wallowing, and wariness. Or even worse, some stumble into false hope, thinking themselves the inheritors of a saving chance, and therein become addicted to the idea of fortuitous lengthening and haphazard salvation, musing that the postponement could be extended eternally (perpetual staying). They pray that a simple accident could in fact be the birthplace of a miracle, as gratitude morphs into greed, which only augments the shock when the new departure-time is set and the guards do come—they are doubly surprised when led out, fools of a disgusting anti-climactic ruse, and one sees this in the manic fluttering of eyelids (the plaintive gaze). Now they realize that this was an uncharitable donation, and that they had been operating under a mistaken outlook all along: that this delay was never about luck, it was always just more torture.

In the second instance (the early arrival), there is also astonishment, this time of the subtraction, since the prisoner had initially been given an established marker with which to reconcile his mortal imagination, a particular striation on the clock with which he somehow sought equilibrium (he had trusted the absolutism of that checkpoint). And now the chronology is violated, the ground swept out from underneath, leaving one to babble the same relapsing words ("not yet . . . too soon"), though this is a delusion of course: they never would have been ready, since they were perceptually robbed of the necessary expanse. This is a bizarre experiment with reason: for, despite having lived in the absurd universe of this prison for so long, subordinated for months or years to its whims and perversions, his own body a testament to the illegitimate union of myth, discourse, and ideology, at this last zenith of the execution-hour somehow he had dared to invest in rationality once again. He was not skeptical when they reported the schedule, and thereby acquiesced to them his last shred of faith (this is what they were after, in any case); they spoke in committed terms about the enterprise and hence lured him into devotion, and with this reliance he was forced to train himself to grow accustomed to the idea of an ensuing destiny. Against all survival-instincts, he acquainted himself with this phase; he regulated his thoughts and turned the supposed hour of his death into a whirlwind or black hole phenomenon, coordinating each breath around this centralized symbol. This stated time was his last metaphysics, and it was shattered (when the key turned too swiftly).

It does not last long, but the momentary encounter between the guard and the prisoner is crucial in its own right, leading one to ask after the cage door opens: do they request that the prisoner stand of his own volition (surrender), do they order that he rise (command), or do they shove him to his feet (brutality)? These are not incidental choices, for each of the three pathways secures a distinct version of authority for the institution and its stranglehold on the reality-principle. The request is employed not to show mercy (no ethical consideration) but to demand total subjugation, for it proves a deeper victory by the prison: that they were able to elicit an unconditional self-betrayal, for now he hands his identity over to the impossible quite willingly, with his wrists hanging lifeless at his sides (incapable of resistance). The command is employed only to humiliate the prisoner with the fact that there is no will or self-determination allowed even amidst the last breath (often the guards will not even look at them, refusing eye contact, as they instruct and charge their target). Still sometimes they stare deeply and longingly into the eyes of the other (this is its own mockery), and the severity of their gaze or the fact of their smiling opens up further realms of inquiry here. Nevertheless, then there is the third option, when the guards approach and handle the body with usual roughness, slamming limbs against their own chests so as to highlight the intimacy of coercion, swapping words for an equally expressive physicality, for this abuse makes apparent the true paradox at work in the execution: that we are in store for an event that strays between hyper-materiality (the pierced flesh) and immateriality (the discontinued pulse). The gateway is corporeal, while the destination is purely abstracted, as one is transported through the unknowable, the beyond, the ethereal, by raw terrestrial force.

But we are not there yet, and cannot skip the trajectory before us: we then follow the poetic imagination into the hallway (the harrowing in-between). The accessories matter here, whether they are chained, whether the manacles are placed across both arms and legs, for it decides whether they are led in shuffling paces or concerted strides (how one walks to death is important). There are many accounts of this journey, how the panorama of the prison underground stretches out before them, and how for once in that voyage they become conspirators of the labyrinth: they hope for more turns, and dream that the corridors are never-ending, they tour the squalor of those serpentines with no superior wish than that they advance forever (there is relative peace on the inside). If only the transitional stage could go on forever (there is calm in the middle passage), one would settle for this purgatory.

Soon enough, one finds the trek leading into a new spatiality—that of the courtyard—whereupon the execution-poets almost always take note of the climate (the ambience is documented to the minutiae). Does one perish in the heat, rain, snow, or fog (is the last sensation one of dampness, dryness, humidity)? Moreover, what are the acoustics of this exposed area (do the shots reverberate, echo, drift upwards, or somehow mute themselves)? Are others watching along the fringes (other convicts, civilians, outside guests—how many eyes are upon this)? Is one tied to a post (does one feel wood upon the back), positioned against a wall (does one feel stone upon the back), or simply marched into some makeshift core without fetters or backdrop (does one feel wind surrounding)?

We must remember, though, that this is a mock execution (we will delve into the real thing later), and so this episode now develops three variations according to the poetic voices who would guide us here, a narrative crossroads of sorts: (1) the solitary execution (where no one dies); (2) the mass execution (where no one dies); or (3) the collective execution of the one (where one dies). The first case follows the chronicle that we have sculpted thus far, as an individual is elected for extermination, plunged into dire internal struggle, left to endure the fated hour alone (how is it different if they have a cell-mate; what camaraderie, resentment, or incommunicability is generated when one is given their death-papers before another?), then is wound through all of the horrendous stages of the ceremony, until staring directly into the firing squad, and some last official words recited, only to hear the barrel click empty or draw blank (the heart stops anyway). The second case changes everything, as the entire population is warned in advance (or at least a large segment) that they have all been selected, and thereby distributing the fear, concern, and outrage among a group. Death, however, does not bring together in the same ways that ideology precipitates unity; rather, it binds them in a common venture, a joint and semi-public situation, but also fractures them into self-involved compartments (one wants their own space for this, and reels at the image of a mass grave), and even worse turns them against one another as each becomes a crouching emblem of the other's demise. To look at the other is to preemptively survey one's own expiring heartbeat (they mirror futurity itself), and so they become a source of distress and even a compradore enemy, one that unwittingly carries out the hate of the prison, mediating its devious mind-games. Nor is the travel to the courtyard the same when one staggers among many, body upon body funneling through the narrow hallways, clamoring in ways that disallow introspection, in an evacuation that looks somewhat like the herding of animals and somewhat like a sacred exodus (a flight-mode caught between beast and angel). And they too are brought before the austere coagulation of the firing squad, where there are usually too many to allow last words, where one feels a strange responsibility to remain quiet (to honor the indefensible sincerity of the pack) but still hears the awkward anomalies of individual reactions floating back and forth (coughing, weeping, divergent breathing patterns), and they do stand out (with harsh resonance). And when it dawns on them that it was nothing more than a show, a piece of jail theater, they are all at once connected in their awe, release, and transient emancipation, a bittersweet solidarity of the death-cheaters—for, together, they participated in the most extraordinary elusion—and their behavior reveals this, as they congratulate one another on their staved-off date. The third case, though, is often the most profound, for here everything follows the same logic as the second mode, where many are stamped for undoing, shepherded before the rifles, and yet only one instrument plays; only one apparatus is loaded, and only one strikes a target. No one knows who will receive the projectile and slump downward, but when it happens, the remaining endeavor toward some form of respect: they either avert their eyes from the crumpled frame, gazing straight ahead or to the other side, or look upon it mournfully, registering sadness on their behalf (in the absence of the other's dear ones), while most strive to choke back their gasps of relief, retracting signs of satisfaction and maintaining righteous stoicism. And when they return to their cells, and to their private thoughts: some are elated (believing justice has been served); some are infuriated (recognizing this charade as a higher injustice than death); some express a weird thanks to the self-restraining killers (thinking their captors capable of spontaneous kindness); some are bathed in moralizing premises (feeling themselves acquitted or forgiven); some are gagged by the wretchedness of the scene (replaying the proceedings as they vomit); while others harbor thoughts of divine intervention (convinced now that the heavens did not discard them). And still others beg for death thereafter, pleading for this not to transpire again (the guarantee), and that they be taken out ahead of time (bartering indeterminacy for certainty).

But there is another, the one behind the poetic imagination we seek here, who takes heed, internalizes the lesson well, and prepares for the next bout (for he knows there will be another time for this). He returns more erudite than before, having learned that he must initiate a complete trans-valuation of what he assumed was his selfhood, and unearths his consciousness with an almost otherworldly goal: he must learn to love the mock execution, must reinforce himself by harnessing a deviant joy, switching the triggers of pain and pleasure and cherishing the excursion to the courtyard (he trains himself to fantasize about gunfire). This way, the next time they come for him, they find no plaything, but rather a laughing volunteer (something close to giddiness), one who would like nothing more than to gamble his mortality and steer right into the crossing (some say he smiles like a flute-player); he craves another round (basking), he jaunts forward and invites the expedition, having cultivated a lust for chance and fortune (to throw dice once more), a thirst for proximal ruin. He wants to disprove his own invincibility, and so they leave him alone, not knowing how to treat this inhuman exception (he is wasted upon their ruthless ways).[5]

Exhalation
(of the breath)

Aer or Fog of War attracts warmachines to War itself; it erases all vision maintained by the eye. Warmachines do not see with eyes, as they have no eyes; they see, detect and sense with their movements, their exclusive dynamism and tactics customized not by their lines of command but by the Fog of War. —Reza Negarestani[6]

Rage exhales itself across the world (to be breathed upon), subordinating whatever comes its way to the strong, quickened intake and emanation. It becomes an airborne property, fogging over established boundaries, it respires and vents itself with a desperate need for exteriority, searching for outlets wherever they may reside.

*The lines reveal: that the enraged will gouge out their own eyes so as to live in miasma (battle-gnosis).

Narrative III: Simulated Legacy (the Child's Command) . . .

Some poets tell of their encounters with those nearest to the executed, having sought them out so as to impart certain wishes in the aftermath. But this is no ritual of grieving; it is a recruitment, intended to multiply the poetic circles through well-crafted inflections of sorrow (they will bring others to the forefront). It is not about showing deference to an emotion, but rather consists of vivid generations of a mood (one should not cope, one should conspire). The mere fact of Being is enough to make innocence a useless concept here; they may not have asked for the sacrifice, but will accept its repercussion at the hands of this new envoy (the demise of one is the invitation of many).

There are several chapters in this procession, but it commences most distinctly within the recesses of a poetic imaginary: for it is not uncommon to see the names or pseudonyms of slain men and women littering the tops of pages in such books, perched beneath the titles of each piece (a hanging epithet). But these are no dedications; each volume contains its files, forming annals in a library of the crucified, as the poet charges himself to record exclusive stanzas for each deceased. He does this only so as to integrate them into a specialized necro-taxonomy of his own, associating them with his own word-plays, substituting their "real" identities for poetic classifications, memorizing them in accordance with his own terminologies, and thereby turning an individual into an aesthetic epitome (they take on a remarkable fictive power now, as rumors, parables, and sagas). This is not witnessing, not testimonial, but rather self-integrating convulsion; he runs images of the fallen in his mind, bringing them into a meditative daze whereby he continually arranges his mosaic of

anecdotes. This is not a one-dimensional solipsism, but rather the swallowing of the executed within a textual channel. They must be assimilated into
a delicate interior language, one of the poet's making, so that he can assume
ownership of their death's potential—unless they become particles of a literary idiom, re-woven into eccentric tongues, then there is nothing subsequent
to the oblivion of the prison (vanity). Nevertheless, if he persuades himself of
the corpse's integrity, able to write the slaughter, then those upon the list have
found their courier, for one only truly labors for that which shadows, ventrilo-
quates, and even amplifies one's own cause.

There are reports that these literary figures, upon being discharged, would
sometimes wander from town to town as dispatch riders for the martyrs, seeking reservations with the extended branches of each dead name. The poet
would make the sojourn to find the relatives, across ornate cities and rural
areas, tracking them down one by one (there is an unspoken dedication here).
The more time reaching these appointments takes, spent on horseback or as
a passenger in train compartments, the more the poetic imagination becomes
adamant toward the now-apparitional identity represented in the work.
And, upon arriving, they would evaluate these toppled homes, diagnose the
mentalities within, and collect themselves accordingly: the enunciation of a
death-notice, after all, is deeply performative. This poetic consciousness then
conveys its new version of the event, and never reluctant to distort, exaggerate,
elide, omit, or implant (whatever works), for the approach is instructed by the
following axiom: "that if it *could* have happened there, it might as well have
happened."

There is one such encounter of singular importance, between the poet and a
young girl wherein the latter questions the reasons for her uncle's untimely fate.
It is crucial that she says the first word (the listener must mouth the opening
of the rite), and he waits until she asks, so that her curiosity might then bring
it all down: she wanted clarity, he gives her blinding light; she wanted honesty,
he gives her mind-bending translucence. She becomes a confidante, and the
price of this hearing-act is pure extroversion (no more private thoughts, only
lucid actions). The poetic figure spins his narrative web, encapsulates her in
a new storytelling, rinses her in epic rumbling images of the uncle's action,
and thereby makes her an agent of transmission. This is predatory inspiration,
as she finds herself at once enlivened and infected by this figment; the poet
sculpts a memory-turning-imperative, one that tints, dyes, and consumes the
present. And he ensures this task by including one factor: he slings the death
upon the young girl's living reality, enumerating all of the small points that
make up her universe (her dolls, her hands, her stone pathway), so that nothing is spared, and staining them with the uncle's blood (he says he died for
them). The poet loads these otherwise neutral elements with the likeness of an
iconic struggle, and thereby troubles her domain (the obligation); he creates

a virtual kinship whereby the executed supposedly perishes for the sake of her tiny world (not for great abstract ideas but for tangible little things), such that every existing dimension is then thrust into a precarious coupling with the inexistent, as he strips down her belongings one by one to the molecular level and resituates them in a literary spectacle of haunting. This is the annexation of her sensitivity, toward the creation of an infinitesimal ally (the poet wants the child on this side); he usurps her trust in the neighboring world and gives her the traits of her uncle's supposed world-view instead, orchestrating the metonymic force of adjacency to leave her symptomatic (this is how epilogues become prologues). Once entrenched in this modality, she will never be the same again, and cannot return to the once-harmless serenity of her previous condition; she becomes the precursor and takes custody of the poetic simulation, feels increasingly disconnected from those around her (trading the love of many for the new love of this one), and eventually strikes out and beyond (into the war-universe), charged not by blood-ties but textual allegiances learned during this one meeting with the poet (to be willing to risk everything for a character). And over time she will add her own specific thickening layers to this hologram, modeling it to suit the charge with innovative striations, as she encompasses, chisels, and hosts the projected persona of the uncle (never the other way around). This is how one becomes an instantiation of vicariousness, in all its strongest manifestations.[7]

Deceleration
(the arrested)

As it were for a second everything became one. The final faint was enchained to the faint of all beginning the start of the beginning and the end of the final the instant of the coming out of the live from the dead and the dead from the live. —Yusuf Idris[8]

Rage determines its own mode of deceleration, guided by a perception-contrast whereby one sees movements ahead of their happening (anticipating trajectories), and phenomena somehow elapse in longer strips (the surrounding world in dispulsion). Rage is always thought to move so fast (darting), but it is in fact everything else that moves so slow (lingering), adjourned beneath a kind of proleptic flash: one arrests existence, postponing its momentum, leaping over its progressive strings before their realization, in order to expedite one's own thoughts and actions (this is how one arrives too soon).

*The lines reveal: that the enraged will mix the blood-lines of the living and the dead.

Narrative IV: Dead-Man's Writing (Concocted Survival) . . .

Some poets tell of a practice of writing as the executed (in the guise of the other) so as to shield the fact of their demise, taking up the name and thereby outrunning the intended deterioration. It starts back in the prison when news reaches that one has been taken, for that night the others all sit and solidify an underhanded consensus: that they will adopt the rhetoric of their former colleague and commit forgeries of his poetic expenditure. This is not a reckless incorporation, but rather an urgent emulation caused by a state of emergency; for every one that falls, the remaining must take another mask upon themselves, continuing the disrupted chain of insight, keeping their numbers steady in a collaborative effort to sustain, resuscitate, and prolong their kind. From this point forward, they will control the collection, publication, and dissemination of the supposed work of this executed one, sending concocted communiqués to the waiting masses and devising ways of explaining his absentia (narratives of plausible disappearance). To achieve this, they not only teach themselves his philosophy, and with it the minor aesthetic turns that evince such perspectives (investigating the style of the expired), but must continue to expand upon that literary ethos (new books from beyond the grave). Replication is not sufficient for the purposes of vivification: they must grow his thinking further through improvisation as well, guessing at the next pathways, thematics, and subject-matters that he could have attempted (otherwise the imitation is exposed), and thus inscribing the unwritten texts that "might have been." By motioning ahead, out hustling time, and filling the void of a cut-off future, they slow down the registering of his death in the real (it remains unofficial if it is not thought of).

Blackout
(diffusion)

Here, by the downslope of hills, facing the sunset
and time's muzzle,
near gardens with severed shadows,
we do what the prisoners do,
and what the unemployed do:
we nurture hope

A country on the verge of dawn,
we have become less intelligent,
because we stare into victory's hour:
no night in our artillery-glistened night
our enemies are sleepless,

and our enemies ignite the light for us
in the blackness of shelters. —Mahmoud Darwish[9]

Rage obtains a mechanism through which sight can be willfully obliterated, drowning out whatever opposes the purpose, such that it sees only what it needs to see, finding endless unanimous justification wherever it turns. Never the unconscious, only periphery-seeking rays (born from another soot). This selective focus, this myopic skill, renders the blackout through which an individual can emerge victorious against the remainder, for it congregates its own self-serving illuminations, and tosses the rest into the pitch-dark (diffuseness).[10]

*The lines reveal: that the enraged will grant themselves the intelligence that comes without thought of victory, renouncing shelter and hope, never waiting for the enemy to provide the lantern.

Narrative V: False Promise (the Betrayal-Letter) . . .

Some poets tell of the given proposals for release, in some fashion always illusory, defective, or retractable (nothing comes for free, and the trade more often benefits power). This is perhaps the most genuine test of temptation, not in paradisiacal gardens where all desires are satisfied (hyper-indulgence), shame is kept beyond the peripheries, and only a single forbidden act casts a shadow across the plateau, but rather in some bare subterranean cell where all desires are prohibited, where shame marches relentlessly (stripping down its subjects), and the only way out is often through the seeds of a single forbidden act. Devious wardens love to invent opportunities for treachery, monitoring the ever-soaring value of the outside and calculating how much each is willing to divest for the sake of a fleeting glimpse of exteriority: will they name others, facilitating a moment whereby some former associate is picked from the alleys and dragged into this same condition, switching places and thereby passing off one's own destiny, or will they even participate in the ridding of a fellow inmate (some are made to watch [unchosen voyeurism], others made to issue the varying orders of maiming [pseudo-authority], and still others are told to pull triggers themselves)? At the very least, even if the answer is "no," they were made to weigh the option for a while, and certain thoughts make one irredeemable, once they enter the realm of possibility (all that is required is a split-second hesitation). At that point, it is viewed as another economic inevitability: one merely needs to keep asking (only so many times), all the while escalating the misfortunes, and someday the response might stumble into darker territories.

And so a particular story begins: that, upon yet another seamlessly tedious day, one of the prison-poets had a confessional letter laid before him, delivered by the caring hands of his own father. Presumably, this parent could no longer tolerate the undefined timeline of his son's sentence, where there is no second trial, no visitation, no word of life or death, and so he raced to all corners of the political matrix, calling forth every contact and significant connection that he had spent decades hoarding, himself a low-level military officer, in order to secure a pardon. After months of persuasion, supplication, bribery, soul-selling etiquette, and even the extortion of ill-born favors, the father is granted a short document by the monarchy, one that offers liberation in exchange for a public assertion of betrayal (stating that the poetic figure had undermined his nation, his society, and his king). It is an apologetic notice, one aimed to broadcast the regret (sincere or otherwise) of the caught. Nevertheless, the father is beyond grateful (tear-stained), and rushes to the prison gates, demanding to be allowed entrance as he displays the official certificate of the king, exhibiting its contents to each bureaucratic station, and barreling past the guards, through hallway after hallway, in search of his dejected child. As he gallops through these straits, one conduit after another, he cannot prevent himself from beholding his surroundings (the poverty, the cheerlessness): it far exceeds even his worst conceived notion, one of the few instances when reality outruns imagination. And then he arrives at the cage of his son, its appearance like all the rest but magnified exponentially by virtue of their bond, and the father sneers at the destitution of such living-quarters. He finds our protagonist standing to one side, leaning across the wall, and somehow manifesting no change in demeanor at the sight of his long-separated father (they have since drained the capacity for surprise), and so the latter charges in, reveals the letter quickly, his voice infused with thrill, explaining the self-evident stipulations and remarking on the oblique journey by which it was attained.

The young poet keeps close watch of the father's mouth (its stress, its aging), never searching after the paper that he has not yet even glanced, and selects his own next words with complete automaticity. Now one might presume that this episode contains but one of two options: either he compromised himself, took the pen that once produced dissidence so as to inscribe resignation, or that he fearlessly postured and negated the deal before him. But he did neither: instead, he stared back at the man in front of him, and with perfect calm asked what prison he was speaking of. The father clutched the sheet in confusion, stuttered a while, and in a concerted effort to clarify the monumentality of things made reference to the institution enveloping them both at that moment. The poet reassured his father that this was his house. The old man then, in growing frustration spilling into anger, made reference to the chains upon his son's wrists. The poet reassured his father that these were his bracelets. The old man fired back, calling attention to the nefarious guards standing right outside the cell doors, telling his son that he had some concept of what they did to him by day and by night in this place. The poet reassured his father that they were his servants, and that they worked for him.

One is astounded or skeptical before this recitation, for it appears to signal either an untold bravery or a pure charlatanism (weak readers will only find trauma, repression, and disavowal here). But the key is at once more grandiose and more modest (one should not admire or dismiss): it is a matter of perceptual sorcery. No, he was not helpless, he was eloquent; he was not disenfranchised or oppressed, he was vigilant and self-aware; in the final scope of things, the prison did not happen to him, he happened to the prison (it belonged to him). After all, today no one remembers the guards, or the wardens, or the government officials who justified the actions, but entire countries still whisper the name of this poet.

Hence one genre breeds another, for such twisted propositions cannot go unanswered; the state's writing-act deserves its own counter-message, an incantation addressed back to the father. This is one of the poet's first experiments with "the anthem," a fiendish style that mobilizes syllables and construes an ultimatum like no other, and which holds its status as one of the most existentially oriented of Eastern utterances, one that melds hysteria and protest (for reasons to become clear).

The first anthem stems from the encounter noted above, as the poetic imagination becomes aggravated enough to chastise the father (and the bleak reality of which he has become the messenger). He warns the father of an age of darkness, mirage, and deception, and reprimands him for failing the test of nobility and succumbing to the will of the enemy. This is no metaphor: the father has arrived to make him stray from his path, poisoning his perception, and the poetic figure reminds him that the bolts and shackles would fall from his body with just one word or one casual waving of the hand (this depth is a self-convened travail, his own provocation). The anthem then moves into its next dimension, as the poetic figure begins to recount legends to the father, summoning the names of ancient others who had withstood the unbearable (and thus winning eternal life), all the while the ordinary men and women lamented their lack of rights from the safety of their mattresses. He substitutes this genealogy of extraordinary warriors for his father's own faint bloodline, repairing alternate heritages, establishing a superior cross-historical vow for which there is no tendency to moan (one is proud to attain such lowliness). He proves that this perceptual magic (seeing the prison as his own temple) is a willed insanity, a subjective schism backed by centuries of an elite tradition (those who fight to have nothing), and thereby rectifies the impression of total lack, destitution, and insubstantial breath (there is fertility here).

And still, the anthem must go farther; it emphasized the vibrating axis of disagreement, but must now also become a force of implication (lofty words suddenly grow more precise), ensuring immediacy through biting, pointed accusation. He reminds the father that he too is cut from their cloth, though now turning his back, receding into estrangement, and asks what has happened to him, indicting his closed eyes, copper dreams, paper crowns, and wooden thrones. He reminds him that he never worshipped gold before, nor cared for gold-threaded robes, and yet now builds the foundations of his existence on flooded ports, trading with wind-sellers. He reminds him of the strangeness of his own story, and how swords of vengeance have been thrown down upon the streets, as the killers of knowledge triumph amidst the burning of books. And then, he reminds him not to look so coldly upon the horizon, and calls out by name the certain province where his comrades rolled in dirt and blood. There is such audacity here, as the poet hurls allegation upon allegation, scolding the father for having come under false pretenses, for having prompted an occasion of disgrace, for having dared to bring the specter of repentance to his altar, for privileging untruth over radical illusion and asking him to exchange his silken honor for forged coins and an animal's saddle (counterfeit being). No, instead he will invalidate the roles and teach the father a lesson, demanding that he refrain from further pathetic advice, and even more that he acknowledge a geographic-genetic rift between them: that the father take the path of tranquillity and refuge (the saving of life), and the poet the path of danger and conflict (the exalting of life). In this respect, the anthem is about reconquest.[11]

Many years later, the same figure would revisit this textual mode, though now allowing it to dwell in a mystified deterritorialized imagination. This anthem is situated upon a desolate beach, where two individuals (once again the poet and the father) roam aimlessly toward the breakwater, at which point a storm gathers and an emergent voice penetrates the air (with unearthly timbre). From across the ocean, a boat (half-coffin, half-bed) glides toward them, and at its helm stands a skeletal rower with bleeding pores, a scythe used as oar, a crow upon his shoulders (digging its talons), and requests the company of the most tired. The elder responds to this cryptic sailor, attempting to cheat passage for both in some frail negotiation (that "we are both tired"), though he has no leverage and thus cowers inward (away from the salt-infused waves). An interim monologue takes hold, amid insinuations of war, disgust, siege, and sorrow-ravaged bodies. But then the poetic consciousness differentiates itself (as the one who left), venturing ahead (with unyielding steps), and offers payment by entering the ship, taking the station of the rower (emissary of the outside). Such is the effective fulfillment of the anthem: to initiate a challenge at the threshold, to transform closed spaces of terror into open arenas of power, to accumulate rage in opposition to despair, and to capture the deed to reality in the name of unreality's infinite estate.[12]

Ecstasy
(of the drums)

In a well-lit loneliness, I have cried with you for those who are alive.
And in a darkened graveyard, I sang with you the most radiant anthems,
For those who died this year were the most in love among the living. —Ahmad Shamlu[13]

Rage shares an overlapping corner with ecstasy, since both research the aggravation of the heartbeat, and both offer a façade of uncontrollability. One must beware the moment when the poetic imagination enlists the sound of drums, for they signify at once a foretelling, the savage forewarning of what comes, as fate tightens, and a palpitation, the advent of a vibrant influx. These are the ones who claim that everything is involuntary, who hearken to hidden pipers, ringmasters, and puppeteers, who speak of their own bodies as if they function autonomously (as insurrectionary agents), and voices in the head that snake and motivate (leaving clues, hints, and ill-conceived plots), as if something foreign grows within them (not of their own), who blame the insidious percussion for their own will to pulverize.

*The lines reveal: that the enraged are capable of sobbing, though never universally, only for those whose vitality exceeded all others.

Narrative VI: Absurd Reunion (Tragicomic Deformity) . . .

Some poets tell of seeing one another again on the other side of the prison, often taking place years later and in safer foreign countries (many have become exilic). What is perhaps most surprising about these reunions is the conspicuous amount of levity (and music); they are not nostalgic affairs, nor do they revolve around forms of commiseration, but rather they are configured around jest, wit, farce, and tragicomic displays. No one sulks there nor hides their deformity, but each makes hilarious use of it (strategic revulsion): when they play cards, the one without fingernails always wants to be the dealer, highlighting the imperfect digits, just as the burn-victim always lights a cigarette, drawing cross-temporal parallels of smoke, and the one-eyed figure gazes too long at everyone, winking often with the vacant non-cycloptic socket, and the one with glass-generated cuts running up and down the arms always rolls back the sleeves and handles wine bottles. They draw festive attention to the injured zones (with such ease), flaunting what would sicken most, but which here become quaint indexes of recreation, leisure, diversion, and amusement.

Thirst
(the devoured)

During the day I am an ordinary man
who carries on his ordinary duties without complaint
like any sheep in the flock, but at night
I am a vulture ascending a mountain
and my prey rests under my claws. —Sargon Boulus[14]

Rage arrives at a nexus where it is able to procure three reins of impossibility: that of the passenger, the merchant, and the hangman. This is where thought becomes a pack, one that shares its food, and consciousness is capable of conveying itself from one condition to another in cylindrical fashion: to be the intermediary (of the purchase), to monitor the exchange (between here and there, possession and dispossession), and then to conclude the transference (between living and dying). This is the access-point to thirst: to splinter experience, to snap its continuity and place itself across specific crevices where it can be devoured (the passenger entrusted to the vehicle, the merchant to the item, the hangman to the rope).

*The lines reveal: that the enraged take on the daily guise of the average ones, without protest, though all the while biding their time before the ascension to predatory tastes.

Narrative VII: Open Wounds (Recurring Lesion)

Some poets tell of those who would continually re-open their gashes, methodically retracing the lines and edges, seeking permanent freshness, and, in this regard, disallowed the sealing-shut and drying of tissue. They preferred the wound to the scar, for the latter would leave an inaccurate representation of their state: the event was not done yet, and so any emblem of closure would prove imprecise (one cannot afford complacency). Instead, they sought a vista of ongoing carnage, without the escapism of a falsely healing body, avoiding the pretense of a biological defense in exchange for the exaltation of a biopolitical vulnerability. Beyond this, the more one delineates these rows of streaked flesh, following their elasticity and frontiers, the more they become one's own, allowing the reorientation from a sadistic to a masochistic axis (less pathological than practical). The first time belongs to the guards; by the ninth time, though, earned by right of self-decided reiteration, they form the columns of one's own toughening profile.

Instability
(the strayed)

On the altitude of the wound
I was on the wing.
And the altitude of the wound
silenced my name amid the blue chances
every instant in my blood's resistance.
Lying by my red I saw,
in the circulation of the rain's saliva,

images of vultures
who wore angel boots
and prowled by my red. —Yadollah Royai[15]

Rage is an unstable becoming, always prone to some detour, an off-path and miscarriage (it will not move in straight lines), nor does it exhibit a hierarchy of dwelling-places: it will live anywhere, down lost streets and in abandoned warehouses. This makes it an almost unbeatable intensity, since it strays into ragged and unkempt back-rooms, having recanted all oaths to the pristine delusion of what is deserved. The overcome figure does not worry about what one is owed (no pleading of cases); rage will take for one what is necessary.

*The lines reveal: that the enraged seek the incline where their wounds will run most freely, flushed outward to bait certain sharks, if only for their adoration of red colors.

Narrative VIII: Penultimate Wishing (Alternative Destroying Image) . . .

Some poets tell of a narrative ritual wherein the prisoners gather when one of them has been taken for an extended time (abnormal duration) and begin to sketch all the possible modes of interrogation, excision, incision, and anguish that might be ratified upon the missing one. They imagine their extracted ally in terrible straits, they conjure the near-worst images of the other, each a clandestine alternative to death, discussing the types of wailing, bleeding, aching, weeping that would still provide signs of potential continuation. The longer they are away, the more unruly, unclean, and withered their suggestions become (sometimes this is how one advocates life). For this is the discomfort of the lesser abuse (soreness is still better than numbness), to track the sordid paces right before the precipice (the something that might be happening instead of the likely nothing that has taken over), through which the other prisoners stand firm against closure and maintain their counterpart.

Overwrought
(the elder)

Yet, I feel
such rage here on the earth's
backbone, learning the sweetness
of all hidden and forbidden
things.
I scrawl the history
of time's beginnings. —Adonis[16]

Rage leaves subjectivity overwrought, relaying alongside itself a quiet necromantic principle: it ages consciousness quickly, leaving one a weathered entity, etched and inveterate, yet who alone has the penetrating wisdom to summon the fallen, to call upon the de-voided and the downcast, to rally the provinces of the departed. This is a spectral acumen, one that fortifies itself by virtue of the fact that rage also enjoins the disconcerting birth of the elder: namely, that upon entering this state, another surfaces, though this one born a split-second before oneself, and therefore also condemned to die a split-second before. This elder experiences the chain of things an instant prior, and thus knows that all the divinations fail, knows that the future will not hold. Thereafter, all writing is laden with this prophetic downturn: the one whose prophecies are disbelieved, whose prophecies arrive too late, whose prophecies cannot save, whose prophecies cannot be read or translated, spoken by the one who cares nothing for the people, and who cannot tell which are accurate or false. All that is left is the script of senility (the shaking hand), textualities of strain and curvature.

*The lines reveal: that the enraged will recognize similar impulses in the marrow of the earth itself, and will leave manuscripts verifying the sweet convergence of such furies.

Narrative IX: Forsaken Desire (the Silhouette) . . .

Some poets tell of a mispriced inheritance when asked if they enjoy their own artistic artifacts. The response is one of metamorphic simplicity, revealing the discrepancy between past and present: that there was once someone who would have wanted to read such things, but in order to be capable of drafting them, one had to become something else (there is no retroactive winning). This is a silhouetted response, whereby the one who would have adored such lines no longer exists, having turned into the stern creator unable to desire or appreciate the work—for one knows too well the costs that it entailed, and the transformation has depleted the sieve of self-gratification.

Hate
(the across)

But after the rape
of the light of morning's laughter,
suddenly,
hatred filled me.
After the springs were buried alive,
after the watercourses' destruction,
the flame swept through me.
After the pillaging of the shadow

and the sundering of the spikes of wheat . . .
after the murder of the doves . . .
I was charged with a sharpened hatred,
blue as the edge of death itself! —Taha Muhammad Ali[17]

Rage patrols the continuum, the disgraced in-between, and reconfigures the older definition of hate, such that a more chaotic alignment would move across things rather than against them (draping). To hate across world, not against world . . . as if it were only an insistent surface along which to unfold the exercise of violence, the formulation of a new theory of space (where one allows punitive thoughts to swim). For this thing called "world" is no true adversary, not implicated in some serious exchange; it is not to be resisted, it is simply in the way, and therefore must be cleared. It stands between the envisioning and fulfillment of the enraged mind, relevant not existentially but spatially by virtue of its positional interference. Thus existence falls only as a matter of circumstance, as a consequence of its being-there (upon the stage), a casualty of location, for rage must commandeer authority over the middle. Debris is a matter of necessity, of almost indifferent requirement (that it has to sweep the road). The world is not extended the privilege of authenticity, it is not conferred the right to presence here, it is not a depth, but rather becomes an axis along which to incite the unruly venture (vehemence).

  This poetic imagination thrives upon the instantaneous culmination of hatred. Hatred as a cylinder of force, murderous and unyielding, released as a visceral extension of the one who wants more, never an act of nihilistic mourning but a venomous affirmation, never a regression but a ceaseless proliferation, a spiraling inward/outward (and ever optimizing). Hatred as the brutalization of what is (all-encircling intolerance), forever set to will finality against the standing ways, to pull apart without even looking upon the objects of destruction (for none are exempted) . . . reflexive cycles of encounter and mutilation, the intoxicated dismemberment of the species. Hatred as fuel, as the entitlement to exalted creation and re-creation, a ravenous streaming of possibility borne by talons (where language becomes tearing), rampant excitation and provocation. Hatred as passion for the other life, and thus rapture in this reality's subjugation, howling amid unfathomed consummations of blood-lust . . . to break its back and sever its veins, to drive it to its knees and make it bow, and therein to extract a last gasp, the eternal admission of its defeat and conquest (dishonored), if even for an instant alone. Hatred as the vehicle of Man's free-fall into lethal depths, the race now driven under (within the throes), a sacrifice to rake the sacred, to suffocate the absolute, and thus to speak in languages of imposition (those that govern the plummeting). Hatred as the velocity of impulse, the strength of a single hunger for expression, tightly sustained in martial strides, and now loosened from the recesses of an interiority seeking gratification from every sector (wrenching all against itself), leaving only the insurmountable compulsion of the task, and the echo of rent garments across all regions. Hatred as the escalation of a supra-subjective wanting, incarnating the personal desire of someone who then trips over their own drive, ever straying closer to the borders of an impersonal obsession, its power conveyed by an infatuation-gone-awry. Thieving the demonic from its underpass, suffusing its scornful dominance across the fault-lines of world, leaving an existence chronically showered, unnerved, treacheries spread across the open, it marks the paradox of irresolution and conviction, the elite allegiance of inconstancy and imperative, chance and force in simultaneity, as the ultimate circularity of the chaotic will, the concentrated movements of the immeasurable. Hatred as a rare occasioning of seduction, the steeling of a wager with extinction, the allure of an unspoken oath (with scowling), and the implicit inescapability therein, drawing existence toward the unveiling of imminent disaster, at once fierce and steady, treading with slow yet scorched paces. Hatred as the sudden taste for pain, its torment now set in assault as machines of pressure (wracking), tumbling legions set upon the glass cages of the real . . . and in the aftermath of this interminable present, an epoch of sublime terminalities.[18]

*The lines reveal: that the enraged are left brimming by virtue of the pillaging of neglected and trifling entities, that they rave mostly against the defiling of the springs, the shadows, the spikes of wheat, and the doves.

Narrative X: Refused Blindfold (the Disconnect) . . .

Some poets tell of the refusal of the blindfold, referring to those who would rather look outward than have the shroud tied across their eyes as the execution unfolds. There are photographs of such individuals smiling, cackling, dancing, chanting, scoffing, or making no expression at all, but they are almost always staring into the lens (which is in the same direction as the death-squad). This is not only an issue of cognizance, but, even more significantly, of cursing; they deny the contentment of a blind death so as to unleash an aura of damnation. They want no screen between them, no visor to block the staunch promotion of the hex, for they must harass the sanctimony of the event with incoherence, to confirm the unsurpassable disconnect and the shifted relation (counter-surveillance: to watch power in turn). The only question is: can one really stop one's eyes from closing (the flinch) when the sound of gunfire busts forward? For if one can only sustain that locked gaze of hate throughout, even amidst the piercing, then the odium might just last forever.

Hostility
(the uneven)

The night moonlight rained down damnation . . .
Of us one whose chain was heavier some,
Damned his ears and moaned: "We must go."
And exhausted we said: "Damned be our ears.
And our eyes too. Go we must." —Mehdi Akhavan-Saless[19]

One can best understand hostility as a system of entanglements, connections, fusions, wires, strands, strings, threads, and tapestries, which reigns as a coalescence of seams and ridges (stitching) that then takes on the focus of a lash (flogging), and which leaves its score, an infinity of the marked, the branded, and the gashed, amidst the junction of rows and striations and the all-encompassing risk of their undoing. This concave gathering of ranks reflects not what existence is or is not, never a mimetic statement of its current status, but rather what it could never be (the trellis), what it has never fathomed (the outline), and yet which now makes its way, as that which it cannot tame or own, that which cannot be subordinated by a calling, though now treading in its midst (to mirror what it cannot become, yet which looks for it).

Beyond this, hostility offers limitless manifestations to tempt, with scope beyond comprehension: the kind that is born of stillness and that of rushing, that of coldness and of furor, of silence and of the scream, of the apex and of the pits, hidden and unveiled, that cascades the past, that avalanches the present, and that bombards the future, the kind of gentle complexities and that of bare simplicities, that drags Being toward combustion or toward void.

It is only through the practice of hostility that one develops a taste for specificity, for the attentiveness of the gymnast, the dancer, the calligrapher, the trapeze entertainer, for the understanding and arrangement of tones, articulations of the slight difference, for the lesser variations between states of the uneven. One learns that: annihilation has no equivalence with death; the desolated and the devastated are not identical but rather carry disparate potentials; to eviscerate is not the same as to break, nor to dissolve, nor to obliterate; eruption and disintegration are attained by divergent paths; and an eradicated space bears one atmosphere and the extinguished space another and the exploded still one more. The violence wavers between such impressions, between these fine, reeling lines, if even just barely.

*The lines reveal: that the enraged will clot their own sensorial abilities when necessary for departure, overlying their wits in order to make the exodus.

Narrative XI: Phantom Treachery (the Impostor Ally) . . .

Some poets tell of impostor allies in their midst, sympathizers sent into these detention units to pose as dependable functionaries of the complex. For, upon entering the resistance movements, the elder leaders of the undergrounds would often order the new members to pursue one of three professions: (1) to become professors (so as to recruit young minds to the front lines); (2) to become military officers (so as to access weaponry, thieve martial secrets, and subvert counter-revolutionary offensives); or (3) to become prison guards. The last category was the minority faction (not all had the constitution for this request), and the rationale clear enough: it was not so as to aid in some naïve attempts at escape (there were rarely any breakouts), nor was it to minimize the toll of physical abuse (most were so apprehensive about being detected that they would overcompensate, hitting harder than the actual practitioners), but rather it was merely to uphold the stark principle that it is better to be mutilated at the hands of one's own. Some have spoken of this rigorous pact, of what it means to take blows by a fellow companion, and how both must master the art of restrained expressions (one side cannot show sympathy, and the other cannot look pleadingly for help, held together in a ring of non-divulgence). Some were pushed as far as to take limbs, or to carry out executions, and they were revered by the knowing prisoners for practicing such duties (it is difficult to will the despicable). No blame, no censure, only undying respect for allowing them to suffer without full estrangement, and without sating the blood-lust of the authentic guards, for one would rather perish in a surreptitious state of nearness with the like-minded.

Here betrayal becomes the currency of tribute, and care masquerades as treachery, wound through the confidential glance, as the captive says: "cut me so the others lose their turn, and do it well so that none find out."

The Interlace
(manipulation)

Now I am not within the chains and prison of the enemy,
For I could break the ties if I so wished:
With the touch of the hand the chains will fall from my legs
With the touch of the hand I can remove the bolt from the door . . .
I have remained out of the heights of my own faith,
Such that the phoenix would lose its feathers at this altitude.
What pain is it if you yourself are provoking the pain?
What prison is it if you are there of your own choosing? —Ahmad Shamlu[20]

Rage can escort those it contacts into an atypical state, an influence that contagiously hooks and re-arranges the foundation of others' identities, bothers the routine disposition and wrests outward a different manner. One must hound the other into carrying on as if they were someone else (to corner them), if even for a minute, offering a stimulus that brings a flash of transmutation. This is the apex of manipulation: to come close enough to lace the drinks with some personality-altering tablets (to have never done this before), and to pressure the encounter so as to leave no option but dramatic undulation (to start the rippling that stirs the deluge). It is a long-held Eastern saying that if a scorpion is surrounded by a ring of fire, realizing it has no escape route, it will eventually sting itself, and it is no overstatement that rage follows this paradigm of interloping and eloping actors.

   *The lines reveal: that the enraged are provocateurs of seemingly subordinated lives (if only to then allow an upward exertion).

Narrative XII: Forbidden Smuggling (the Anomaly) . . .

Some poets tell of a near-paradoxical moment of collusion, wherein a lone prison guard decides to copy down the writings of the incarcerated and smuggle them out to the undergrounds. It is a disturbing fact that some of the pieces which survived, composed in the aridity, seclusion, and remoteness of those cells, could only find their way beyond, reaching back into the world, through the exertion of select torturers. These are the same men who each evening would come down those tapered corridors and spend hours carving into sinews, nor did they stop their atrocities for having taken this outlawed work to the rebel-groups (who are actually the incorrect inheritors)—if anything they intensified the ensuing hurt in order to compensate for their counterintuitive actions. But something happened within this horrible fortress, the glint of a crisis, and this single aspect must be interrogated further: from where does this new compulsion stem, and what is the self-imposed accountability of the persecutor to the poetic experience? Why do they deviate (for even a provisional term), passing from the watchtower to the hideaway, from zones of surveillance to those of covert disadvantage? These were exceptional turns, no doubt, occurring in truly slim proportions, but every once in a while such a convoluted interplay would slip through the prison format (the reordering of instincts).

   The ingenious source of this capsize, the dim-lit reasons for this slight yet consequential participation of the guards in the transference of illegal words, their defiance of the very formulae they upheld, is not for any of the logical reasons that one might expect. There was no sudden fluctuation of conscience (good and evil are obsolete in such spaces), not even a minute redemptive concern (guilt is too sentimental), nor was it the product of some transgressive envy: that, after a while, in the presence of such insurgent types, the guardians themselves developed some desire to inhabit criminality (slinking). Nor did they bear some tacit reverence for the tradition (they could not care less about literature, and rightfully so). No, the allure came from elsewhere.

   The fact is that, for such an incredible conspiring to actualize itself, turning the self-proclaimed oppressor into a carrier of illicit language, there can be no identification (sameness would lead nowhere). Thus, it is not that personal information was shared, details of human commonality given back and forth, a reciprocal banter of origins, customs, dreams, families, or calamities, and thereby facilitating some embedded trust; the principles of compassion, pity, and empathy have no weight here. Moreover, equivalence only results in a stalemate, altering nothing but the surface-appearance of subjective interaction, and thereby supports continuation of what is; there would be no great incongruities in the prison itinerary if they began to discover resemblances in the face of the other.

Once again, for this to work, for the guard to transcribe the diabolical poetics of the prisoner and sneak it to the appropriate destinations, for there to emerge a contemplative zone where such an act could even appear viable, there can be no intimacy. This is not a partnership; it is not built on some foundation of understanding between bandits (such idealizations are crooked). Instead, like all miraculous phenomena, knowledge must be foregone in the wake of awe—it is not that the guard comprehends the poet's thought, but precisely that it remains incomprehensible. The onlooker is arrested, struck by the appearance of something truly alien (it does not belong there), and thereby lending the text a grandeur, sublimity, and even wrongness (out-of-line). The reaction is one of amazement; the poetic experience, coursing amidst such bare circumstances, breeds distance and confusion (why is this happening now?), making it at once untouchable and magnetic (who would perform in such ways?). It is a sign of difference, indirectness, and ahistoricality that then must be preserved; like some massive ancient statues of lost gods, symbols of unknown religions and primordial coronations, disconnected from the present reality and yet looming still upon the land, one is hesitant to wreck them. One cannot act decisively against strangeness. And so these fugitive texts, with their own lexicon, are repositories of obscure wisdom; the guard senses this, and moves to save them. Universality would have singlehandedly allowed those words to fade upon the cell walls (one does not imperil oneself over general truths); otherworldliness alone made them strive (one goes above and beyond for the exquisite).

The more archaic, unnatural, and irrelevant the poetic expression becomes, the more it wins over its surroundings. It is a crucible of inexplicable achievement within a seemingly degraded state, proving that, though the poetic figure is wrapped in their machinations, something remains inaccessible to them, some magnificence, and he writes through it (in an almost extra-planetary dialect). As a result, both style and content are of startling importance, for the guards would find no such motive were they purely revolutionary ideological scripts—any referential text, diametrically engaged with the prison itself, would be ignored without question (they are not interested in what they already know). Rather, only a poetics that says nothing straightforward about the prison (traveling elsewhere), that even maneuvers into apolitical, foreign, and extraneous realms of imagination, will attain an influence. The writing-act must blow unfamiliarity into the air, must circumvent all context, eliminating any evidence of "being-within" and instead competing for unrelated visions (to become enigmatic). In this way, the guards are stunned, knocked back into perplexity; they never ask the poets to interpret their words, they do not enter into discussions; they leave the riddles unsolved, and maintain the fact of extreme silence and disparity between them. They often will not even tell anyone of what they have done (the subsidiary errand), including the poets themselves, who learn only later, once released, for it is not so much a pact than a possession. Conspiracy requires multi-leveled consciousness, whereas our topic is something closer to raptness.

This is its own category of idolatry: the guard stares at the lines, their shapes and contours, himself not a believer, interlocutor, or student but knowing that others have invested conviction in its messages (a half-acknowledgment of indefinite power). He knows that some young supporters have even used these rhymes as their last words before military tribunals, whispering or shouting them before unswerving judges, an ark for their departure. Some have found their answers here, making this an esoteric inroad to some kind of fatalistic energy; and the guards do not want to be on the wrong side of destiny (it is the only thing they still fear).

Then again, there is always the question: which of these banned textual exports were chosen to weather and traverse the prison fences (were they arbitrarily lifted) and which were left there to rot (were they arbitrarily forsaken)? Such editors as this. Either way, it instills an everlasting sense of incompletion in the reader of these pieces (this was not all that was said there); only a few partial leaves have been torn from the book.

To close this intriguing slide of consciousness, it might be worthwhile to note that the occasional protection of a poetic work by the guards was both temporary and limited. Not only did the torture-chamber resume its rhythms, never missing a beat, never passing on an opportunity, but the hypnotic effect of the poetic moment that has been documented here did not even save some of its authors from more inexcusable shows of discourtesy. There are, after all, entire abysmal sections of mass cemeteries where the heretical, the scandalous, and the unwanted are thrown, and it is conventional practice for there to be numerous decrees surrounding these wastelands: hatred must follow these former prisoners even after death, and so nothing is allowed to grow there, no planted things permitted, nor any individualizing signposts (all headstones will be overturned, all flowers removed). There are stories of parents and grandparents who place makeshift rocks in guessed-at locales across these fields, haphazard metaphoric designations that grant them some delusion of consistency while visiting their dead children, and even these are vandalized. And so the guards remain diligent in bringing this emptiness to constant fruition: after all, they were not cured or enlightened; they will indeed trample the unmarked gravesites of their opponents, allowing them no stable resting-place even years later, and no offerings from the devoted, and yet aware that at least once, when they carried some samples on an exemplary night, they aided in the longevity of a third side.

The Undone
(reign)

I write, then I cross out, to discover whatever I have forfeited,
To discover the words for such volatile thoughts.
I scrape at the rear of my skull,
My finger resembling a cylindrical rod
So as to unbraid, knot after knot, these entwined fibers.
In my dust-saturated mind
your face's colors have gradually dwindled.
I shut my weary eyes in order to meditate upon what remains. —Simin Behbehani[21]

Rage is a dictatorial energy that nevertheless dooms its own autocracy, as a totalitarianism-becoming-undone. We are therefore brought back to the minds of crazed kings who would set fire to their own capitals, who order generals to mow down the grass and crops of their own land (allowing no harvest, no reaping), who throw their subjects into ever-ripening discord, who cannot stand the prosaic manner of reigning and therefore applaud the rise of messianic competitors, throne-seekers, cult rivals, and coup-engineers. It is through rage alone that one rules anarchically, tempting the effervescent appropriation and re-appropriation of the palace, dueling and unseating one another at will, and thereby injecting the erosive into whatever dominion exists (short-lived bastions).

*The lines reveal: that the enraged labor under complexity, that they kick against braided ideas (tethered at the base of the skull).

Narrative XIII: Dropped Body (the Pit) . . .

Some poets tell about episodes of complicity and then redress, wherein one prisoner is mandated to harm another so as to supplement the violation. In one particular instance, one was said to have been taken into a room where his compatriot was strung up by ropes (across the stomach) over a pit filled with spikes, nails, and other patinated tools of impalement. These sticks are an obvious equipment, assembled in vertical columns so as to threaten the suspended figure above, and the ditch below is its own abyss. The other standing prisoner is then handed the cable to which the aerial body is secured and instructed to hold it for as long as possible, and no doubt he sits there, flexing the tendons, strapping the lifeline across his own shoulder, back, and torso in order to hold the pivot. But this is only a feigned godliness, indicating a losing bout with the unpreventable, and futile efforts soon become clear as the trench below collects another (misused gravity). Hence, the next time one is asked to partake in such a venture, one knows better than to grapple with the obvious; instead, one looks at the guards and simply delivers the outcome instantaneously, with no satisfaction to divide between them (one should look at all the definitions of the word bereaving). One drops the body before the single ticking of the clock, without second thoughts or signs of altruistic distress but with complete impassivity (there is no crossroads), walking back to the cell just as quickly as one was brought to this juncture.

Immanence
(of the blood)

They killed me once
Then wore my face many times. —Samih al-Qasim[22]

Inasmuch as rage hardens consciousness, it also confers itself into classes of liquidity, often amidst the outflow (hypovolemic becomings), fostering a stream of images in exsanguination. We must avoid the timeless linking of blood to birth and death, purity and impurity, and to ignore its eminent use in rituals, sacrifices, oaths, and atonements, for it can also be set forward to disrupt the structures of consecration as a force of applied immanence. To this end, rage and blood pledge to one another in an alternative thaumaturgy, for it is only through precipitation, moisture, and wetness that the former can pursue its ordeal and duel for the palm of the world—to become "what remains within," one must first make an overture toward empirical planes of trickling, dripping, and dissolution. Thought itself becomes waifish and runs, from the needles, then carried across by pale rivulets, by the canals of Being's intimate laceration.

*The lines reveal: that the enraged shall be impersonated, puppets of incorrect emulation, murdered off only so as to become timeless properties of the replicators.

Narrative XIV: Blood Draft (the Lettering) . . .

Some poets tell of writing in blood upon the prison walls—most often with one's own, sometimes with another's—and note the consequences of printing in this plasma-script. The reasons as to why one might compose with this interior instrument are self-evident: in an otherwise parched world, where creative supplies are withheld, it is a matter of availability, nothing more, and so one consigns oneself to this abject ink (spraying language). Still, one wonders whether it alters the prose, these residual patterns, and what bold strokes and split-reeds emerge therein, inciting their own anthology of proverbs, hieroglyphs, and plagiarisms.

Prism
(atrophic space)

This doubt and hesitation had turned all his thoughts into frightening shadows which followed him everywhere. Especially at night, when he turned and twisted in the cold bed. Alone, no matter how much he wanted to think about spiritual worlds, as soon as he fell asleep and his thoughts grew dim, a hundred demons would tempt him. —Sadeq Hedayat[23]

Rage is an attractive core, a nucleic point that draws everything toward itself, making its own chest the targeted center of the world's antagonism. This is the crux of an atrophic space, however, a lair enfolding and closing in from all sides (the house is telescopic), as if erected by a devious carpentry and struck by foul weather each night. Thus, to consult with rage is already to stroll through the district for which everything must pay its toll, and in which everything must take a furtive tour, as nervous guests of the prism.

*The lines reveal: that the enraged are least comfortable when in states of relaxation, that they pollute their own bedding and convert their own sanctum into sites of jeopardy.

Narrative XV: Turned Back (the Gravesite)

Some poets tell of the funeral ceremonies of the executed, and in particular the gesture of one figure who climbed the cemetery's hill one day, looked upon the casket of the acquaintance, and turned his back to her grave. Over the decades, there have been several interpretations of this gesture: some take it as a flagrant denunciation of the social ceremony itself, an affront to the masses who had convened for the sake of traditional self-exhibition, who dared to recite fruitless prayers on behalf of one they no longer truly wanted part of (otherwise, they would have joined her years before), there to bargain for their own petty sense of loss; some take it as a rejection of her death, disowning the finality of the eliminated body (being placed beneath) and staring outside instead, toward an open horizon; some take it as a symbolic demonstration of standing guard, watching over her form and image with immortal patience; and some take it as an affirmation of her singularity, that no matter how close they had come, still she remained elusive, ungraspable, and self-possessed (without souls to claim).

Chapter 6

Assassination: Writings of War

Warfare
(the imaginary)

Terror (the wayfare)
Incantation (the paroxysm)
Inscription (the engraving, of the bones)
Current (circulation, of the ropes)

Arena (animality, the creature, the caged)
Raid (engulfing, the overtaken)
Empire (honor)
Fatality (devastation)
Apocalypse (of the ultimate)

The assassin is among the most prominent figures in play throughout new Middle Eastern literature, signaling not an expanded interest with some remote persona but a perspectival shift whereby writing itself is increasingly upheld as a kind of assassination. The author thereby becomes a patron of this ascendant ethos: where all is betrayed but the excess of the desert, all breath drawn toward the chasm of an extinguished sky . . . where thought becomes a sorcery of death, and consciousness turns to murder. By calling forward the assassin's intellectual pose, the text positions itself within the center of violence, sifting through evocations of massacre, devastation, and flame with one command in mind: to ravage the entirety. A writing that is at once the garrison state, the janissary, and the fifth column (lines that disaggregate). Without doubt, it is a harmful apotheosis that treads these literary imaginaries, as words become incarnations of defacement and a lone someone transfuses epic collision with all that has dared to be (from the outer reaches).

In this light, the assassin can be seen as the true prodigy of contemporary Middle Eastern thought—the one that: acquires and learns what is already intuitively possessed; develops the doctrine into the instinct; heeds the master; bows before a nameless teacher, though never becoming the disciple; launches the emergent against the embedded, as a lengthening substance that deposes normality (to praise the outlandish); receives adoration and yet dislikes what one does, loathes the gift, despises the inborn talent, but nevertheless guarantees the realization of the art-form.[1]

Warfare
(the imaginary)

Gliding into dance rather than reality
I surrender celebrations to the garden of black roses
The one distinction I feel is that of the lost battle ax buried in the grave
There were ants and there were secrets hidden within them
Stains from cruel whips. —Namik Kuyumcu[2]

The philosophical registers of the East bring a different understanding of war, one of atmospheric combat . . . this wrong arisen, arisen wrong. On this side of the global experience, war embodies the hallmark of imagination, a perfect extremity-zone and alchemical mix of totality and infinity that knows no equal, the threshold at which all realms coalesce and entangle, a terrain of liquid interlacings that warn of the jagged collusion of states. Poetic thought thereby becomes a diacritics of infuriation (to rake the underpass brutal). And so there is a need for the elevation of war, the proliferation of its endlessness, an affirmation and aggravation of its disaster . . . to make it pound harder, faster, more savage, more twisted than ever before . . . to enter into the heart of its atrocity and refine the mechanism, to prey across its inner circles and provoke the hurt beyond its own ability to endure . . . to escalate war to its breaking-point, to deepen the incision and enshroud it in impossible pain, an excruciation unto itself, where torture grows tortured of its own.

There is movement in war, serrated waves of riot and extinction, and the law of the infiltration-arch, speed ripped across itself, toward the immanence of onslaught. And there is stillness, the immobility of forms that collapse, the even descent to earth, the lithium-curve of bodies, calligraphy of the death-arrested, ragged and motionless.

There is force in war, the aggression that treads across, eyes centered on confrontation, unflinching as it advances into proximity with the everything. And there is distance, the sudden remoteness of the mind, the withdrawal and the indifference, and even intimations of mercy, as hands recede back toward the undisclosed.

There is the howl in war, the fractured invasion of noise, sounds that wrack and perforate, the shriek of metal against metal, metal against flesh, and the coarse inhale and exhale of condemned breath. And there is silence, the deafening in the midst of action, and the unsafe quiet of that moment before what must come, the devastated quiet of the moment after, the erasure of resonance, when the last echo wanes.

There is alliance in war, the demarcation of sides, and with this the formation of a swarm, a legion of assault. And there is solitude, the crystallization of the lone, the secluded, the inner now barricaded against the outer, aligned with nothing beyond its own, cast toward isolation, enclosed and turning within itself.

There is obsession in war, desire and hunger borne across a thousand axes, that which exists for excitation alone, seethes addicted to the next beginning, the next end. And there is exhaustion, satiation beyond endurance, the hatred toward all wanting, and toward all continuation, and with it the muted outcry for no more.

There is excess in war, the insurgency of presence, the saturation of drive, of heightening and the unbound, beyond the last edge. And there is oblivion, the incarcerations of the nothing, and the aridness that follows, the evacuation of air, the pale carrion of the field, emblems of deprivation, inescapable and haunted, and the disappearance of an epoch.

There is ecstasy in war, the seduction of the combat-trance, itself a lethal synthesis of enchantments, a new fever consecrated, amidst the delirium of arms, when wrath turns to rapture. And there is torment, pain that scathes all degrees, from warped despair to agony vicious and unforgiving, from the gaze of supplication, stranded and downcast, to the tares of damage, soul-hideous and lashing.

There is the eternal in war, the inexorability of its influence, its unbroken grip on time, engraved into the back of existence, at once immemorial and ceaseless . . . the primal and the futuristic circulated through an apocalyptic present. And there is the vanishing, the fading and the waste, transience leveled across the lines, and the unspoken overthrow of temporal regimes.

There is hardness in war, sunken and grave, coldness that deadens the expression, seals the face into the permanent acidic, an age of vitriolic sedimentations, and the synchronicity of muscle. And there is frailty, erratic and indefinite before each merger, that of the diaphanous experience, vulnerable to the mania of a thistle, as the surface screams before the touch.

There is the will in war, the regimentation of vision, and the precision of its machine, the deep manipulation of its elements, severe and rigid. And there is the chaotic, an instinct without origin, uncontained in the face of regulation, and with it the reign of chance, the anarchy of the unformed.

There is the raid in war, the sudden contraction of space, that which circumscribes an arena of conflict, and with it the suffocation and enclosure of an unforeseen violence. And there is the limitlessness, the opening of space, and the refraction of borders.

There is contamination in war, itself a prism of impurity, torsos that mirror the violated, chests marked of the contagion. And there is innocence, the displaced laughter of the as yet untainted, the unstained, and the poetics of forgetting.

There is assurance in war, the raw immediacy of the event, its concreteness, its undeniability, its irrevocability . . . that one cannot turn away. And there is illusion, the emanation of the unreal, the blurring and the lie, and the awareness of the mirage that encircles.

There is awakening in war, the carved awareness of the one who has over-witnessed, the transparency of a worn consciousness, once exposed to the wrong shades, and now delivered to the stranglehold of insomnia, its terror and its seamlessness. And there is obscurity, the secrecy of its madness, its lapse and its distortion, and the vertigo of its imbalance.

There is honor in war, the irradiation of a stance that withstands all menace, that holds its word beyond all penalties, and that punishes itself at the first trace of trembling. And there is betrayal, the desertion of the one who searches outside this sphere, whose thirst is a corridor to treason.

There is self-exaltation in war, resurrected upon the right to seize, to capture and to kill, entitled to take what is already stolen. And there is self-sacrifice, the relinquishment to blindness, at once destitute and abandoned, undefended before being and non-being, the forfeiture of world.

There is fatality in war, the all-engulfing risk of disintegration, ever dragged and caving toward ruin. And there is the immortal, return of the survival-instinct, and the interminability of its legacy of hurt.[3]

*In light of the above excerpt, one should also contemplate the connection between assassination and gliding, dancing, and a language of black flowers.

Terror
(the wayfare)

We inhaled with difficulty amidst the rank air of a plague, and
                                             pouring sweat
within a pointless struggle
                    we continued shovelling
in the wasted area of a putrid sea
that from one end to another
was clothed in corpses
          whose eyes
                still
from the terror of the great storm
                remain open. —Ahmad Shamlu[4]

Poetic assassination requires an affinity for terror and its disparate grades:
(1) the chase (to write that which makes one run away); (2) the fraying (to
write that which scrapes the nerves, leaving composure within tatters); (3) the
equatorial pools (to write of the space that causes snarling, groaning, arthritic
effects, and the sly belief that floating further inward somehow brings one
closer to the outside); and (4) the predicament (to write of the tension between
possibility and fatality, at once generating the desire for escape and the fact of
the inescapable). This is the forking nature of the wayfare, where emergency
takes charge, and the struggles of consciousness are now transposed upon the
terms of the very thing that assassinates consciousness: to vie for one's right to
existence in accordance with its creed and from within its territory.

*In light of the above excerpt, one should also contemplate the connection
between assassination and pointless revolt, fearlessness within rankness, and
the shaking of the netherworld (beyond inferno, beyond perdition).

Incantation
(the paroxysm)

*The first invisible writing of modern times! From now on I shall write the way sculp-
tors sculpt! Hereafter I shall write with a hammer! From now on I shall write with
claws! From now on I shall write with a rake and an eraser! Plain Text, It's decided!
Understood! Concluded!* —Réda Bensmaia[5]

The incantation is a genre central to this creative imagination . . . where words
are confiscated, caving toward the dejected . . . for it follows a paroxysmal language (that which does not bother to translate itself for the other, though it makes
things happen to the other). In addition, the incantation turns the saying away

from the sign and toward its impulsive physicality, responsive yet non-emotive—tears as pain without sorrow, nothing more, the sigh as fatigue without regret, the scream as horror without trauma—all restored to the level of a sphinx's action. There is no one left, for one has become an onyx space of seizure, without soul (only riddle), and the body just the place where things transpire.

*In light of the above excerpt, one should also contemplate the connection between assassination and invisibility, sculpting, and textual clawing.

Inscription
(engraving, of the bones)

There was a narrow tablet (the crypt-stone's downward-moving inscription) meant to be cut in a wave-like outline from a marble unlike that of the crypt-stone itself. Grass has sprouted all across the gravesite—and, within this grass, there is a hatchet. —Yadollah Royai[6]

One often stumbles upon the overlooked inscriptions of the cutthroat. The intent: inscrutable transformation. The gateway: willed madness. The location: deep tissue. The gauge: spinal trembling. The risk: sudden death. To write the obvious, for they fear the obvious.

These are documents that experiment with the countless registers of pain, cast in multiple forms of: void (impossibility), depth (opacity), paralysis (indifference), quarantine (stigma), fragmentation (disunity), porosity (openness), implosion (absorption), disorientation (obliqueness), overflow (limitlessness), amputation (decay), fragility (susceptibility), transparency (crystallization), expulsion (purging), deprivation (loss), dread (despair), strangulation (waste), magic (bittenness), malformation (dysfunctionality), reception (hyper-sensitivity). A landmine topography of sensation, each an irruption between flesh and nerve.

As for the complicated question of engraving, one can picture the white page as a subtractive sculpting, a filing-down to reveal the potential maxims, reminding one of the chalk of bones, and the negative images laid in copper plates (to write backwards).

*In light of the above excerpt, one should also contemplate the connection between assassination and tablets, tombstones, and the sudden environmental growth of unnatural things (hatchets within grass).

Current
(circulation, of the ropes)

While I escape the pandemonium of voices,
With ropes stretching across the wind
They render me perplexed, somewhere between aid and the unaided. —Yadollah Royai[7]

Such Eastern literatures often speak of currents, and of the shudder that runs its course through the body in waves (vanquishing trajectories). This notwithstanding, such circulations are selected in order to create a slicing dissonance in time, shot through the moment so as to insert discontemporaneity. This is how the assassin extricates himself from time's grip, slipping across the ropes of an ahistorical tiding, leaving bemused all who would risk engagement (for he is not in the now, but rather its nemesis). He becomes the one who is always expected (from the exterior path), though his appearance is hoped against (the prayer of non-arrival).

*In light of the above excerpt, one should also contemplate the connection between assassination and the voice, the wind, and the baffled pose of the helpless that it etches upon the other.

Arena
(animality, the creature, the caged)

It was the first time I had seen wild animals. Those who were awake in their cages kept walking back and forth like this, just like this. At that time also I had become like those animals. Perhaps I thought like them as well. I felt within myself that I was like them. This listless walking about, circling round myself. —Sadeq Hedayat[8]

The assassin equates the present world with the arena, whereupon an abrupt entrapment of Man can be undertaken: the logic of the spectacle is one of vicarious death and reconfirmed life, wherein the masses exploit the sacrificial victim at the center in order to flood themselves with the fictive sensation of survival, a false enlivening (for they have won and lost nothing), though this delusion of immortality can be turned against them (to remedy their glamor). For it is precisely at this instant, amidst the onset weakness brought by the conceit of Being and the conceived invincibility therein, that the frenzy of the crowds can fall to the steadiness of another type, one who makes the arena the frontier of their undoing. The assassin, as a constant template of violence, does not require the primal shock of this event, does not crave the unearned rush, and can therefore move upon the cheering hordes without detection (to render caged).

Strangely enough, part of this reversal-strategy of the arena is predicated upon the incursion of the creature (as that which might pounce): these are the undecidable entities, immobile forms that one nevertheless believes have the capacity to move (suspect animus), sightless forms that one believes have the capacity to watch (suspect vision), forever afraid that the stillness will rupture, though for now they remain waiting (the scarecrow, the automaton, the vagrant, the dead). Most fear the recovery of the disregarded.

*In light of the above excerpt, one should also contemplate the connection between assassination and pacing, listlessness, and the circularity of the kept mind.

Raid
(engulfing, the overtaken)

Our desert aloneness is not easy . . .
Beware!
Here the sun is a bush of smelting
and light is a waking whip
and the sea-like thing
that flows
from the edges of rage and sand
in the veins of raiding
is the warmth of men's blood. —Esmail Khoi[9]

Poetic assassination relies upon the premise of textual raiding: a theory of looting, invasion, encroachment, movement-as-insection. Space turned mercenary, following the prowler's rhythm: war beyond the law, without words, blood itself as code, and the new instinct to permeation. Infinite enemy-state (where all is imperiled), with no translation of a judgment, simply the ecstatic presence of engulfing forms, and the modest warmth of being overtaken.

The assassin is a figure renowned for specificity, for the particularized attention to the single target, which then raises the question: how might one transfer this acuity to the world itself? When such methodologies are predicated upon difference, contrast, and selectivity, how does one make a whole existence distinctive (since it presumes to be everything)? Where does one look, how does one follow, upon what feature does one concentrate, when the totality reflects the marked object? This is why the assassin figure shares a bond with radical imagination: for, in order to specialize, one needs to elicit a comparative gap, a criterion of discrimination, which in turn leads to the creative projection of alternative worlds. In essence, one must invent a host of outsider spheres if only in order to discern, recognize, and then mine this reality (exactness requires variation). The assassin is thus the consummate dreamer (because the guild demands it).

*In light of the above excerpt, one should also contemplate the connection between assassination and desertion, aloneness, and the interflow of sun, light, and sea (to form whips).

Empire
(honor)

And might he actually become a citizen of her empire? Or when he made his next visit, would he shoot himself in the head on one of its darkened platforms? All this raging, clamoring and bitter violence—was it a sign of imminent death or of new birth? —Ghada Samman[10]

All empires begin with the demarcation of a sensitive border, and the subsequent flirtation with this slightening barrier, coming infinitely close without touching (the thinnest separation). And there is a cost to crossing, not the same as transgression, but another toll (a certain pain in the approach).

The relevance here lies in the fact that the assassination-outlook then distends itself (exogenic status), internalizing each domain as its own (to chase after, to hunt down), to strive and impose upon all areas of experience, interiority ejected beyond itself with infinite entitlement. Borne by an amalgamation-compulsion, by the enforcement of a widening hunger, it traverses all limits, seeking uncontrolled battle, from the narrow straits of self-containment to the vastness of an outlaw immanence, thought and action fused together as a spreading ivy, actualizing principles of unstoppable infiltration. Thrash as precision. Night-perished.

This radical imagination progresses not with a utopian drive to universalization but with the horizontality of a rampage, a continuous lashing-beyond, emission, and accumulation, the master-theft of space (to consume tirelessly). Empire as captor, as a volatile holding of the disparate provinces, wanting all, taking all, and yet guarding nothing (the epoch of the forsaken). Trespass and aggression, incision and conquest . . . and then the desertion (all-traitorous). Apprehension of the known, it surrounds and saturates (with no named leader), searing pathways across the built-up world, stabbing into the body of what is there, and therein chiseling away at its assurance (blurring the maps), as the will cloaks all it touches, carving its intangible wrath into the myth of existence, scything across the everything. Vampirism, unregulated volition, resuscitation, and projection of the coverer (to impair the boundaries), the era of anti-actuality whipped across all spheres (histrionic dispatching), a trajectory of stolen earth, toxic to ontological certainties: the zero-world as the jumbled opening of space, the threat as the re-territorialization of space, annihilation as the ignition of space, the sharpening as the acceleration of space, rage as the great riling of space, assassination as the bleeding of space, and empire as the exotic reconfiguration of space. Here thought transforms into a perpetual conquest, leaving itself vulnerable to the recurrence of conflict-without-cause, just the steady parade of inception, agony, promulgation, and occupation (interfaces of instinct and anger), and the uninterrupted challenge of chaos to itself.

Furthermore, this world-assassination effectuates its own concept of honor, one that is linked to temptation: to construct the inkling to lose a world, whether through forfeiture or havoc, to insinuate the path, to shift the mood, to speak the word or impulse that brings a scenario closer to its own evacuation. Honor as an insertion of the wanting-no-more of this.

There is an immaculate rigidity at work in the creation of imperial bodies, one that realigns consciousness itself across the persuasions of the formless and the unformed (one wonders which is the more elite incarnation of warfare, which the perfect taking-machine). The formless is that which has gone through, that which has endured the tyranny of form, has walked alongside it with unbearable proximity, inhabiting its treacheries and incarcerations, and has since abandoned its captivity (the pure fugitive). The unformed is that which has always stood outside the chains, a foreign element, an unknown impulse, reckless and untamed, invulnerable so far to the trappings of form (the delirium of the one who has had no part in this). So which nears closest toward the cause of a poetic infliction, cutting deepest into world? Both are possessed of advantages and chinks: the formless, though having overcome itself, remains susceptible to the resetting of trauma, plagued by the recollection of its past, its wounds, the suffocation it once withstood; it can therefore be defined by its loss, owned by what has taken place, allowing for degeneration into lower types of vengeance. The unformed, however, has never seen the inside of its enemy's camp; it has never breathed its oxygen, never learned its motions, studied its profane ways, never become what it would destroy, remaining vulgar, raw, and transparent in its bristling. It therefore lacks the stealth, secrecy, and quietness of the formless; it also lacks the immunity that the formless has won for having tread within the walls, its original distance at once a source of power and of fragility; it can be infected, inasmuch as its own outcast instinct can contaminate a world that has never seen its presence (savage on all sides, it can bring a damage unforeseen to life and itself). The formless is a thief, a stalker, marked by subtlety, balance, and elusion, while the unformed is a storm, a scream, marked by thorn and lawlessness. The first is shadowy, and thus it preys (amorphous, imperceptible); the second is carnivorous, and thus it strikes (tingling, gnawing). The resolution is this: to privilege the supreme aspects of both becomings, the force of one countering the lapse of the other at all times, though to attend to this possibility one must block the extant holes. The formless must be willing to go without memory, to initiate the permanent erasure of its own history, such that it becomes "the formless-without-past" when necessary; similarly, the unformed must shield itself against the new barricades, the enclosures it has never fought before, and thus toward which it could still be lured and sealed away. In this way, it must be willing to betray the possibility of its own impending tomorrow, ripping from its hands any vision of an imminent world, handing itself over to a self-detonating knot of the present, and thereby becoming the "unformed-without-future" when necessary. Once combined, these two styles invoke the most compelling version of the marksman-turning-emperor.

*In light of the above excerpt, one should also contemplate the connection between assassination and visitation, suicidal dismount, and the clamoring sign of the newborn (to hold court on the platform).

Fatality
(devastation)

In a world that becomes ever blacker as one gets to know it better
A companion of dispossession wherever one is
All colors turning to black in the face of war
It's from such a history of bone and marrow that I come
We've paid our debts to the final grave-digger
And we owe not a cent to the seamstress. —Namik Kuyumcu[11]

Fatality, through its flair with excess, word-breaking, and paradox, brings the settling of the debt: it hails the most scattered sites and wrenches them before a forensic committee (where all events wear the tunic of eruption). This inspection draws a line in the sand, separating the rest from a rare post-identity who lives and dies by stoning, for it is the latter's elitism that bends things into relinquishing, upheaval, and irretrievable outburst. All perception perceives the end, all desire desires the end. Such is the culmination of the assassin's expenditure: the proliferation of terminal pressure . . . where nothing asks to be spared, where no one asks to be saved from altercation.

To will the inversion of Being's self-serving approach, the counter-ploy of making things unearthed . . . and the disposal of the weapon, to rid the instrument from view (the text, the thought, the self that lies behind). Beyond dialectics, to train from distance (the archer's dimension), to appear removed even in immediate range, calm in the knowledge that one has taught the real to incapacitate itself.

The tripartite operation: annexation, menace, the unfitting . . . that each instant is first stolen away, thieved from its own essence, then driven to an unavailing point, and then made uncomfortable to itself. To plague, through invariability, until existence is forgotten. All desire a poison that wrings its sponge through the mind, all thought an exercise in trans-impurity. There is no being, only contagion, only a beast, half in clay, half in world, the arms of a fatality-machine. Betrayal, infliction, convulsion, end of world. No innocence allowed, now circling in the breath of evil. The visitation of this, the last imperative, drowned in war.

And this also leans into the meaning of devastation that we seek: the height and vanishing-point of infatuation, held too close to the skin . . . to want something to the extent of frustration, exasperated union, where its sustenance becomes impossible (untenable love).

*In light of the above excerpt, one should also contemplate the connection between assassination and companionship, color, and the sentiment (lodged in the marrow) that one owes nothing to the weavers, collectors, and reapers of this existence.

Apocalypse
(of the ultimate)

On the last evening of this earth, we sever our days
from our trees, and count the ribs we will carry along
and the ribs we will leave behind, right here . . . on the last evening . . .
And I am one of the kings of the end . . . —Mahmoud Darwish[12]

Why introduce poetics at the end of the world?

Assassination incites the apocalyptic in order to clear way for three tests (each its own distinct inquest): (1) to make words at the ending border, to rain creation in the face of finality, to galvanize the arms at the hour of the world's demise, to undertake the tragic paradox of building across the threshold of a damned moment, in order to see whether one is capable of failing well; (2) to wager for the possibility of the influx of alternate existences, to investigate the potential transition, to test the word of the reckoning (does it hold, is there truly nothing more?), to erase the regime of existence in the wake of the emerging untold (to fight on behalf of the possibility of another spell); and (3) to attempt to devise the one factor that could withstand the fall of world, that could persist beyond the breaking-point, that makes it past (striving farther than the known). These are ultimate demonstrations of courage: to see whether one can still maneuver creatively at the end of time (opposing futility); to bet that there is another material vitalism beyond this reality (opposing totality); to experiment with the formulation of the unstoppable, eternal thing (opposing finality).

These are also ultimate demonstrations of despair, rising across three planes: (1) to despair over that of which one is capable (that one is in awe of one's own hands, and the magnitude therein); (2) to despair that this process must soon finish, and one is coerced into departure (that one wants another round, still ravening for adversity); and (3) to despair over the inability to mourn (that one cannot weep, plead, or kneel any longer).

In its own dank ironic turn, this apocalyptic tendency is about survival most of all: for the assassin does not merely function to provide the catastrophic will, but also struggles for awhile on behalf of the world (and of the human), just long enough to induct and expose it to the full bearing of the disaster (they should not miss what will befall their ways). Thus it prolongs this panting reality, with seemingly generous quantities of patience, so that its edifices can experience the complete awful fate in store (a blackened destiny breathes, torn across itself).

> . . . when knives sway, starved beyond the uneven . . .
> (something more than what it says)
> . . . when slain echoes tremble still, driven toward insignificance . . .
> (something less than what it says)

> . . . shards of desperate fury, stranded across the
> desolate . . . (something other than what it says)
> . . . imprisoned depths, now thieved of exile . . .
> (something different than when it was said)
> . . . convulsions of the quickening, sacrificed across
> barren walls . . . (something too late to be said)
> . . . bodies enveloped in abrasion, hostage to forsaken
> shrouds . . . (something said to only one and no other)

This topic concludes with an attention to the catalogue of evocations, jargons, and endnotes through which such an Eastern poetic consciousness reminds itself (words that in this become blood and shade). There are certain terms that one might find in an assassin's journal—neologistic pairings, charged verbs, and archived objects, each with its own chapter, heading, definition, and ornate mode of citation (the diction of a hired gun), including such phrases as: irradiation, seething, impermanence, locking, dominance, aggression, unbalanced passages, inviolable calling, emblazoning, death-coughs, battle-drums, spears, oblivion, incendiary perishing, ransom notes, phantom gazes, wolven instincts, unrelenting famine, dementia, suspension, recurrence, perforated sight, burial-seductions, forgetting, desertion, lethal haze, disquiet, prismatic dissonance, impossible awakening, rogue hours, night-wrenching, exorcism, and inhaled punishment.

*In light of the above excerpt, one should also contemplate the connection between assassination and severance, counting, carrying, and the hollow glory of last kingship (to rule over the final evening).

Chapter 6.5

Interlude: Of the Factions, of the Barriers

I. Fanaticism
(the ranks, bewilderment,
the murder-treatise)

II. Esotericism
(the protected, restricted
wisdom, the murmur)

III. Unfamiliarity
(the newcomer, the satellite, the idiom)

IV. Treason
(the traitor, duplicity, the façade)

V. Complicity
(the carrier, bondage, the pact)

VI. Confidentiality
(the implanted, intimacy,
the suggestion)

VII. Offering
(the grieving, decline, the altar)

VIII. Schism
(the barricaded, recursion,
the episode)

IX. Profanity
(defilement, the oath)

X. Intimidation
(the imperiled,
|the apotheosis)

XI. Abuse
(greed, the rave)

XII. Derailment
(the displaced, melted time/space,
the projection)

XIII. Disguise
(the strata, layering, the skin)

XIV. Subtraction
(scarcity, the hole)

XV. Withdrawal
(the arid, separation,
the drought)

XVI. Neutrality
(the anonymous,
the atonal)

XVII. Disturbance
(the seamless, warping, the miasma)

XVIII. Misfortune
(astonishment, the shallow)

XIX. Replication
(the laden, the rite)

XX. Impersonation
(fragility, the inland)

XXI. Quickening
(immobility, the transfusion)

XXII. Unreality
(the allusion, the inquest)

XXIII. Blankness
(the amnesic, incompletion,
the defect)

XXIV. Allegiance
(the coalition, the gang, the swarm)

XXV. Vice
(the ground, the ceiling,
the sky, the fault)

XXVI. Misguidance
(the wayward, the wayside,
the tongue)

XXVII. Premonition
(the messenger, the handle,
the signpost)

XXVIII. Rivalry
(the fractal, intrigue, the ring)

XXIX. Iconization
(the emblazoned, animation,
the post-symbolic)

XXX. Stigma
(the shunned, intolerance, the dregs)

XXXI. Spite
(the underhanded, retaliation,
the vise)

XXXII. Aging
(the decomposed, the undead,
the throes)

XXXIII. Evening
(the unlike, the vigil,
the vial, mist)

These are wrongful solicitations, the signs of an unusual expertise: to organize the gradients of misleading (the process by which writing becomes unsure) . . .

These are expensive texts, those of the dampened, the convicted, and the riotous.

These are the sayings of thirty-three poetic barriers . . .

I.

There are others here, *orders of fanaticism*, for whom there is only the command, torrential speaking, language that becomes necessary, that exemplifies the one fervor, and which serves as a slave-agent, language that cannot be swayed/penetrated by another language, for which all is proof and justification. They act as *the ranks*, those who ask what it means to take one's turn here, and to stand in rows. These are the ones of *bewilderment*, those who reel in disbelief and uninvited inspiration, those who know not what they write, assigned to a vicarious task. Thus they bring *the murder-treatise*, the work that murders truth, and the one who came looking for it (to be on the list).

II.

There are others here, *orders of esotericism*, for to carry the esoteric is to become a translation of its vanity; never so loud (one does not yell here), never so quick or brief (one does not swat at the margins), but rather coated, as an object heartless, an object of burden, as words grow serious and weighted, taken by frost. They act as *the protected*, those who leave thought in sheltered quadrants (the well, the village), where one delves through what is most gaunt (the skeletal, the least), through what is not careful (the gallery, the switch), where one seeks counsel with those who are outstretched and gaping (the interrogated), and with those who extract what is owed (the professional). These are the ones of *restricted wisdom*, holding the arcane, the archaic, and the jealous insight. Thus they bring *the murmur*, the side-lament for what cannot be brought back, the incurable, resounding what is unresurrected (there are borders past which things become lost causes).

III.

There are others here, *orders of unfamiliarity*, those who draft the strange equation: that to conceive a thought is to open a fatal door, one that leads onto two possibilities: (1) that it is then set loose to kill (often beyond our hands); or (2) that one invites it to turn back and glance its maker, as the penalty of inception (to be maimed by the very image one gives rise to). What does it mean that a reflection could revenge itself against its origin, the one who conveyed it to the surface now buried beneath its surface (theo-punishment)? To become degraded, whether through fast reaction or slow drain on the mind, wearing away at the nervous system. They act as *the newcomer*, those for whom descendance is a slaughtering, those of imagined ancestry, who turn everywhere into the elsewhere. These are the ones of *the satellite* (this is the last place one goes, and these the last thoughts of their kind). Thus they bring *the idiom*, unidentifiable slang, where writing becomes the gutter-talk of the undesirables, leaving only varied inkstains, the dismissed handwriting of the illiterate.

IV.

There are others here, *orders of treason*, for whom language invalidates, as keen indications of reversal. They act as *the traitor*, sent to betray, divulge, and elicit the mistrust of all who perceive them, and for whom disloyalty alone is sacred. These are the ones of *duplicity*, who speak as another, in the cloak of another, with the mouth of another (never who they say). Thus they bring *the façade*: to dam the text, to climb and fall from the top of its wall, to deny passage, antitransgression, where the witness is obligated to the disappearance of what was seen.

V.

There are others here, *orders of complicity*, for whom there is an influence, those of infinite consent, who permit the intent of another, who cater to external motivations. They act as *the carrier*, those who involve, collude, and transport, who hunch and stoop, found crouching beneath the domes of power. These are the ones of *bondage*, where bowing becomes a mean-slit gesture, gives access to the knees, the ankles, the heels, where one chips away from beneath—for lowness should not be underestimated, and humiliation its own harmful vantage and entrance-point. Thus they bring *the pact*, site of impoverished agreements, for whom writing is a backhanded payment (the will to bribery).

VI.

There are others here, *orders of confidentiality*, the unrecorded dialogues, without the right to expression, for whom no chronicle exists, who tell one another by covert tokens, by sermons of denial, and for whom there are always two secrecies: the secret the other knows about (withheld information) and the secret unknown to the other (injected information). They act as *the implanted*, those at once of the stronghold and the contrivance. These are the ones of *intimacy*, the closeness that extends too far, into void, the interior removal, who allocate the private fear of disclosure. Thus they bring *the suggestion*, the opposite of apotropaic utterances, for they do not ward off but rather bring in what is wrong, invitations to displeasure (the image that gathers bad luck).

VII.

There are others here, *orders of offering*, where one must beware the gift, where one cannot afford what is given, where debt gathers, sold to limitless proposals (the hands are not free here). They act as *the grieving*, those of spinning loss, the half-obliterated, by distance or waning, where full mourning never comes to pass. These are the ones of *decline*, that which can still be recaptured, though doubtful. Thus they bring *the altar*, with presentations of the unprivileged, where consciousness kneels and forfeits its own.

VIII.

There are others here, *orders of schism*, for whom indentations become channels, for whom imbalance and division become maximal lusts, the deconstitution of sects, articulations of the gulf. They act as *the barricaded*, where thought becomes hindrance (anti-procession), subordinating itself to a cosmology of levels, rifts, and striations. These are the ones of *recursion*, backward and forward, narratives of poor arrival (where time is raked across), of overdue hours, those that wrench resemblance against sameness, turning what is nearest toward the dissimilar. Thus they bring *the episode*, to stratify and pull between, as an impenetrable infirmity, the impassable window, mocked by translucence.

IX.

There are others here, *orders of profanity*, those who are tied to slander, who slur the name, neither to disband nor to oppose the sacred but to leave it endlessly coated (where the forbidden resides in a thin film). These are the ones of *defilement*, where materiality worsens the situation, hardens the abstracted, covers the onlooker in rancid tiers. Thus they bring *the oath*, that which demands upholding, at the life-cost of all who remain disavowed, that fastens destiny to a hideous point, though all swear without realization, sightless to the implications that await.

X.

There are others here, *orders of intimidation*, for whom language gives fear, instructs a certain paleness, contrarian presence, that which looms, envelops, and deters. They act as *the imperiled*, where the mind becomes endangered by what blankets it, what hovers over. Thus they bring *the apotheosis*, deified writing, language that acts of its own will, for it answers to nothing, where the celestial forfeits shape and strings itself as pulsation.

XI.

There are others here, *orders of abuse*, for whom there comes the ladder, vertical coercion, mortality-from-above. These are the ones of *greed*, the unstoppable hand, who ensure the collection/shackling of transcripts, the anthology that is never enough, that slakes itself continually, cannot finish its work, and takes ever more, becoming an instrument of capture, and thereby enlivens what it confiscates. Thus they bring *the rave*, its false smoothness, simplicity that masks complexity, holding back what is too quiet, where the blockade takes over, restraining what is more than silence, as stammering and nonsense grow sadistic.

XII.

There are others here, *orders of derailment*, who practice in the misalignment of stars, the substitution of maps, and the eradication of checkpoints (*against* the vehicle). They act as *the displaced*, who treat texts as refugee camps, words as peripheral populations, who seek the disorientation of the knowing passenger, toward abyssal destinations of non-reflection. These are the ones of *melted time/space*, for whom heat is an avenue of escape, to the spilling and leakage of thought, and for whom writing is a scientific premise of thawing/congealment. Thus they bring *the projection*, for which there remains a perpetual recasting, to then screen itself across all other dormant surfaces, superimposing its visage upon the errant.

XIII.

There are others here, *orders of disguise*, who claim fictitious innocence (all the while . . .). They act as *the strata*, with its host of lethal objects: the diagram, the belt, the column. These are the ones of *layering*, for whom admissions are wrapped in innumerable decoy articulations, hides that form casks, anti-confessions that form the sleeve of naked limbs. Thus they bring *the skin*, whose coverings deceive, the fingerprints removed so as to remain untracked, impenetrable, and still bottomless (to become total wound).

XIV.

There are others here, *orders of subtraction*, those of illicit business, whose talent is to scale away, leaving under-formed, for whom the most chilling removals and replacements are common (to seek the emaciation of thought). These are the ones of *scarcity*—the strict, the sobered, the expressionless: the ones of grave and austere plans, the non-temperament (what winter is this?; what futural asceticism?). Thus they bring *the hole*, where to know is to lapse, to meditate is to fall through, and to search is to find the text that invites slithering.

XV.

There are others here, *orders of withdrawal*, those of final negation, whose flight is no retreat but rather a cancellation: to rescind the middle-ground, and by extension the right of return. They act as *the arid*, for whom the companion is disbanded, for whom nothing is shared (not even the partition), for whom the forest and the journey have been mislaid once and for all. These are the ones of *separation*, who train in misrecognition and counter-solidarity (ultimate misanthropy). Thus they bring *the drought*, where one must give no water, but rather leave the other dying of thirst, handed over to the generosity of desiccation.

XVI.

There are others here, orders of neutrality, those who sleep through the event and overlook the creation/destruction around, where there are no original authors, no immemorial figures, no sentiment even, only found texts (the scroll). They act as *the anonymous*, where the name goes missing, at once chosen and overthrown by the alias. Thus they bring *the atonal*, where sound reminds the arteries of their sick crusade (hailing, neo-extinction).

XVII.

There are others here, *orders of disturbance*, whose function is to redden, to conceive the dim-lit incident that might foam, stretch, and shower. They act as *the seamless*, amidst consistent plays of decapitation, for whom words aim forever at the neck, as the chieftains of a now-dissident, headless generation. These are the ones of *warping*, writing that sweeps the length of the stonecutter's forearm, that chisels and procures the downward turn (the slope). Thus they bring *the miasma*, atmospheric corruption, where newfound agonies are transmitted by the air.

XVIII.

There are others here, *orders of misfortune*, who behold the revolutionary paradox of shock and anti-shock, those who keep obscene count, presiding over a blacksmith's calculation of seconds. These are the ones of *astonishment*, who deal out cards of genuflection and salivation, unwanted awe, in militaristic flows. Thus they bring *the shallow*, thought that seeks but one function: to trample, amidst the desecration of graves, the overturning of vaults, the excavation of crypt-sites, and the washing away of the epithet (there is nowhere left to gather and weep for the age).

XIX.

There are others here, *orders of replication*, whose stomachs breed unfeeling children, for whom the most young are already the most ancient, and for whom the art of derivation calls forward a still-undetectable pain. They act as *the laden*, those for whom all are named beggars, made to barter with pathetic holdings, to sell details for souls, and hence binding the supplicant within the heaviness of the revelation. Thus they bring *the rite*, its crescent of monotonous imitation, its cold spawning, where to release is to seal closed, to shut down the precious anatomy of the moment.

XX.

There are others here, *orders of impersonation*, those who bring to life only to turn to stone, where thought is petrified, consigned to a steel arabesque (the chimera, the caricature). These are the ones of *fragility*, for the brittle ones harbor the unkind, as the delicate body becomes a box with unsafe contents (one must be scared of gentle appearances). Thus they bring *the inland*, where the invasive will seeks its landscape, a black-sand coastline, announcing this one eternal axiom: that all violence is spatial.

XXI.

There are others here, *orders of quickening*, those who delight in the folklore of acceleration, mythological speed, to model speech-acts after the velocity of legends. These are also the ones of *immobility*, where extreme pace hits the wall of entropy, becoming those who remain locked, in techniques of holding, strung up before inertia, who take thought toward its first dead-end, the uncrossable quarter, to set crude obstacles (no longer possible to turn around). Thus they bring *the transfusion*, where some things are depleted, then aided once more, only to be bled out later (and, when spilled, what does it mean to reabsorb/partake of blood that has since circulated through the enemy?).

XXII.

There are others here, *orders of unreality*, those who control the minimal degrees of shading: the illusion (that launches), the mirage (that promises), the reflection (that lightens), the hallucination (that misrepresents), the simulation (that twists), the memory (that falsifies), the story (that beguiles), the vision (that worries), the dream (that soothes), the nightmare (that concerns), the fantasy (that dissipates), the apparition (that skulks). These are the ones of *the allusion*, for whom nefarious references lead all thought, slung to whatever intricate mentioning, and for whom vague manipulations of the half-statement take precedence. Thus they bring *the inquest*, the havoc of the minor question, where ambiguity goes uncleansed and methods can only insinuate the dire turn ahead.

XXIII.

There are others here, *orders of blankness,* those who pass the plain discs of rejection, ire, and futility between themselves, for whom meaning surmounts nothing, pours into useless cisterns. They act as *the amnesic,* those for whom select particles of the happening have been sliced out, for whom the non-recollection persists, crowding the valley of mind. These are the ones of *incompletion,* the partial lesioning, for whom all projects strand themselves in undeveloped intentions. Thus they bring *the defect,* that which grasps the fixed price of imagining, the penalty wrought somewhere, for here one flings open a territory, a component, that must be harmed, that must accept the consequence of this venture. It was not there before, no soul, no unconscious, but rather delivered amidst the invention—it is the priority that arises only to be burned down, whenever the engagement. This is the underside of contemplation: to be stabbed with each new envisioning, though only in the second heart, never the first, for it cuts into the one that is stored elsewhere, the victim-organ built just for this. Such writing is the record of this flesh now viciously grazed, a writing sanctioned in rough country.

XXIV.

There are others here, *orders of allegiance,* who crystallize in group dominations, squadrons, and patrols, and for whom a collective perplexity stands (the pandemonium of "the several"). They act as *the coalition*: to gather numbers, where words become masses, valued in exponential drifts. They act as *the gang*: to harvest foul interiorities, where words commiserate in their soiled mission. They act as *the swarm*: to swallow alive, where words bear the signature of the encircling many, set to administer a public hanging.

XXV.

There are others here, *orders of vice,* who induce atomic habits, exacerbated by the carceral (morbid enclaves). These are ones of *the ground*: to lessen the surface, to sink the earth, toward unnoticed descent. These are ones of *the ceiling*: to throw the listener upward, toward encasement. These are ones of *the sky*: to lead into the courtyard, before the clearing, between the independence above and the regiment below. Thus they bring *the fault,* concoctions of worship, disappointment, and lead, where texts take on heaviness, as language falls across the shoulders.

XXVI.

There are others here, *orders of misguidance*, who profit from the strained conversion, compulsory metamorphosis, and hyper-metaphoric transition. They act as *the wayward*, of vast fatigue, upon whom one finds the deepening birthmark of exhaustion (some faint here, some sway, still others subside completely). These are ones of *the wayside*, where thought becomes debris (the shipwreck), building anti-gallows upon anti-gallows, its own archive of the difficult, the dispassionate, and the disliked. Thus they bring *the tongue*, through which one must convene the session, and yet where all is misspoken (counter-lyricism).

XXVII.

There are others here, *orders of premonition*, where to listen is to follow, to follow is to become convinced, and the convinced are no longer spared (unfounded examples). They act as *the messenger*, who assembles the shells of post-reasoned arguments, enhancing the seduction-routes of the missive through embellishment, elaboration, and hypnosis (the caretaker). These are the ones of *the handle*, as that which must be twisted, must give way to contortion, to the morose logic of rotation. Thus they bring *the signpost*, where thought snakes, hoards, stockpiles itself, where the nocturnal accumulates, squanders daylight, and leaves behind the incommensurate (darkening-sensation).

XXVIII.

There are others here, *orders of rivalry*, caught in lawless competitions, those who taunt, ridicule, and rile the spirit (the foreground of retribution). They act as *the fractal*, rebel-edifice, for whom dissension is orthodoxy, and where one keeps company with salted types. These are the ones of *intrigue*, for whom envy, conspiracy, and interference rule the scene (what deals have been made?). Thus they bring *the ring*, that which asserts a decadent equivalence: to see everything in its death-tics (all is merely borrowed).

XXIX.

There are others here, *orders of iconization*, where thought becomes valiant through bronzing, becomes the statue of misdirected faith (pseudo-prostration). They act as *the emblazoned*, for whom the center is conflagration, for whom thought cradles its burn-victims (the mysticism of a living hell). These are the ones of *animation*, those who mix the once-connected, though no longer, whose associations tailor/combine different faculties of the charlatan. Thus they bring *the post-symbolic*, to disembowel eloquence, where representation is now obstructed, no longer admitted into the arc of the possible (with the vanishing of the original comes the celebration of the impostor).

XXX.

There are others here, *orders of stigma*, those of the once-slighted, of great caution (the unworn). They act as *the shunned*, those of anti-glory, where nothing triumphs (of what repulsion can one speak?). These are the ones of *intolerance*, unauthorized teachers of the foundation, who roam illegitimate academies, with bastard etymologies, critiques, and modes of interpretation, and for whom every year conveys a millenarian stroke. Thus they bring *the dregs*, those who realize the evil in cups, bowls, and further vessels, those who make others drink, of cheapened liquors, for taste is the only sense that condemns entirely.

XXXI.

There are others here, *orders of spite*, for whom all discourse reviles itself (within terminologies of discontent). They act as *the underhanded*, those of ultimate cowardice, for whom every turn emits the heartbeat of awful things (the eyes are telling here, taken by honest fright). These are the ones of *retaliation*, where to remind is to terrorize (backlash). Thus they bring *the vise*, flouting what is already at the cusp/the verge, for which all deserves tightening.

XXXII.

There are others here, *orders of aging*, those of compulsive dwelling, for whom color tells the tale of how long one has been there, how long one stays, and how long one has left (to read the complexion). They act as *the decomposed*, incurring mortification: where consciousness is mangled, and perishes soon after. These are the ones of *the undead*, excessive terminality, remnants of the overkill (no one abstains, from whatever infringement). Thus they bring *the throes*, where language becomes tantrum and miraculous.

XXXIII.

There are others here, *orders of evening*, for whom sundown marks the closure of all temporal gates (the settlement). They act as *the unlike*, those who become unrecognizable, before others and oneself. These are the ones of *the vigil*, who endure lateness, raising an improbable flag (the unbeaten text). These are the ones of *the vial*, those who store words/concepts in glass containers, watching the amount, heeding the myriad levels, remedies, and doses (the tonic). Thus they bring *the mist*, where thought fogs over, drops the curtain (toward grayness), where it steams, lingers, and drapes itself as the sadness of an expectant world (astray-through-illumination).

Chapter 7

Conclusion (Of Those Who Have Become Jagged): Reckonings of an Eastern Violence

LATENESS
Pained Forgetting (the unrecollected)

SHATTERING
Poetic Excess (suprahumanity)
Poetic Anger (universal fury)
Poetic Assemblage (cleaving)
Poetic Consumption (feeding)
Poetic Unworlding (evisceration)

DROWNING
The Outlander (derivation)
The Survivor (dirge)
The Barbarian (prediction)

WRECKAGE
Non-Mourning (sorrowlessness)
Trance (expression)
Seriality (estimation)

DAMNATION
Hereditary Malice (the interdiction)
Hyper-Suspicion (the exemption)
Deep Progeny (the sliver)

DYSPHORIA
Simulation of the Dissimulation (curiosity)
Dissimulation of the Simulation (the unmentioned)
Weariness (infectious malaise)

CONTAMINATION
The Fairy Tale (exodus)
The Superstition (willed foolishness)
The Folk Song (sonic dilapidation)
The Temple Dance (teasing)

COLDNESS
The Inverted Wine-Song (anti-boasting)
The Refugee (circumambulation)

DARKENING
The Lunatic-Atlas (fictional maps)

We end at the end of the world, yet with a fresh compulsion: to track the increasingly post-apocalyptic narratives of the Middle Eastern new wave. For one should see the collective culmination of such violent tendencies in practice, strewn across their most fatalistic encounters (and ask what is then forthcoming). These are the intersections of various dawnings, those that must nevertheless shift out of a catastrophic perception of the world (some of the poets here burn cities). It is in this regard that the Middle Eastern backdrop provides an entrance-point into a cosmological reckoning, an existential turn of grim, confrontational, and excessive proportions (some of the poets here flood cities). To theorize this disquiet and render a multidimensional overview, one that carries the writing-act to a critical outer boundary, this conclusion evaluates a vast array of the most prominent examples of such cosmological dismay. By navigating the intricate contours of these textual realms and their distinct conceptual frameworks—those of "damnation," "dysphoria," "shattering," "coldness," "drowning," "wreckage," "lateness," "contamination," and "darkening"—one comes to understand where all prior demarcations resolve themselves. Ultimately, these omens/portrayals coalesce toward a novel threshold of experience, one for which the East surfaces as a vital foreground in the revelation of a disastrous age (some of the poets here betray cities to endless winter).

It is from within their radical unrest, difference, and alienation that one witnesses a further complex gesture on the part of these poetic circles: namely, the attempt to envision a writing-act that extends farther than the confines of reigning historical, social, and political codes (into a post-apocalyptic beyond). Far from the rituals of everydayness, they generate the stage for a creative banishment, an irrelational vantage that situates the authorial figure in a permanent elsewhere; no doubt, this must increasingly become the dominant intellectual and artistic position of an Eastern postmodernism, one of disconnect, incommunicability, and even antihumanist undertones (so as to go beyond the real). Through its recurring experiments with estrangement and solitude, its simulations of cataclysm, depictions of rage, lyrics of malformation and transformation, anatomies of torment and delirium, we come to see how the Eastern moment in fact occasions a captivating will to destruction, transfiguration, and escape. In the final stride, these avant-garde movements (of those who have become jagged) allow a forceful redefinition of consciousness to transpire, turning our contemporary roads into tragic-ecstatic domains with obscure implications for yet another counter-future. Thus, one can only commence this process by contemplating the different techniques through which such voices attack the cities of the real (each has their preference), leaving a constellation of metropolitan sieges. Nine cities brought down.

Prelude: The Poetics of Foreshadowing

*I remember well the moonlit night that my father placed me on a bay mare and bade
me farewell with these words: 'You are going [to Tehran] to study, my son, but—do not
forget! You are a man of the highlands, and you must be strong!' By these words my
father meant that, as I grew up, I should remain attached to the hunt, the gun, and
the struggles of the countryside, and not be spoiled [by the city]. Having thus spoken,
he stood there amid the silhouettes of tall boulders surrounding the ridge, and faded in
the background as my horse took me over the passes.* —Nima Yushij[1]

Perhaps one should have listened to the poet's father, to his warnings of the
city crowds and their stained ways (to reject the banners). But it is too late for
this now; instead we are left with a fearsome legacy, as the words of our vision-
aries collect themselves by an undesirable doorway (such is the dwelling-place
of those who have surpassed even otherness).

We begin again in this rising zero-world, where cosmopolitan idealism falls
to cosmological rage, where intellectual plurality falls to schizoid conspirato-
riality, where knowing goes too far (becoming catastrophic), where enlightenment lasts too long (leaving a generation of insomniacs). There are no more
revolutions here, since the concept of rebellion has been transplanted by infliction; there are no more martyrs here, since the concept of sacrifice has been
transplanted by reckoning. These poetic constellations have long rehearsed
the death of Man (less a vendetta than a mercy-killing).

Within their slow-cutting verses, impossibility takes on a descriptive matrix:
a texture, tactility, color, temperature, rhythm, lightness, hardness. Thus one
can speak of a poetics of the mal-sutured (the riveted), a language of touch-
stones . . . and we see in their eyes that they were sent to delegate the cursed
image (the whirlpool, the dead-end, the three drops of blood) . . . a textual
bastion of recoil and scowling (impersonations of purgatory).

There is an escalation of melancholic blood: as estrangement outlasts itself,
turning into despair, and despair outlasts itself, turning into hate, and hate
outlasts itself, turning into vengeance, and vengeance outlasts itself, turning
toward the ripe obliteration of self and world.

Nevertheless, before these cityscapes are cast down, one after another, before
the poets compete in the demonstration of cosmological fires, one must first
understand a central lesson: that the old allegorical model between the historical and the poetic is an inverted falsehood. At this nexus, it is not that the historical event sets its precedent, enveloping the scene, and then the poetic voice
rushes forward in the subsequent moment to record, represent, or clarify what
has elapsed; rather, the most immense historical episodes (invasions, famines,
epidemics) are themselves but lighter signals of an oncoming poetic shift. The
hierarchy is therefore righted: that these street-conflagrations are themselves

allegorical tellings (microcosmic flares) of a more overarching textual-existential event. One does not read poetry in order to interpret genocide; one uses the genocide in order to interpret poetry, for the latter gesture (when it finds its target) is more far-reaching, complex, and dangerous than any byproduct of historical everydayness. Wherever the design of reality is split open or razed, one should look for a writer in the surrounding area, the one growing stronger and more eloquent along the perimeter, for this is the handiwork of an emergent consciousness (the one who speaks like no one else before). One must differentiate the species; one must recognize which comes first, and which extends farther in significance. Historical winds can only hearken to poetic storms.

City 1. The Poetics of Lateness

A deep silence fell upon the tower. The moon was slowly rising and its cold glimmer gradually outlined the inside of the sanctuary. The round enclosure was divided into cobbled rectangles, in each of which lay a corpse, already rotten or on the verge of decomposition. White shrouds covered the bones and stuck to the flesh. —Sadeq Hedayat[2]

Where does it lead, when a writer starts from beyond (and thus long overdue)?

This one assaults the city through lateness: he stacks time, in iron casings, in a terrible density through which thought itself is subdued (the stakes are suddenly so low). There is only negative embellishment; one cannot request anything (nothing helps), one cannot seek audience (there are no ministers), one cannot nest here (homeland has no meaning); one can only make donations to the wasteland, one can only find some corner in which to turn oneself into a relic (to join the stockpile), becoming merchandise for the undertaker. And so, there is one beginning premise at work here among the undying:

1. Pained Forgetting (the unrecollected)—This is a disconsolate temporality at work, behind which stands a writer who projects the cityscape into a long-postponed ditch, a decreasing limbo (even the middle-ground is unsteady, being sucked down) where lost souls somehow become even more lost causes, those who have been late-lamented (or not lamented at all). There is only a tower it seems (an anti-monument), the selected burial-place of Being itself, where the living have placed their fallen, honoring them once in order to forget them forever, bequeathing them to the loneliness and ever-looming silence of the mausoleum. This is our first vision of the city, a white non-spiritual cove where the undead roam, wonder, and converse about the absence of conversationalists, a warehouse of half-sentences and obsolete regrets. The architectural makeup of this space only enhances the time-frame, a post-ontological storage-facility where the now-disrespected are placed into rectangular compartments

and ringlets, lodged in an unofficial afterlife where Zoroastrian priests recite mandatory psalms over the bodies of those who have become weightless, slackened, and unclaimed. There is no urgency in this port (just sighing, swimming, philosophizing), this feudal estate of the insubstantial, as they council one another over the absence of a verdict, sneer at their celestial meagerness, and take aim at unresponsive divinities like snipers. They are the victims of the balance, facing the dried-out horror of the intermediate, left to the flocks of vultures and hyena packs that swarm around the tower (this is its own fellowship). Nor are these lateness-preying forms of animality the only threat (there are other rapacities), for even memory serves a dissident function beneath these rooftops, as recollections of former lives do nothing but exacerbate their anger against the impenetrable vault of heaven. And so, in this first city, Man becomes an effigy of self-dissolution, and hangs himself through the afterwards.

City 2. The Poetics of the Shattered

Turned blue in fury, a claw
shatters
within it
tornado's being turns to dust
twists in the grip of the
valleys
hatred tears the beads off the
string
it splits open
the dreadful sea-gazing castles
the swamp of steel rushes
the dagger of its eyes freezes the
throats of creeks
You and the white
you and the eternal tunnel. —Hushang Irani[3]

Where does it lead, when a poet splinters the realm of articulation (the profession that bids the broken misreading)?

This one assaults the city through shattering: where ideas grow ostentatious (the hyper-affair), forming a literary chandelier, something meticulous and heraldic that nevertheless moves toward overreaction, a whirling textuality where one incorrect word rolls into the next. This is a matter of futural innocence—where ever-adding complexity exonerates one from consciousness (he does not know what he is saying, since the saying is falling apart)—a site of experimental temper and speed, where images are taken to the almost-nonsensical brink, and communication turns guttural, beastly, sound-based, no longer the language of creation but of the creature. A runaway artistry, where meaning hurls itself against the rocks.

For this to work, for the city walls to crumble beneath the weight of claws, tornados, and steel swamps, the poetic identity itself must inhabit a certain five principles of monstrosity:

1. Poetic Excess (suprahumanity)—look to the horrific exaggeration of the human form here, the unnatural incarnation of the poet at an extreme fringe (gone too far), as an intensification of thought, evolution of body, and irradiation of spirit that then unsings the world (explosive transportation). In this way, it represents an incredible culmination (fatal heights), taken beyond its own given boundaries, forcing us to turn toward what is outside ourselves (insubordination).

2. Poetic Anger (universal fury)—look to the obvious depictions of wildness, the acidic tantrum, typically beginning from some singular violence (an original, specific violation—i.e., that something hideous happened somewhere) that then transforms, grows, and spreads into an indiscriminate violence (a death-wish for everyone). In this way, it universalizes its frustration over this first wrong and thereby spills its wrath across all it touches, forcing us to re-contemplate questions of fault and guilt, for we are reminded that *they* did not draw first blood, that *they* are not the atrocity, but are merely responding to and reciprocating the impediments of Man. After all, man betrayed the poets first, injected damage into their verses, and they simply terrorize in turn, through reciprocal fury, though as better practitioners of this vituperation, now turned against in an awful mirroring that is not clearly an act of justice or injustice.

3. Poetic Assemblage (cleaving)—look to the true secret of its invincibility, that it is not one being but rather an entire configuration, a collection of toxic elements, sutured together by different parts, molecular dimensions, cellular compartments, unknown legions, and therefore unstoppable and self-reproducing. It has no center because it is a knot of factional parties housed within one voice (disguised multitudes); there are always many identities being strummed, lending the poetic imagination an unbeatable versatility (the complex)—this is why Man, as a unified being, loses in every confrontation, fails every showdown, because he is outnumbered by an intricate constellation of enemies appearing to be one. Fragments cannot be terminated.

4. Poetic Consumption (feeding)—look to the ever-present mentioning of the throat, its own ravenous machinery of hunger, thirst, and desire, turning all into desperate characters of vampiric obsession; the poet becomes captivated and fascinated by its prey, gravitates to things and seeks exceptional closeness to its target—it wants pure proximity, to the extent that it internalizes/swallows the other. Through this gesture, though, it has a contagious effect on the viewer—its own overpowering will to devour our world makes it at once a figure of complete repulsion (we are disgusted by its obscenity,

its abomination, its aggression and grotesque outer shell) and at the same time complete seduction (we are mesmerized, awed, and enchanted by its arrival). One becomes attracted to the savagery at work here, attentive to language as an intestinal business (for we still hope to find our way into the labyrinth of the poet's stomach).

5. Poetic Unworlding (evisceration): look to the obscure threshold between being and non-being, presence and absence, appearance and disappearance, reality and unreality (the occupant); the fact that this poetic consciousness can negotiate so many realms simultaneously allows it to overcome the crisis over mortality, for death holds no currency for those who do not crave existence, those of dynamic annihilative potential, those of supreme intelligence who rule through self-evisceration. Are they not the next inescapable regime to come after our own human fable has collapsed?

City 3. The Poetics of Drowning

I am not of these debased city-dwellers
I am the pain-filled memory of the mountain provinces
Who from the misfortune of being within your city,
Has been left afflicted as time passed.[4]

> *someone is dying in the water,*
> *someone is continuously flailing*
> *on this angered, burdened, dark, familiar sea.*[5]

With my poetry I have driven the people into a great conflict; good and bad, they have fallen in confusion; I myself am sitting in a corner, watching them; I have flooded the nest of ants. —Nima Yushij[6]

Where does it lead, when a poet floods the homes of all but his own (clouded worlds)?

This one assaults the city through drowning: where the body is halved (liquid division), an equator drawn across (first the legs, then the midsection, then finally the neck, mouth, and eyes). The head is safe for a time, long enough to contemplate the incident, while everything below is plunged into chance (outspoken humiliation). To attain mastery over this technique, however, such that language itself evinces a perpetual drowning, the poet must coordinate three modes of consciousness in succession:

1. The Outlander (derivation)—the first action is to construct the image of some supposed antiquity (the dreamed advent), where one belongs to a hallucinogenic race, and then spins this idyllic delusion into panic. This is no typical nostalgia, but a tightly wound excuse for the poetic imagination

to then turn adversarial; atavism justifies everything here, as his adhesion to the far-off cradle of the provinces becomes a will to tirade against the cityscapes. The poet must now assume the status of a protector, saving the impressionable (the ones left behind) from what befell him (the one who was taken under), as his bitterness becomes the lone motivation. There is no likening with the others (beyond remedy), only the vertical blame of the outlander—the more he alludes to the old altitudes, the more his present suffering concerns itself, and thus the mountain falls into a lethal dialectic with the cement.

2. The Survivor (dirge)—the second action is to lament the experience of one's own drowning, to speak of the modern city as a cruel beach (the false mainland), an anti-home where the poet once sought inter-human salvation and was denied, left to choke upon the salt waters. This unfaithfulness is indisputable: he succumbed to the great pressure of the tides, extended a frantic hand towards the shore, and received nothing in turn (beyond rescue). And the total lack of response in turn, one of carelessness, avoidance, and non-assistance, is the genesis of a misanthropic imagination like no other (he wants repayment). More than even this, though, the poet now returns to the city as the survivor (for he was not fully undone), and sets his sights greedily upon the next site of risk (making his own requiem pertain to the rest); he has acquired an odd taste for such extraordinary occasions of sunkenness, and hence seeks other players for this zombifying game (insistence).[7]

3. The Barbarian (prediction)—the third action is to reflect upon the existential-aesthetic image of a city immersed, to envision the scope of a torrential rush against the capital: where the buildings are left covered, the squares overlain and streaming, the alleys and windows flooded through (the rush). Here the poetic instinct turns barbaric, the one of anti-civilizational campaigns, who predicts the fulfillment of his own epic grudge, victimizes through downpour (where all are eligible), and renders the people helpless before over-exposure.[8]

City 4. The Poetics of Wreckage

Rain will destroy the south of the city
Rain
      will destroy
            the south of the city . . .
And I, amazingly, am not sorrow-stricken.[9]

      At this moment
      I am expressive and explosive, like wrath
      and, like wrath, I am capable . . .[10]

The south of the city will be destroyed
and there's no reason to feel sad—
the tumbling of water will destroy the south
and the south's destruction
will destroy the north. —Esmail Khoi[11]

And where does it lead, when a poet builds the era only so as to watch it denigrated (rainfall)?

This one assaults the city through wreckage: he flirts with causation and sequence, subsuming things into a domino-logic, using language as over-enunciation, a kind of training, preparation, and repetitive inscription of a destiny (preemptive rustling). It is a developing charade, one spurred by pronouncement (the more it is said, the more it is sure to happen), so as to make the poetic ethos unequivocal, a statement torched across the city gates. To gain this convinced mortuary-tone, its calculations now immune to reanalysis, three axioms must be followed:

1. Non-Mourning (sorrowlessness)—where one stamps the declaration into an unfeeling chant, watching over the rubble, the tearing-asunder of locales, with cool expectation. The poetic imagination must extricate itself (uncoupling), soaring beyond the grief-afflicted and commending its own neutrality.

2. Trance (expression)—where discourse seeks chilling objectivity, the eloquence of a force, convening an impersonal moment that still says "I" but means something closer to "it" or "someone," showing kinship with the explosion of a capable mood, a post-psychic transference into the deed, the phenomenon, and the result.

3. Seriality (estimation)—where thought forms a repercussive string, manipulating the geometry of effect, importing and exporting bad intentions, and leaving the targets interchangeable . . . such that when one sector deteriorates, the others are ground into a similar fine powder. The poetic imagination sends its stress to one side, with the knowledge that its shock-wave will reach all directions (north-becoming-south, east-becoming-west), caught in a flawless band of instigations and debris.

City 5. The Poetics of Damnation

I damn you, on my descendants and on my father.[12]

I have tired of an agony not of my own
I have resided upon an earth not of my own[13]

In the city with no street, they thrive
In the decomposed web of alleys and dead-ends
Coated in furnace smoke and smuggling and the yellow-scarred
A colored frame in the pocket and a bow and arrow in the hand
The children of the depths
The children of the depths. —Ahmad Shamlu[14]

Where does it lead, when a poet foregoes the last trace of mercy (pure rancor)?

This one assaults the city through damnation: he forms an aesthetic fist and uses lineage as a weapon, where certain genealogies entitle (the anointed), breeding acolytes, and other genealogies eject (the scattered), breeding apostates, and still others strain the calendar so as to breed a new elitism (the magnetic). These hordes are born across three installations:

1. Hereditary Malice (the interdiction)—the poetic imagination must summon both its ancestors and its offspring to discredit the present, differentiating its own roots so as to stimulate the feud (the specialization of one side leads to a slick uniformity of caskets for the other side). The relatives prevail, at the expense of everyone else, eliciting a confidential dynasty and tradition of reproach.
2. Hyper-Suspicion (the exemption)—the poetic imagination must undertake a paranoiac shedding, for it is valorized by going without (so that there is no serenity). This is a crucial intermission, where the most grandiose and intimate segments are disavowed (the loss of anchors)—one's misery and rapture, life and afterlife, are brought into refusal (namelessness). None of it can belong anymore.
3. Deep Progeny (the sliver)—the poetic imagination must praise its latest children, unleashing the emergent ones through rhapsody (they form their own citadel). Once prisoners, though now crawling upward, they are specialized in accusation, talented interlocutors of the defamed, and use their gifts to will the schematic and the circumstance of counter-waste. There are other pieces in which weeping fairies are wrested forward to behold a city of chains, wolves, and snakes, only then to confirm the same literary inevitability: that the lullaby will succeed the canon. And this leaves the sliver, a thriving sixth zone that replaces the uncared-for future: to have found a part beyond the last rows, beyond our chartered extremity . . . that there is still more room, extending the limit of prospects, an aisle of potential thought which he dispenses only to his connections. He has synthesized a thin extra compartment, two steps after Being, that will make all else inferior.

City 6. The Poetics of Dysphoria

A rain-soaked owl screams out in the street
Beneath a tall wall a man's life wears away
Who knows what is happening within the dark heart of the night?
The foot of the night-slaves is caught within the chains of sadness

> *I am imprisoned by the shadows of the night*
> *The night is imprisoned by the cold net of the sky*
> *I must walk step by step with the shadows*
> *Every night is a dark and maddened city.* —Abbas Saffari [15]

And where does it lead, when a poet dims all light (many night-prisons)?

This one assaults the city through dysphoria: where shadows spare no one (simplified desolation), and where, though there are continual showers, everything remains dehydrated. This is a stratospheric conspiracy (aesthetic set-ups), to coercively extract the other's outcry, a manipulative sadness and narrative of aversion, where the goal is nervousness, resentment, and weeping (to make harrowing). Thus the poetic imagination must accentuate the following three modules:

1. Simulation of the Dissimulation (curiosity)—to pretend what one hides, diverting attention from the withheld trait by secreting a falsified version, shielding it behind a second story and title, though here with the precise intent of heightening the travesty (the next fake is more touching, and causes greater distress). Or, in other cases, to pretend *that* one is hiding, raising interest that leads to inquisitive, prying questions, sowing agitation, jealousy, and burden in the other by referencing some novelty (premature evidence).
2. Dissimulation of the Simulation (the unmentioned)—to hide what one pretends, blanketing the lie and covering over those external traces that might publicize the fraud, whether attained through reticence (saying nothing), glossing parables (weaving new myths into the property), or the excommunication of the insiders (eliminating all who have participated and could spill the contents of its fictive origin). Or, in other cases, to hide *that* one is pretending, using duplicity (vague information) in order to create the polysemous city, a place of camouflage, veiling, ignorance, murkiness, and self-censoring.
3. Weariness (infectious malaise)—to make the city-dweller give in to idleness, negligence, and absolute relaxation, so flung between substandard correlations that the will to knowing grows increasingly miniscule, leaving a depressive slope and fatigue-akin-to-madness. There are only the downtrodden, as one becomes nothing more than the tired insanity around them.

City 7. The Poetics of Contamination

After you, we betrayed one another.
We erased with lead pellets,
With exploded drops of blood,
the mementos written on plastered walls.[16]

> *When my faith was hanging*
> *by the weak thread of justice*
> *and in the whole city*
> *the hearts of my lamps were*
> *being torn to pieces,*
> *when the childlike eyes of my love*
> *were being blindfolded by law's black kerchief,*
> *and fountains of blood were gushing forth*
> *from the distressed temples of my desire,*
> *when my life was no longer anything,*
> *nothing but the tick tock of a wall clock,*
> *I discovered that I must,*
> *that I absolutely had to*
> *love madly.* —Forugh Farrokhzad[17]

Where does it lead, when a poet invents a sensual betrayal (to disrobe the clientele)?

This one assaults the city through contamination: where the industrial stronghold becomes the anthropomorphic enemy of the garden (lushness vs. hegemony), such that the inhabitants themselves are no longer important (for the walls are graphic). The cityscape is at once the concealed bedroom and the nemesis of her night-partners, turning affections traitorous and thereby justifying her erotic revenge (upon the marble); it facilitates and then interrupts the forbidden encounter. And so, she will upset the law (pyrotechnics vs. prohibition): she guides the city into aromatic disgrace, scandalizes its parks and litters its alleys with sin, nakedness, lust, vice (within the loins) . . . the body becomes phosphoric, a hidden cove of flings, enticements, stunts, and subterfuge (where all are patronized). There are at least four modes within which this poetic imagination circulates:

1. The Fairy Tale (exodus)—to use good to lure evil (sending the little ones away), where innocence is baited, escorted into precarious woods, and marred by unseen three-headed beings (the storyteller's commingling formula of departure, enthralling, and deathliness). A genre of mutual captors.

2. The Superstition (willed foolishness)—to use evil to lure good (tricking the mind into low comfort), where the more youthful, seemingly playful sister of destiny is called forth (the counting of beads), with the calming appearance of triviality and harmlessness (the recitation of silly rhyme-schemes), though exacting a grand gesture of its own: to systematize irrationality.

3. The Folk Song (sonic dilapidation)—to use good to lure good (forcing communion through resonance), where the citizens are brought together by musicality, chimes, stringed instruments, and acoustic familiarity, only to find that this domestic tune ultimately leaves all homeless (it unifies temporarily, all the while scratching at the foundation of the organic, until the old courtyards become uninhabitable).

4. The Temple Dance (teasing)—to use evil to lure evil (across indulgent cliffs), combining the scarlet influence of movement, gazing, and complexion in order to stigmatize the city, one illicit physiognomic slum enough to spoil everything, as the spectacle of impurity gathers the impure (obsessive percolation).

City 8. The Poetics of Coldness

And fortune's lantern, dead or alive,
is hidden not within the anguish of death
yet within the thick tomb of darkness
Comrades, go and bring the wine,
for night and day are one.

> *The weather is heart-wrenching,*
> *the doors closed, heads buried in their collars,*
> *hands hidden, breath cloud-like,*
> > *hearts tired and tormented,*
> *the trees like crystallized skeletons,*
> *the earth low-spirited, the sky's roof low,*
> > *the sun and moon enveloped in haze.* —Mehdi Akhavan-Saless[18]

Where does it lead, when the poet turns everything frigid (the seasonal coffin)?

This one assaults the city through coldness: where there is no vindication of the worst winter morning, and where all language turns to feigned lyricism—here the writer embodies the second coming of the ancient mystic, the medieval romantic, the classical artisan, though now trapped in the wrong age, transposed onto an untimely front where his humors are crippled, face-to-face with an inconsiderate epoch, where his disposition is unmatched and found eccentric. He seeks the prior moment of bottles, taverns, wine-bearers, and the vintage; he seeks the loudness of the hedonic quadrants, but finds nothing left to toast but the arctic end of time (without celebration). And so, there are two thematic pillars behind this once-gallant image:

1. The Inverted Wine-Song (anti-boasting)—to be met with failing intoxication, donating one's spirit to a regretful era, attempting the informal slang of past rituals but finding oneself slapped back (without hospitality), where there are no dealers, no fountains, and virility is undercut, where what was once privileged becomes unhealthy (the empty bowl).
2. The Refugee (circumambulation)—to go scouring (beating upon closed doors), chasing the lost animus (without cynicism), but finding only rifle-shot, ammunition, cheated friendship (among the smothered), for there is no harbor within this period of dismissal, no stations, shopkeepers, or warm neighborhoods. Here one can do no better than to become the vagrant (forever requesting), the one of groping hands, for there is not even one shack left into which one can make retreat (the city houses nothing).

City 9. The Poetics of Darkening

I have been to the darkened city . . .

> *. . . where the madmen howl unbroken*
> *and night-born desires tear at the purity of a vacant sky*
> *. . . incensed by lies of the massacre . . .*
> *and where even the air hurts . . .*

I have been to the darkened city . . .

> *. . . where a mercenary haze envelops each misfortuned arrival*
> *and vision descends into formless impressions*
> *. . . entangled in an arsenal of jagged façades . . .*
> *and where all fires endure the same sentence of hellish vanishing . . .*

I have been to the darkened city . . .

> *. . . where trembling alone is possible*
> *and arrested hungers lance the frame*
> *. . . impaled across sharpened staves of desecration . . .*
> *and where bodies writhe to be held . . .*

I have been to the darkened city . . .

> *. . . where the nothing draws its passage across legions of the soul-slain*
> *and the nowhere calls upon each visitor by name*

. . . kneeling before a cycle of terminal plagues . . .
and where strands of thoughts, once untamed, now turn towards desolation . . .

I have been to the darkened city . . .

. . . where careening winds engulf each sound in an execution
and coarse chains reveal the crimes of shattered men
. . . a stranger's exodus into annihilation . . .
and where the shadows of forgotten streets go to mouth their last rites . . .

I have been to the darkened city . . .

. . . where the condemned cling to stones in an extravagance of destitution
and afflictions wrack dim-lit assurances of rising again
. . . ever unentitled to healing . . .
and where all who enter must pay for the violence of wanting . . .

I have been to the darkened city . . .

. . . where death-moans pierce the quiet
and blood is law
. . . carving dishonor into an aristocracy of wounds . . .
and where chaos walks as a blind man, barely able to stand . . .

I have been to the darkened city . . .

. . . where machines of desertion reign cold
and rogues march unshamed before an interrogation of scythes
. . . intensities caught fast within the prism of a defenseless pain . . .
and where scar-streaked convictions come to forge a world of thorn and dust . . .

I have been to the darkened city . . .

. . . where soldiers turn to supplicants before barren altars
and innocence alone is found guilty
. . . incisions of despair engraved upon the shoulders of a lone survivor. . .
and where iron screams clasp themselves to silence . . .

I have been to the darkened city . . .

. . . where, beyond the rows of arid currents, there is no more
and downcast searches close in a steel-lattice of slashed throats
. . . all rights suspended in the mania of deprivation . . .
and where passions twice-disgraced now lash themselves in agony against the ground . . .

I have been to the darkened city . . .

. . . where once ungoverned infusions subside towards grieving,
where divinities starve and breathing yields to profane rhythms,
and the black rains pound,
and the hours recede . . . and fade . . . and burn

Epilogue: The Lunatic-Atlas (Fictional Maps)

How does one proceed once the many cities of the real have fallen, whether by lateness, shattering, drowning, wreckage, damnation, dysphoria, contamination, coldness, or darkening? Space itself remains (the flags are not irreplaceable), and new opportunistic iterations invite the Eastern poets forward as they entertain browsing thoughts of dislocation and relocation: one says that his "house is a cloud,"[19] another speaks of a "vacuum with neither God nor fire,"[20] another projects herself across a "deserted stairway" and a "sky concealed from me by the hanging of a curtain,"[21] while still others point to a "vector of light and pride."[22] There are no well-wishers here anymore, since there are no easy or straightforward trips (a thousand obstacles) . . . and yet still in search of another beginning.

Hence, the creative eye lunges outward to supplant the old topologies with omitted, lost, and undiscovered sites, this time resulting in a fantasy-cartography, a lunatic atlas of missing lands. One hires peculiar types to chart the stars (astronomic henchmen), whose insight lies somewhere beyond divination, exploration, and ambition, who can flush out the misplaced scrolls and document the next steps with improper materials (odd substitutes for inkwells and parchments). This is how poetic genius becomes a nautical discipline, finding the sea-routes to: mobile and disappearing realms, ruinous states buried beneath the new cities (catacombs), forsaken paradises from which there is no return (the errant, the detained), rumored spheres where no one has ever been (the unfound) and those no one has seen but the teller (the once-visited). This is how the authors of cosmological reckoning begin and end their compendium of violence, one that is also an encyclopedia of the inexistent.

And so, it is in this respect that we come to fathom the East as no less than the imposition of a post-apocalyptic mood.

Notes

Preface

[1] Maurice Blanchot, *The Writing of the Disaster*, trans. A. Smock (Lincoln: University of Nebraska Press, 1980), 1.

[2] Ahmad Shamlu, "A Separation," trans. J. Mohaghegh from *Majmu'eh-ye Asar-e Ahmad Shamlu* (*The Collected Works of Ahmad Shamlu*) (Tehran: Zamaneh Press, 1381/2002), 814. [Hereafter *MAAS*.]

[3] William Burroughs, *Burroughs Live: The Collected Interview of William S. Burroughs, 1960–1997* (New York: Semiotext(e), 2000), 736.

[4] Mahmoud Darwish, "Winds Shift Against Us," in *Unfortunately, It Was Paradise*, trans. M. Akash, C. Forche, S. Antoon, and A. El-Zein (Berkeley: University of California Press, 2003), 18.

[5] Walter Benjamin, "Critique of Violence," in *Reflections*, trans. E. Jephcott (New York: Schocken, 1986), 249–51.

[6] Adonis, "This Is My Name," in *A Time between Ashes and Roses*, trans. S. Toorawa (Syracuse: Syracuse University Press, 2004), 45.

[7] Edmond Jabes, *The Book of Questions*, trans. R. Waldrop (Middletown: Wesleyan University Press, 1983), 61.

[8] Taha Muhammad Ali, "Thrombosis in the Veins of Petroleum," in *So What*, trans. P. Cole, Y. Hijazi, and G. Levin (Port Townsend: Copper Canyon Press, 2006), 13–15.

[9] Fernando Pessoa, *The Book of Disquiet*, trans. R. Zenith (New York: Penguin Classics, 2002), 62–3.

[10] Khosrow Golesorkhi, "Morning," trans. J. Mohaghegh from *Ay Sarzamin-e Man* (*O My Homeland*) (Tehran: Entesharat-e Negah, 1373/1995), 7.

[11] Jorge Luis Borges, "Happiness," in *Selected Poems*, trans. A. Coleman (New York: Penguin Books, 2000), 441.

[12] Ghada Samman, *Beirut Nightmares*, trans. N. Roberts (London: Quartet Books, 1976), 2.

[13] Paul Virilio, *Pure War*, trans. M. Polizzotti (New York: Semiotext(e), 2008), 175.

[14] Namik Kuyumcu, "Dreams of Beavers and a Black Knife," trans. J. E. Carpenter and S. Karantay in *Contemporary Turkish Poetry: A Selection* (Istanbul: Bogazici University Press, 2006), 218.

[15] E. M. Cioran, "On Mission," in *A Short History of Decay*, trans. R. Howard (New York: Arcade, 1998).

[16] Nazim Hikmet, "Since I've Been In Jail," in *Poems of Nazim Hikmet*, trans. R. Blasing and M. Konuk (New York: Persea, 2002).

[17] Georges Bataille, *The Unfinished System of Nonknowledge*, trans. M. Kendall and S. Kendall (Minneapolis: University of Minnesota Press, 2001), 232.

[18] Sadeq Hedayat, *The Blind Owl*, trans. D. P. Costello (New York: Grove, 1957), 105.

[19] Friedrich Nietzsche, "On War and Warriors," in *Thus Spoke Zarathustra* in *The Portable Nietzsche*, trans. W. Kaufmann (New York: Penguin Books, 1977), 159.

[20] Joyce Mansour, *Screams*, trans. S. Gavronsky (Sausalito: The Post-Apollo Press, 1995), 43.

[21] Gilles Deleuze and Felix Guattari, *A Thousand Plateaus*, trans. B. Massumi (Minneapolis: University of Minnesota Press, 1987), 400.

[22] Suleyman Cobanoglu, "The Game of Jereed," trans. M. Kenne and S. Paker in *Contemporary Turkish Poetry: A Selection*, 246.

[23] Comte de Lautreamont, *Maldoror and Poems*, trans. P. Knight (London: Penguin Books, 1978), 31.

[24] Kucuk Iskender, "West Side Story," trans. S. Karantay in *Contemporary Turkish Poetry*, 236.

[25] Gaston Bachelard, "Cosmos of Iron," in *The Right to Dream*, trans. J. A. Underwood (Dallas: Dallas Institute of Humanities and Culture, 1989), 39.

[26] Manouchehr Neyestani, "Factory," in *An Anthology of Modern Persian Poetry*, trans. A. Karimi-Hakkak (Boulder: Westview Press, 1978), 162.

[27] Arthur Rimbaud, *Rimbaud Complete*, trans. W. Mason (Modern Library: New York, 2003), 195.

[28] 'Abd al-Wahhab al-Bayyati, "The Birth of Aisha and Her Death," trans. S. Boulus and C. Middleton in *Modern Arabic Poetry* (New York: Columbia University Press, 1987), 173–4.

[29] Michel Serres, *Genesis*, trans. G. James and J. Nielson (Ann Arbor: University of Michigan Press, 1995), 54.

[30] Samih al-Qasim, "Slit Lips," in *Victims of a Map*, trans. A. al-Udhari (London: Saqi, 1984), 53.

[31] Gerard de Nerval, *Selected Writings*, trans. R. Sieburth (New York: Penguin Books, 1999), 40.

[32] Nosrat Rahmani, "Friday Afternoon in the Fall," in *An Anthology of Modern Persian Poetry*, 78.

[33] Jean-Francois Lyotard, *The Inhuman: Reflections on Time*, trans. G. Bennington and R. Bowlby (Stanford: Stanford University Press, 1988), 182.

[34] Forugh Farrokhzad, "The Wind Will Take Us," in *An Anthology of Modern Persian Poetry*, 141.

[35] Michel Foucault, "A Preface to Transgression," in *Language, Counter-Memory, Practice*, trans. D. Bouchard (Ithaca: Cornell University Press, 1977), 34.

[36] Mahmoud al-Buraikan, "Man of the Stone City," trans. L. Jayyusi and N. S. Nye in *Modern Arabic Poetry*, 191.

[37] Franz Kafka, *The Blue Octavo Notebooks*, trans. E. Kaiser and E. Wilkins (Cambridge: Exact Change, 1991), 13.

[38] Mehdi Akhavan-Saless, "The Return of the Ravens," in *An Anthology of Modern Persian Poetry*, 93.

[39] Jean Baudrillard, *The Transparency of Evil: Essays on Extreme Phenomena*, trans. J. Benedict (London: Verso, 1990), 106.

40 Fu'ad Rifqa, "Mirrors," trans. S. Boulus and S. Hazo in *Modern Arabic Poetry*, 388.
41 Antonin Artaud, *Selected Writings*, trans. H. Weaver (Los Angeles: University of California Press, 1988), 85.
42 Manouchehr Sheibani, "Candle Mass," in *An Anthology of Modern Persian Poetry*, 44.
43 Octavio Paz, "Introduction," in *Miserable Miracle,* trans. L. Varese and A. Moschovakis (New York: New York Review Books, 2002), ix.
44 Nima Yushij, "Sorrowful by Night," trans. P. Losensky in *Essays on Nima Yushij: Animating Modernism in Iranian Poetry*, ed. A. Karimi-Hakkak (Brill Academic Publishers, 2004), 150.
45 Alphonso Lingis, *Dangerous Emotions* (Berkeley: University of California Press, 2000), 134.
46 Sargon Boulus, "Siege," trans. S. Boulus and A. Elliot in *Modern Arabic Poetry*, 187.
47 Unica Zurn, *The Man of Jasmine*, trans. M. Green (London: Atlas Press, 1977), 33.
48 Orhan Pamuk, *My Name is Red*, trans. E. Goknar (New York: Everyman's Library, 2010), 310.
49 Blaise Cendrars, *Moravagine*, trans. P. La Farge (New York: New York Review Books, 2004), 41.
50 Réda Bensmaia, *The Year of Passages*, trans. T. Conley (Minneapolis: University of Minnesota Press, 1995), 59.
51 Julia Kristeva, *Powers of Horror*, trans. L. Roudiez (New York: Columbia University Press, 1982), 1.
52 Reza Negarestani, *Cyclonopedia* (Melbourne: re.press, 2008), 182.
53 Henri Michaux, *Darkness Moves*, trans. D. Ball (Berkeley: University of California Press, 1997), 175–7.
54 Nader Naderpour, "Blood and Ashes," in *False Dawn*, trans. M. Hillmann (Austin: University of Texas, Austin, 1986).
55 Samuel Beckett, *Stories and Texts for Nothing* (New York: Grove Press, 1967), 139.
56 Bedouin Proverb.

Chapter 0

1 Ahmad Shamlu, "The Pitch Black of Sightlessness," trans. J. Mohaghegh and A. Lawandow from *MAAS*, 967.
2 Ahmad Shamlu, "At the Threshold," trans. J. Mohaghegh and A. Lawandow from *MAAS*, 971.
3 Ahmad Shamlu, "Self-Entanglement. . . ," trans. J. Mohaghegh and A. Lawandow from *MAAS*, 969.
4 Shamlu, "At the Threshold," 972.
5 Sadeq Hedayat, "Three Drops of Blood," in *Three Drops of Blood*, trans. D. Miller Mostaghel (Surrey: One World Classics, 2008), 9.
6 Ibid., 11.
7 Ibid., 9–10.

8 Ibid., 10.
9 Ibid., 11.
10 Ibid., 9.
11 Ibid.
12 Ibid., 10.
13 Ibid.
14 Sadeq Hedayat, "Dead End," trans. P. Meade in *Sadeq Hedayat: An Anthology*, ed. E. Yarshater (Boulder: Westview Press, 1979), 104.
15 Ibid., 112.
16 Ibid., 113.
17 Ibid., 117.
18 Hedayat, "The Whirlpool," trans. B. Spooner in *Sadeq Hedayat*, 67.
19 Ibid., 74.
20 Hedayat, "The Mirage or the Shadow Incarnate," trans. S. Danesh in *Sadeq Hedayat*, 166.
21 Hedayat, "The Doll Behind the Curtain," trans. A. Karimi-Hakkak in *Sadeq Hedayat*, 136.
22 Hedayat, "Fire-Worshipper," in *Three Drops of Blood*, 43.
23 Hedayat, "Dash Akol," trans. R. Arndt and M. Ekhtiar in *Sadeq Hedayat*, 47.
24 Hedayat, "The Benedictions," trans. G. Kapuscinski and M. Hambly in *Sadeq Hedayat*, 79.
25 Hedayat, "The Stray Dog," in *Three Drops of Blood*, 58.
26 Ibid., 60.
27 Hedayat, "The Broken Mirror," in *Three Drops of Blood*, 61.
28 Hedayat, "Laleh," trans. B. Spooner in *Sadeq Hedayat*, 182.
29 Ibid., 183.
30 Hedayat, "Davud the Hunchback," trans. H. S. G. Darke in *Sadeq Hedayat*, 176.

Chapter 1

1 Shamlu, "Resurrection," trans. J. Mohaghegh from *MAAS*, 836.
2 Adonis, "Psalm," in *Selected Poems*, trans. K. Mattawa (New Haven: Yale University Press, 2010), 23.
3 Ibid.
4 Ibid.
5 Mahmoud Darwish, *Memories for Forgetfulness*, trans. I. Muhawi (Berkeley: University of California Press, 1995), 4.
6 Adonis, "This Is My Name," in *A Time between Ashes and Roses*, 93.
7 Nima Yushij, "The Corpses of Death," trans. J. Mohaghegh from *Majmu'eh-ye Kamel-e Asha'ar-e Nima Yushij* (*The Complete Collected Poetry of Nima Yushij*) (Tehran: Mo'asaseh Entesharat Negah, 1996), 335. [Hereafter *MKANY*.]
8 al-Qasim, "Bats," in *Victims of a Map*, 61.
9 Darwish, "When the Martyrs Go to Sleep," in *Unfortunately, It Was Paradise*, 22.
10 Sun'allah Ibrahim, *The Committee*, trans. C. Constable and M. S. Germain (Syracuse: Syracuse University Press, 2001), 28.

11 Esmail Khoi, "A Rendezvous between Life and Hazard," in *Edges of Poetry*, trans. A. Karimi-Hakkak (Blue Logos Press, 1995), 76.

12 Negarestani, *Cyclonopedia*, 90.

13 Mahmoud Darwish, "Dense Fog Over the Bridge," in *If I were Another*, trans. F. Joudah (New York: Farrar, Straus and Giroux, 2009), 160.

14 Hushang Golshiri, *The Prince*, trans. J. Buchan (London: Vintage: 2006), 153.

15 Mahmoud al-Buraikan, "Tale of the Assyrian Statue," trans. L. Jayyusi and N. S. Nye in *Modern Arabic Poetry*, 188.

16 Mansour, *Screams*, 13.

17 Farrokhzad, "The Wall," in *Sin*, 12.

18 al-Buraikan, "Tale of the Assyrian Statue," 190.

19 Adonis, "Singular in a Plural Form," in *Selected Poems*, trans. K. Mattawa, 158.

Chapter 2

1 Samman, *Beirut Nightmares*, 153.

2 Metin Celal, "135 Wake-Up Service," trans. S. Karantay in *Contemporary Turkish Poetry*, 216.

3 Darwish, "The Night There," in *Unfortunately, It Was Paradise*, 23.

4 Bensmaia, *The Year of Passages*, 106.7.

5 Darwish, *Memories for Forgetfulness*, 128.

6 Hedayat, *The Blind Owl*, 2.

7 Moussa Wuld Ibno, "City of Winds," in *Modern Arabic Fiction*, ed. S. Jayyusi (New York: Columbia University Press, 2008), 922.

8 Kamal Sabti, "Poems from Jungles," trans. L. Jayyusi and N. S. Nye in *Modern Arabic Poetry*, 393–5.

9 Adonis, "This Is My Name," in *A Time between Ashes and Roses*, 113.

10 Hedayat, *The Blind Owl*, 44.

11 Yushij, "*The Ship*," trans. J. Mohaghegh from *MKANY*, 499.

12 Naguib Mahfouz, *The Dreams*, trans. R. Stock (Cairo: The American University of Cairo Press, 2000–3), 4.

13 Farrokhzad, "The Return," in *Sin*, 18.

14 Negarestani, *Cyclonopedia*, 108.

15 Adonis, "The Crow's Feather," in *The Pages of Day and Night*, trans. S. Hazo (Marlboro Press, 2000), 31.

16 Bensmaia, *The Year of Passages*, 100.1.

17 Yushij, "Hey People," trans. J. Mohaghegh from *MKANY*, 301.

18 Antonin Artaud, *Selected Writings*, trans. H. Weaver (Los Angeles: University of California Press, 1988). There is some connection between this idea of the unbearable and the treatment of pain in Artaud's work, whereby he writes: "We whom pain has sent traveling through our souls in search of a calm place to cling to, seeking stability in evil as others seek stability in good. We are not mad, we are wonderful doctors, we know the dosage of the soul, of sensibility, or marrow, of thought. You must leave us alone, you must leave the sick alone, we ask nothing of mankind, we ask only for the relief of our suffering" (102).

Nevertheless, the Middle Eastern version does not seek some eventual release as its goal; if anything, health is related here to gushing.

19 Shamlu, "May My Prison Be No Enclosure," trans. J. Mohaghegh from *MAAS*, 691.

20 Shamlu, "Nocturne 2," trans. J. Mohaghegh from *MAAS*, 185.

21 Shamlu, "A Scream," trans. J. Mohaghegh from *MAAS*, 358.

22 Samman, *Beirut Nightmares*, 152.

23 Adonis, "This Is My Name," in *A Time between Ashes and Roses*, 57.

24 Shamlu, "Poverty," trans. J. Mohaghegh from *MAAS*, 347.

25 Shamlu, "The Path After the Bridge," trans. J. Mohaghegh from *MAAS*, 501.

26 Khoi, "Tavern Poem 3," in *Edges of Poetry*, 72.

27 Darwish, "They Would Love to See Me Dead" in *Unfortunately, It Was Paradise*, 21.

28 Mansour, *Screams*, 42.

29 Mahmoud Darwish, "Going to the World" in *Journal of an Ordinary Grief*, trans. I. Muhawi (Brooklyn: Archipelago Books, 2010), 133–4.

Chapter 3

1 Sargon Boulus, "The Knife Sharpener," trans. A. Lawandow from *Ḥāmil al-Fānūs Fi Layl al-Dhi̇āb: Qaṣā'id* [*The Lantern Carrier in the Night of Wolves: Poems*] (Köln: Kamel Verlag, 1996), 17–21.

2 Negarestani, *Cyclonopedia*, 189.

3 Boulus, "The Knife Sharpener."

4 Ibid.

5 Maurice Blanchot, *The Space of Literature*, trans. A. Smock (Lincoln: University of Nebraska Press, 1982). There is some connection between this idea of the ritual and the treatment of the someone in Blanchot's work, whereby he writes: "When I am alone, I am not alone, but, in this present, I am already returning to myself in the form of Someone. Someone is there, where I am alone. The fact of being alone is my belonging to this dead time which is not my time, or yours, or the time we share in common, but Someone's time. Someone is what is still present when there is no one" (31). Nevertheless, the Middle Eastern version does not seek this possibility only in states of extreme solitude; if anything, one must prove capable of summoning this "someone" forward when most surrounded and encircled by others (so that it moves against them).

6 Boulus, "The Knife Sharpener."

7 Farrokhzad, "Border Walls," in *Sin*, 43.

8 Boulus, "The Knife Sharpener."

9 Ibid.

10 Henri Michaux, *Darkness Moves*, trans. D. Ball (Berkeley: University of California Press, 1997). There is some connection between this idea of disappearance and the treatment of washing in Michaux's work, whereby he writes: "All they wanted to do was to pull him by the hair. They had no desire to hurt him. All at once they ripped his head off. Surely it wasn't on tight. It never comes off just like

that. Surely it was missing something. When it's not on shoulders any more, it's in the way. You have to give it away. But you have to wash it, because it smears the hand of whoever gets it. They had to wash it. Because the one they gave it to, with his hands already covered with blood, is beginning to get suspicious, is beginning to look at them like someone who's waiting for an explanation" (70). Nevertheless, the Middle Eastern version does not speak of it as a sanitizing gesture used to rinse clean all evidence of the violent imagination; if anything disappearance brings further attention to the atrocity.

11 Boulus, "The Knife Sharpener."

12 Ibid.

13 Bensmaia, *The Year of Passages*, 52.2.

14 Yusuf Idris, quoted in "Farhat's Republic," quoted in "Yusuf Idris and the Drama of Ideas" by Faruq 'Abd al-Wahhab in *Critical Perspectives on Yusuf Idris* (Colorado Springs: Three Continents Press, 1994), 156.

15 Boulus, "The Knife Sharpener."

16 Samih al-Qasim, "The Tragedy of Houdini the Miraculous," in *Sadder Than Water*, trans. G. Levin and N. Kassis (Jerusalem: Ibis Editions, 2006), 85.

17 Ibid., 89.

18 Yushij, quoted in "Nima Yushij: A Life" by A. Karimi-Hakkak in *Essays on Nima Yushij*, 17.

19 Adonis, "An Introduction to the History of the Petty Kings," in *A Time between Ashes and Roses*, 57.

20 Boulus, "The Knife Sharpener."

Chapter 4

1 Gerard de Nerval, *Selected Writings*, trans. R. Sieburth (New York: Penguin Books, 1999). There is some connection between this idea of midnight and the treatment of dreaming in de Nerval's work, whereby he writes: "Dream is a second life. I have never been able to cross through those gates of ivory or horn which separates us from the invisible world without a sense of dread. The first few instants of sleep are the image of death; a drowsy numbness steals over our thoughts . . . Little by little, the dim cavern is suffused with light, and, emerging from its shadowy depths, the pale figures who dwell in limbo come into view, solemn and still" (265). Nevertheless, the Middle Eastern version does not uphold this transcendent separation of the invisible and the real; if anything, the sleepers must become absolute insomniacs, dreaming with eyes open, beyond even sleepwalkers, resembling the very figures of limbo that used to dwell only in the resting mind.

2 Bensmaia, *The Year of Passages*, 62.3.

3 Mahmoud Darwish, *State of Siege*, trans. M. Akash and D. A. Moore (Syracuse: Syracuse University Press, 2010), 137.

4 Farrokhzad, "Later," in *Sin*, 16.

5 Shamlu, "Of Your Uncles," trans. J. Mohaghegh from *MAAS*, 233.

⁶ Yusuf Idris, quoted in "Questions of the World of Yusuf Idris' Short Stories" by M. Mikhail in *Critical Perspectives on Yusuf Idris*, ed. R. M. A. Allen (Colorado Springs: Three Continents Press, 1994), 51.

⁷ Leonardo Alishan, "The Black City," in *Flash Fiction Forward*, ed. J. Thomas and R. Shapard (New York: W.W. Norton & Co., 2006), 121.

⁸ Yushij, "Woe and Wellaway," in *An Anthology of Modern Persian Poetry*, 37.

⁹ Farrokhzad, "I'll Be Greeting the Sun Again," in *An Anthology of Modern Persian Poetry*, 148.

¹⁰ Bensmaia, *The Year of Passages*, 126.7.

¹¹ Yadollah Royai, "Seascape 30," in *Modern Iranian Poetry*, trans. Saeed Saeedpoor (San Jose: Authors Choice Press, 2001), 97.

¹² Yadollah Royai, "Manichaeus' Tomb," trans. J. Mohaghegh.

¹³ Yushij, "Moonlight," trans. J. Mohaghegh from *MAAS*, 444.

¹⁴ Bensmaia, *The Year of Passages*, 94.5.

¹⁵ Mehdi Akhavan-Saless, "Namaz," trans. Saeed Saeedpoor in *Modern Iranian Poetry*, 61.

¹⁶ Darwish, *State of Siege*, 133.

¹⁷ Pamuk, *My Name is Red*, 5.

¹⁸ Samih al-Qasim, "Oasis," trans. N. Kassis in *Sadder Than Water*, 81.

¹⁹ Pamuk, *My Names is Red*, 4.

²⁰ Reza Negarestani, *Cyclonopedia* (Melbourne: re.press, 2008), 189.

²¹ Michel Serres, *The Five Senses: A Philosophy of Mingled Bodies*, trans. M. Sankey and P. Cowley (London: Continuum, 2009). There is some connection between this idea of scarring and the treatment of marking in Serres's work, whereby he writes: "And thus means: marked. Emblazoned. Marked: different, designated for torture, a victim . . . Marked: the body of the word, of language, bears the trace or scratch of writing. The life and death of the word bring together the written and the spoken" (211). Nevertheless, the Middle Eastern version does not stray into notions of victimhood; if anything, there is exaltation in the process of wearing these signs.

²² Mansour, *Screams*, 49.

²³ Paruyr Sevak, "Indifference," in *Anthology of Armenian Poetry*, trans. D. Der Hovanessian and M. Margossian (New York: Columbia University Press, 1978), 313.

²⁴ Negarestani, *Cyclonopedia*, 201.

²⁵ Mehdi Akhavan-Saless, "Lament," in *An Anthology of Modern Persian Poetry*, 88.

²⁶ Sadeq Hedayat, *The Blind Owl*, 41.

²⁷ al-Qasim, "The Tragedy of Houdini the Miraculous," trans. G. Levin and N. Kassis in *Sadder Than Water*, 103.

²⁸ Bensmaia, *The Year of Passages*, 84.5.

²⁹ Samman, *Beirut Nightmares*, 7.

³⁰ Mehdi Akhavan-Saless, "Elegy," trans. Saeed Saeedpoor in *Modern Iranian Poetry*, 60.

³¹ Mohammad Reza Shafi'i Kadkani, "The Prayer of Ghastliness," trans. J. Mohaghegh.

Chapter 5

1. Bensmaia, *The Year of Passages*, 74.4.
2. Jean Baudrillard, *Fatal Strategies*, trans. W. G. J. Niesluchowski (Los Angeles: Semiotext(e), 1990). There is some connection between this idea of overthrow and its treatment in Baudrillard's work, whereby he writes: "We will find subtle forms of radicalizing secret qualities; we will fight obscenity with its own weapons. To the truer than true we will oppose the falser than false. We will not oppose the beautiful to the ugly, but will look for the uglier than ugly: the monstrous. We will not oppose the visible to the hidden, but will look for the more hidden than hidden: the secret. We will not be looking for change, and will not oppose the fixed to the mobile; we will look for the more mobile than mobile: metamorphosis. We will not distinguish the true from the false, but will look for the falser than false: illusion and appearance" (25). Nevertheless, the Middle Eastern version does not employ this fatal strategy as a nihilistic end unto itself; if anything, it is an antidote and clearing procedure for the coming of a usurper's consciousness (the assassin).
3. Mamdouh 'Udwan, "Elegy for a Man Who Died and Died," trans. M. Jayyusi and N. S. Nye in *Modern Arabic Poetry*, 463.
4. al-Qasim, "The Will of a Man Dying in Exile," in *Victims of a Map*, 81.
5. This is based in part upon Ahmad Shamlu's "The Hour of Execution."
6. Negarestani, *Cyclonopedia*, 103.
7. This is based in part upon Ahmad Shamlu's "Of Your Uncles."
8. Yusuf Idris, quoted in "Yusuf Idris and the Drama of Ideas" by L. 'Awad in *Critical Perspectives on Yusuf Idris* (Colorado Springs: Three Continents Press, 1994), 158.
9. Mahmoud Darwish, "A State of Siege," in *The Butterfly's Burden*, trans. F. Joudah (Port Townsend: Copper Canyon Press, 2007), 121.
10. Alphonso Lingis, *Dangerous Emotions* (Berkeley: University of California Press, 2000). There is some connection between this idea of blackout and the treatment of excessive thought in Lingis's work, whereby he writes: "Is there not something catastrophic in the very nature of thought? Thought is driven by an excessive compulsion, and is itself an excess over and beyond perception. Thinking is looking for what exceeds the powers of sight, what is unbearable to look at, what exceeds the possibilities of thought" (134). Nevertheless, the Middle Eastern version does not rest with the premise of an inborn, catastrophic nature; if anything, rage is a hard-won state driven by a will to overdosed mindsets.
11. This is based in part upon Ahmad Shamlu's "The Letter."
12. This is based in part upon Ahmad Shamlu's "Anthem for the One Who Left and the One Who Stayed Behind."
13. Shamlu, "Public Love," trans. J. Mohaghegh from *MAAS*, 213.
14. Sargon Boulus, "The Metamorphoses of an Ordinary Man," trans. A. Lawandow from *Ḥāmil al-Fānūs Fi Layl al-Dhi'āb: Qaṣā'id [The Lantern Carrier in the Night of Wolves: Poems]* (Köln: Kamel Verlag, 1996), 67.
15. Yadollah Royai, "Nostalgia 11," in *Modern Iranian Poetry*, 98.

[16] Adonis, "Remembering the First Century," in *The Pages of Day and Night*, trans. S. Hazo (Evanston, IL: Marlboro Press, 2000), 42.

[17] Taha Muhammad Ali, "Abd el-Hadi The Fool," in *So What*, trans. P. Cole, Y. Hijazi, and G. Levin (Port Townsend: Copper Canyon Press, 2006), 129.

[18] Emile Cioran, "Strangled Thoughts," in *The New Gods*, trans. R. Howard (New York: Quadrangle, 1974). There is some connection between this idea of crossing hate and the treatment of preserving hate in Cioran's work, whereby he writes: "You are done for—a living dead man—not when you stop loving but stop hating. Hatred preserves: in it, in its chemistry, resides the mystery of life" (section 1). Nevertheless, the Middle Eastern version does not find its chemical vitality in its ability to safeguard and protect sameness (the source of resentment); if anything, it is sought after as a formula for transfiguration (the source of ecstatic principles).

[19] Akhavan-Saless, "Inscription," in *Modern Iranian Poetry*, 64.

[20] Shamlu, "The Letter," trans. J. Mohaghegh from *MAAS*, 687.

[21] Simin Behbehani, "I Write, Then I Cross Out," trans. J. Mohaghegh.

[22] al-Qasim, "How I Became an Article," in *Victims of a Map*, 71.

[23] Hedayat, "The Man Who Killed His Passions," in *Three Drops of Blood*, 92.

Chapter 6

[1] Gilles Deleuze, "Coldness and Cruelty," in *Masochism*, trans. J. McNeil and A. Willm (New York: Zone, 1991). There is some connection between this idea of the prodigy and the treatment of the masochistic teacher in Deleuze's work, whereby he writes: "We are no longer in the presence of a torturer seizing upon a victim and enjoying her all the more because she is unconsenting and unpersuaded. We are dealing instead with a victim in search of a torturer and who needs to educate, persuade, and conclude an alliance with the torturer in order to realize the strangest of schemes" (20). Nevertheless, the Middle Eastern version does not simply direct its instruction so as to be pointed back upon itself; if anything, it takes its share and more, but confers this knowledge in order to effectuate an outward-moving assassination.

[2] Namik Kuyumcu, "Dreams of Beavers and a Black Knife," trans. J. E. Carpenter and S. Karantay in *Contemporary Turkish Poetry*, 217.

[3] Friedrich Nietzsche, *The Gay Science*, trans. W. Kaufmann (New York: Vintage, 1974). There is some connection between this idea of warfare and the treatment of a warlike age in Nietzsche's work, whereby he writes: "I welcome all signs that a more virile, warlike age is about to begin, which will restore honor to courage above all. For this age shall prepare the way for one yet higher, and it shall gather the strength that this higher age will require one day-the age that will carry heroism into the search for knowledge and that will wage wars for the sake of ideas and their consequences" (2. 283). Nevertheless, the Middle Eastern version does not hang its hopes on future displays of honor or courage; if anything, it converts potentiality into an immediate whip by making ideas offer their automatic, instant payment to consequence.

4   Shamlu, "Quest," trans. J. Mohaghegh from *MAAS*, 594–5.
5   Bensmaia, *The Year of Passages*, 66.7
6   Royai, "The Crypt-Stone of the Martyr," trans. J. Mohaghegh.
7   Royai, "Overflowing 67," trans. J. Mohaghegh.
8   Hedayat, "Buried Alive," trans. B. Spooner in *Sadeq Hedayat*, 153.
9   Khoi, "A Rendezvous between Life and Hazard," in *Edges of Poetry*, 76.
10 Samman, *Beirut Nightmares*, 161.
11 Kuyumcu, "Dreams of Beavers and a Black Knife," 217.
12 Darwish, "Eleven Planets at the End of the Andalusian Scene," in *If I Were Another*, 57–60.

Chapter 7

1   Yushij, quoted in A. Karimi-Hakkak, "Nima Yushij: A Life," in *Essays on Nima Yushij*, 20.
2   Hedayat, "The Benedictions," in *Sadeq Hedayat*, 77.
3   Hushang Irani, "Huh," quoted in "The Space between Voices," trans. P. Vahabzadeh in *Essays on Nima Yushij*, 208.
4   Yushij, "The Story of Pale Complexion, Cold Blood," trans. J. Mohaghegh from *MKANY*, 26.
5   Yushij, "Hey People," trans. J. Mohaghegh from *MKANY*, 301.
6   Yushij quoted in M. Kianush, *Modern Persian Poetry* (Ibex Publishers, 1996), 17.
7   Elias Canetti, *Crowds and Power*, trans. C. Stewart (New York: The Noonday Press, 1960). There is some connection between this idea of the survivor and its treatment in Canetti's work, whereby he writes: "The satisfaction in survival, which is a kind of pleasure, can become a dangerous and insatiable passion. It feeds on its occasions. The larger and more frequent the heaps of dead which a survivor confronts, the stronger and more insistent becomes his need for them . . . Such men can only breathe in danger; to them an existence without danger is stale and flat; they find no savor in a peaceful life" (230). Nevertheless, the Middle Eastern version never drifts too far into the realm of addictive tendencies; if anything, survival retains a trace of playfulness (closer to the domains of contest, pastime, and competition than to need).
8   Michel Foucault, *Society Must Be Defended: Lectures at the College de France, 1975–1976*, trans. D. Macey (New York: Picador, 2003). There is some connection between this idea of the barbarian and its treatment in Foucault's work, whereby he writes: "The barbarian is someone who can be understood, characterized, and defined only in relation to a civilization, and by the fact that he exists outside it. There can be no barbarian unless an island of civilization exists somewhere, unless he lives outside it, and unless he fights it. And the barbarian's relation with that speck of civilization—which the barbarian despises, and which he wants—is one of hostility and permanent warfare . . . The barbarian is always the man who stalks the frontiers of States, the man who stumbles into the city walls . . . He does not make his entrance into history by founding a society, but by penetrating a civilization, setting it ablaze and destroying it" (195).

Nevertheless, the Middle Eastern version does not stop at the destruction of civilization; if anything, the poetic imagination takes us further, into the post-apocalyptic realm where only the barbarians remain and now must decide upon their new world.

9   Khoi, "The North Too," in *Edges of Poetry*, 62.

10 Ibid., 64.

11 Ibid., 68.

12 Shamlu, "Alone," trans. J. Mohaghegh from *MAAS*, 305.

13 Shamlu, "Poverty," trans. J. Mohaghegh from *MAAS*, 347.

14 Shamlu, "The Children of the Depths," trans. J. Mohaghegh from *MAAS*, 805.

15 Abbas Saffari, "Night-Imprisoned," trans. J. Mohaghegh from *Farhad: Jomeh* (Los Angeles: Taraneh Enterprises, 1991), Track 12.

16 Farrokhzad, "After You," in *Sin*, 94.

17 Forugh Farrokhzad, "Window," in *A Lonely Woman: Forugh Farrokhzad and Her Poetry*, trans. M. Hillmann (Pueblo: Passeggiata Press, 1987), 123.

18 Mehdi Akhavan-Saless, "Winter," trans. J. Mohaghegh from *Zemestan* (Winter) (Tehran: Morvareed Publishers, 2000), 99.

19 Yushij, "My House is a Cloud," trans. J. Mohaghegh from *MKANY*, 504.

20 Shamlu, "The Garden of the Mirror," trans. J. Mohaghegh in *MAAS*, 389.

21 Farrokhzad, "Another Birth," trans. A. Karimi-Hakkak in *An Anthology of Modern Persian Poetry*, 151.

22 Khoi, "A Rendezvous between Life and Hazard," in *Edges of Poetry*, 74.

Bibliography

Adonis, Mahmoud Darwish, Samih al-Qasim. *Victims of a Map*. Translated by A. al-Udhari. London: Saqi, 1984.

—. *The Pages of Day and Night*. Translated by S. Hazo. Evanston, IL: Marlboro Press, 2000.

—. *A Time between Ashes and Roses*. Translated by S. Toorawa. Syracuse: Syracuse University Press, 2004.

—. *Selected Poems*. Translated by K. Mattawa. New Haven: Yale University Press, 2010.

Ali, Taha Muhammad. *So What*. Translated by P. Cole, Y. Hijazi, and G. Levin. Port Townsend: Copper Canyon Press, 2006.

Alishan, Leonardo. "The Black City." In *Flash Fiction Forward*. Edited by J. Thomas and R. Shapard. New York: W.W. Norton & Co., 2006.

Artaud, Antonin. *Selected Writings*. Translated by H. Weaver. Los Angeles: University of California Press, 1988.

Bachelard, Gaston. *The Right to Dream*. Translated by J. A. Underwood. Dallas: Dallas Institute of Humanities and Culture, 1989.

Bataille, Georges. *The Unfinished System of Nonknowledge*. Translated by M. Kendall and S. Kendall. Minneapolis: University of Minnesota Press, 2001.

Baudrillard, Jean. *Fatal Strategies*. Translated by W. G. J. Niesluchowski. Los Angeles: Semiotext(e), 1990.

—. *The Transparency of Evil: Essays on Extreme Phenomena*. Translated by J. Benedict. London: Verso, 1990.

Beckett, Samuel. *Stories and Texts for Nothing*. New York: Grove Press, 1967.

Benjamin, Walter. *Reflections*. Translated by E. Jephcott. New York: Schocken, 1986.

Bensmaia, Réda. *The Year of Passages*. Translated by T. Conley. Minneapolis: University of Minnesota Press, 1995.

Blanchot, Maurice. *The Writing of the Disaster*. Translated by A. Smock. Lincoln: University of Nebraska Press, 1980.

—. *The Space of Literature*. Translated by A. Smock. Lincoln: University of Nebraska Press, 1982.

Borges, Jorge Luis. *Selected Poems*. Translated by A. Coleman. New York: Penguin Books, 2000.

Boulus, Sargon. *Ḥāmil al-Fānūs Fi Layl al-Dhi'āb: Qaṣā'id* (*The Lantern Carrier in the Night of Wolves: Poems*). Köln: Kamel Verlag, 1996.

Burroughs, William. *Burroughs Live: The Collected Interview of William S. Burroughs, 1960–1997*. New York: Semiotext(e), 2000.

Canetti, Elias. *Crowds and Power*. Translated by C. Stewart. New York: The Noonday Press, 1960.

Cendrars, Blaise. *Moravagine*. Translated by P. La Farge. New York: New York Review Books, 2004.

Cioran, E. M. *The New Gods*. Translated by R. Howard. New York: Quadrangle, 1974.

—. *A Short History of Decay*. Translated by R. Howard. New York: Arcade, 1998.

Darwish, Mahmoud. *Memories for Forgetfulness*. Translated by I. Muhawi. Berkeley: University of California Press, 1995.

—. *Unfortunately, It Was Paradise*. Translated by M. Akash, C. Forche, S. Antoon, and A. El-Zein. Berkeley: University of California Press, 2003.

—. *The Butterfly's Burden*. Translated by F. Joudah. Port Townsend: Copper Canyon Press, 2007.

—. *If I were Another*. Translated by F. Joudah. New York: Farrar, Straus and Giroux, 2009.

—. *State of Siege*. Translated by M. Akash and D. A. Moore. Syracuse: Syracuse University Press, 2010.

Deleuze, Gilles and Guattari, Felix. *A Thousand Plateaus*. Translated by B. Massumi. Minneapolis: University of Minnesota Press, 1987.

—. "Coldness and Cruelty." In *Masochism*. Translated by J. McNeil and A. Willm. New York: Zone, 1991.

Der Hovanessian, D. and Margossian, M., eds. *Anthology of Armenian Poetry*. New York: Columbia University Press, 1978.

Farrokhzad, Forugh. *Sin: Selected Poems of Forugh Farrokhzad*. Translated by S. Wolpe. Fayetteville: The University of Arkansas Press, 2007.

Foucault, Michel. "A Preface to Transgression." In *Language, Counter-Memory, Practice*. Translated by D. Bouchard. Ithaca: Cornell University Press, 1977.

—. *Society Must Be Defended: Lectures at the College de France, 1975–1976*. Translated by D. Macey. New York: Picador, 2003.

Golesorkhi, Khosrow. *Ay Sarzamin-e Man (O My Homeland)*. Tehran: Entesharat-e Negah, 1373/1995.

Golshiri, Hushang. *The Prince*. Translated by J Buchan. London: Vintage, 2006.

Hedayat, Sadeq. *The Blind Owl*. Translated by D. P. Costello. New York: Grove, 1957.

—. *Sadeq Hedayat: An Anthology*. Edited by E. Yarshater. Boulder: Westview Press, 1979.

—. *Three Drops of Blood*. Translated by D. Miller Mostaghel. Surrey: One World Classics, 2008.

Hikmet, Nazim. *Poems of Nazim Hikmet*. Translated by R. Blasing and M. Konuk. New York: Persea, 2002.

Hillmann, Michael. *A Lonely Woman: Forugh Farrokhzad and Her Poetry*. Pueblo: Passeggiata Press, 1987.

Ibrahim, Sun'allah. *The Committee*. Translated by C. Constable and M. S. Germain. Syracuse: Syracuse University Press, 2001.

Idris, Yusuf. *Critical Perspectives on Yusuf Idris*. Edited by R. M. A. Allen. Colorado Springs: Three Continents Press, 1994.

Jabes, Edmond. *The Book of Questions*. Translated by R. Waldrop. Middletown: Wesleyan University Press, 1983.

Jayyusi, Salma, ed. *Modern Arabic Poetry*. New York: Columbia University Press, 1987.

Kafka, Franz. *The Blue Octavo Notebooks*. Translated by E. Kaiser and E. Wilkins. Cambridge: Exact Change, 1991.

Karantay, Suat, ed. *Contemporary Turkish Poetry: A Selection*. Istanbul: Bogazici University Press, 2006.

Karimi-Hakkak, Ahmad, ed. *An Anthology of Modern Persian Poetry*. Boulder: Westview Press, 1978.

—. *Essays on Nima Yushij: Animating Modernism in Iranian Poetry*. Leiden: Brill Academic Publishers, 2004.

Khoi, Esmail. *Edges of Poetry*. Translated by A. Karimi-Hakkak. Santa Monica: Blue Logos Press, 1995.

Kianush, Mahmud. *Modern Persian Poetry*. Bethesda: Ibex Publishers, 1996.

Kristeva, Julia. *Powers of Horror*. Translated by L. Roudiez. New York: Columbia University Press, 1982.

de Lautreamont, Comte. *Maldoror and Poems*. Translated by P. Knight. London: Penguin Books, 1978.

Lingis, Alphonso. *Dangerous Emotions*. Berkeley: University of California Press, 2000.

Lyotard, Jean-Francois. *The Inhuman: Reflections on Time*. Translated by G. Bennington and R. Bowlby. Stanford: Stanford University Press, 1988.

Mahfouz, Naguib. *The Dreams*. Translated by R. Stock. Cairo: The American University of Cairo Press, 2004.

Mansour, Joyce. *Screams*. Translated by S. Gavronsky. Sausalito: The Post-Apollo Press, 1995.

Michaux, Henri. *Darkness Moves*. Translated by D. Ball. Berkeley: University of California Press, 1997.

Naderpour, Nader. *False Dawn*. Translated by M. Hillmann. Austin: University of Texas, Austin, 1986.

Negarestani, Reza. *Cyclonopedia*. Melbourne: re.press, 2008.

de Nerval, Gerard. *Selected Writings*. Translated by R. Sieburth. New York: Penguin Books, 1999.

Nietzsche, Friedrich. *The Gay Science*. Translated by W. Kaufmann. New York: Vintage, 1974.

—. *Thus Spoke Zarathustra* in *The Portable Nietzsche*. Translated by W. Kaufmann. New York: Penguin Books, 1977.

Pamuk, Orhan. *My Name is Red*. Translated by E. Goknar. New York: Everyman's Library, 2010.

Paz, Octavio. "Introduction." In *Miserable Miracle*. Translated by L. Varese and A. Moschovakis. New York: New York Review Books, 2002.

Pessoa, Fernando. *The Book of Disquiet*. Translated by R. Zenith. New York: Penguin Classics, 2002.

al-Qasim, Samih. *Sadder Than Water*. Translated by G. Levin and N. Kassis. Jerusalem: Ibis Editions, 2006.

Rimbaud, Arthur. *Rimbaud Complete*. Translated by W. Mason. New York: Modern Library, 2003.

Saeedpoor, Saeed, ed. *Modern Iranian Poetry*. San Jose: Authors Choice Press, 2001.

Saffari, Abbas. "Night-Imprisoned." Track 12 on *Farhad: Jomeh*. Los Angeles: Taraneh Enterprises, 1991.

Samman, Ghada. *Beirut Nightmares*. Translated by N. Roberts. London: Quartet Books, 1976.

Serres, Michel. *Genesis*. Translated by G. James and J. Nielson. Ann Arbor: University of Michigan Press, 1995.

—. *The Five Senses: A Philosophy of Mingled Bodies*. Translated by M. Sankey and P. Cowley. London: Continuum, 2009.

Shamlu, Ahmad. *Majmu'eh-ye Asar-e Ahmad Shamlu (The Collected Works of Ahmad Shamlu)*. Tehran: Zamaneh Press, 1381/2002.

Virilio, Paul. *Pure War*. Translated by M. Polizzotti. New York: Semiotext(e), 2008.

Wuld Ibno, Moussa. "City of Winds." In *Modern Arabic Fiction*. Edited by S. Jayyusi. New York: Columbia University Press, 2008.

Yushij, Nima. *Majmu'eh-ye Kamel-e Asha'ar-e Nima Yushij (The Complete Collected Poetry of Nima Yushij)*. Tehran: Mo'asaseh Entesharat Negah, 1996.

Zurn, Unica. *The Man of Jasmine*. Translated by M. Green. London: Atlas Press, 1977.

Index